We were born to make manifest the glory of God
that is within us.
It's not just in some of us; it's in everyone.
And as we let our own light shine,
we unconsciously give other people permission to
do the same.

Nelson Mandela

CONTENTS

THE CIRCLE IS SACRED

SECOND EDITION

STALKING THE SPIRIT-POWERED LIFE

Scout Cloud Lee, Ed. D.

With Carol Ann Washburn Lee, Ed.D.

COUNCIL OAK BOOKS

Tulsa / San Francisco

Council Oak Books
2105 East 15th St. Tulsa, OK 74104

Originally published as
The Circle Is Sacred: A Medicine Book for Women

ISBN 1-57178-136-6

Cover and book design by Carol Stanton
Typography for the second edition by Melanie Haage
Photography by Asia Sayr Ladd on pages 18, 20 – 24, 28, 35, 38,
39, 41, 46, 53, 55, 57, 60, 61, 69, 74, 77-79 (top), 80, 81, 85, 96, 102,
110, 122, 125 (right) –128, 130–132, 136, 140, 143-149 (right), 152,
157, 158, 161-165, 167-168 (top), 170, 172, 175, 179, 198, 208, 215,
224, 230, 236, 241, 246

DEDICATION

The following spirits inspire us.
This book is dedicated to them.

Our mothers and sisters
Pat Spencer, who gives us roots of strength, courage and wisdom.
Faye Washburn, who gives us wings of joy, daring and faith.
Dr. Jan Summers, our mastermind alliance, whose gifts power our dreams.
Sharon Williams, who looks beyond difference to see love.

Our fathers
Wayne Washburn and Ed Spencer, and all the beautiful men
who have powered us to be ourselves.

Margaret Swank and Kapeka Chandler, our role models and heroes.

Greta Gayle Kane and Dr. JoAnne Chinnici, together we live our dreams.

Beth Skye and "Kool," whose love holds the circle sacred.

Cathy Hancock , Lorena Roesner, Mary Stirrup, Lahela Correa and
'Ohana, who lovingly tend and stoke our home fires.

Mariah Kat, and all of our precious sisters who mirror our
teachings and inspire us to "walk our talk."

Council Oak Books, the publishing house that gives wind to new discoveries.

Our animal family and our land, who remain our constant and loving teachers.

One another, in the name of love, playmates for all seasons.

To you, our readers. Thank you!

And always to God, the giver of our breath

These spirits fuel our sacred power.

TO THE READERS

I am grateful for this opportunity to re-visit *The Circle Is Sacred*. The principles behind these words still hold true and over the last eight years have gained in importance.

For thirty-two years I have shared earth medicine with the corporate world and others. I am not an authority on earth medicine. I am a servant to the earth and the laws of nature. With my companions, I offer my gifts through Vision Us, Inc., the Magical Child Foundation, "The Challenge of Excellence" training and camps, Corporate Coaching, The Wolf Song Indigenous Peace Elder's Gatherings, Teamwork 2000 Corporate Trainings, The Circle Is Sacred Gatherings, Reunion Camps, The Leadership Embassy for Excellence, The Lodge of the Stronghearts camps for executives and youth, and The Oklahoma Red Dirt Church.

Each thing has "medicine," "*skan*," "power," or a gift to give. Trees, animals, rivers, clouds, streams — each has a power of its own, just like electricity has its own gift. By understanding the gift, we can work with it. We must seek to embrace the gifts of all of life so that we can work together in harmony. This book is about tracking and appreciating gifts in all of life.

Our elders teach us that each person is a "perfect soul" who reflects the essence of God, the Great Mystery. As I express my insights into the Great Mystery, I trust there cannot exist only one right way. I offer simply a way that best expresses my understanding and insight. Ceremony and ritual are meaningful only when propelled by the creation and integrity of each individual. I speak from my own knowledge, born from within and guided by others' teachings. By bridging ancient wisdom into the creative tapestry of our contemporary lives, we receive a helping hand from our ancestors who have come before us.

We stand inside the dawning of a new millennium. We leave behind a thousand-year reign of warfare. We now know that it is the *tone* that is set at the beginning of any endeavor that divines the *outcome* of that endeavor. Let us together set a tone for "peace on earth" as we move forward in the twenty-first century.

All of us are stewards, here to care take of our own bodies, each other, and the Earth Mother. We are here to fulfill our vision and individual destinies in harmony with one another and in balance with all things. The time of the gun and the rifle are over.

The time of the gun and the rifle are over.

This is a time of great accountability and consequences for our actions. It is time to put the "L" word back into our schools and workplaces—demonstrate love. It is our job to find a way to let our children be happy. This is, in fact, the act of creating community. We have the unique opportunity to return a sense of community into the twenty-first century as we seek friendship with all people and all of life.

Within the Sacred Circle of All-that-is, joy springs. It is within the circle that we experience the wholeness and the holiness of life. Whatever we do to any one thing in the great web of life, we do to ourselves, for we are all one. Knowing this, we enjoy a sense of ease, synchronicity, and ecstasy. We can give our most wonderful gifts.

For the first time in history we are able to connect with our entire planet. The challenge is now to cherish our beautiful earth and recognize that we are part of it.

The values held by children of the twenty-first century are being shaped by mothers and fathers who work outside the home, neighbors who speak different languages, single-parent family structures, teachers who care about the environment, and television that has brought God, angels, and aliens into the mainstream of life.

In the midst of all this change, one fact remains, the fact of our common humanity. Genetically, we are all 99.999% the same. We are all at least fiftieth cousins, members of the same race, the human race. We are truly one team on earth. We are a human team on a spiritual assignment to live peace on earth.

The competitive spirit of American business . . . may well have been inherited from our own warrior lineage and tribal roots.

This time in which we live is called "the Shift of the Ages." We have only to look into our own hands to see thousands of generations before us supporting us to make this shift. We see and feel the shift occurring. This is a time that our ancestors told us about.

In the Challenge of Excellence, we work with successful business people in creating new, non-hierarchical organizations based on indigenous peoples' ideals of personal independence, integrity, equality and open forums. Just as our ancestors knew the balance of flora and fauna, they also understood the delicate balance of relationships and power. In the twenty-first century, business is creating a global family. The values learned through camping and wilderness experiences are extending into the corporate world of training. The competitive spirit of American business that views business as a game to be played with integrity and zeal may well have been inherited from our own warrior lineage and tribal roots. We see companies with this spirit thriving when others fall.

Within our ancestral memories lie solutions to modern-day problems. In our circles, we honor the "good medicine" of all our ancestors and call it back in order that we might send our children forth in the future, holding hands and singing of peace on earth.

In his book, *Respiriting the Workplace*, Jack Hawley writes inspiringly of leadership in the twenty-first century. Leaders must have a respect for others so intense that it becomes open reverence. This respect extends to all. The key to the ninety-nine is in how we treat the one.

I am delighted to see educators honoring intuition and emotion as primary ingredients in the learning process. Artists are among our greatest visionaries and are providing inspiration via painting, sculpture, literature, dance and music. Earth healers from many cultures provide models of holistic health that acknowledge the influence of attitude upon disease. In the face of escalating medical costs, we are now humbly turning back to earth and herbal healing for our wellness. Sacred traditions such as yoga and Tai Chi are now widely practiced in our culture, and in our current ecological crisis, we are turning back to native concepts of living in balance with the land.

In Oklahoma my companions and I have created "The Ranch," a training and retreat center nestled in the beauty of earth's bounty. Here, and throughout the world, we facilitate encampments and trainings for corporations, youth, women, families and individuals. We focus on leadership and teaming principles that have survived into the twenty-first century and we have a deep reverence for all of life. We look upon the ordinary and recognize the miracle and majesty of life. We gaze upon a cloud floating and we appreciate that without the cloud there is no rain. Without the rain, there are no trees. Without the trees, there is no breath. We feel the sun warming the passions of our hearts. We remember and experience the power of living close to our earth and each other. We revisit a style of leadership and empowerment that respects each thing equally and gives voice to the All-that-is. We gather and we empower our authentic, perfect individual selves.

Our differences allow us to see in all directions.

We say, "Thank you, Great One! We love you. We love all your creatures and their beautiful fur and eyes and feathers and scales."

We come to open our hearts to the great love that binds us all together. Each of us faces a slightly different direction, giving each a unique perspective within the circle of life. Our differences allow us to see in all directions, and this seeing is our protection and our joy.

The teepee lodge, in which each pole represents a nation, manifests a time when all nations will be tied together. The teepee's pegs symbolize the earth's children and remind us to make our every act good for the children out seven generations.

At The Ranch animals, insects and plants are to be treated with the kind of respect one customarily accords to high-ranking adults, for life is a circle and everything in it has a sacred place. We again lift our women high and revere their ways of peacefulness, harmony, cooperation, and concern for the general health and prosperity. When the women's hearts turn to dust, the people perish. We celebrate our men who hold their women high and power their dreams.

Likewise, the welfare of our young and our elders is of paramount importance, for therein is held all wisdom and our future. We watch closely, but let the child be herself. Then we know that her eyes will not turn in anger at the one who pulls her back, but toward the calling of her heart's desires. We learn not to defeat her natural desire to test and explore. We watch her learn the place where warmth becomes burning.

As children we naturally chose ones to lead us who were the most trustworthy. It's time to return to this practice, to regain our freedom and our magic.

We climb high outside our comfort zones and know the deeper comfort of courage.

In our workshops and leadership camps at The Ranch, we carve our own coup sticks, lances and staffs and carry them into the gaming field where we find that moving keeps one from getting dull and stupid. We learn to marvel not at the one who kills, but at the one who heals. We learn to value human life more than property and we experience first-hand being the scouts for our clans—the eyes, the ears and the hearts of the people. We learn the value of the peace chief and the one who stands her lodge at the center of the village.

We play with our horse herds, set up games of stealth, hunter/hunted and the counting-of-coup, in order to grow our prowess and our spirit bodies. We climb high outside our comfort zones and know the deeper comfort of courage. We learn the value of laughter and play before any serious business. We see that those who deny their power for winning any game in life weaken the spirit of the games they enter.

We sweat together in the Lodge of the Stone People. Sweating is prescribed for any ailment and is as old as life. We speak the truth as we hold our feathers and pipes and watch the horse of our breath ride our thoughts, spiraling out to the world around us. We laugh and tell stories to sweeten the our days and nights. And we no longer call people primitive who cry out for forgiveness to the dying tree or polluted waters.

We notice that when we praise the wildflowers for growing on the hill, they multiply in abundance and brilliance, that when we admire the deer for letting us see them, they bring their whole families close to entertain and delight us. We learn that when we spend our total attention investing in the beauty in all things, we become wealthy with beauty in and around us.

Passing the "talking stick" we discover many options. We come to value the indigenous people's belief in transformation, whereby an individual can adopt a new identity, a new set of beliefs and take a new name at any stage of life. We practice the "giveaway" and see that life returns abundance in accordance with what we give.

As we come together, our hearts are filled with courage and hope for renewal. More importantly, our wills are singularly focused on acts of power and beauty that are good for the whole of life.

We use our circle to focus our *intent*, understanding that we are each designed to follow our passion and sense of adventure. We nurture the dreams of each in the circle. The most effective prayer is not a request but an *affirmation*. We learn to master the force of our intentions, knowing that we get what we intend. What we intend, we feel. What we feel causes the vibration that attracts to us that very expectation. We learn to abandon all thoughts of failing and to control our emotions by becoming masters of our thoughts and even more so, our feelings. The more we uplift others and lend them our good energy, the more we follow the Divine Plan and The Law of Nature. It is our birthright to hold a vision and bring it about through our creative power and our emotional intelligence. Our heart's desire and soul's aspiration alone guide us along our path. We learn to ask for help when we need it. Within the circle help is available.

We learn to focus, knowing that *energy flows into our attention*. We get that thing that is the object of our focus. We know that we never get anywhere when our thoughts are watching one thing and our eyes another. We learn to discipline our thoughts to "be here now." Power lives in the *now*.

There is nothing more powerful than a well-formed ritual. In the absence of ritual our souls run out of food and social problems occur. Traditionally, elders have required that the young be initiated because they needed to remember their role and value to the community. Without recognition and instruction, initiations do not complete themselves, creating both a fragmented community and individual malaise. Young people seek passage into adulthood and meaningful community, and when we fail to provide this for them, they create their own "rituals." They get "stoned, boned, and zoned," and ultimately to end up "cloned," because they've lost their individuality. Within our circles we create rituals of bonding, celebration, renewal, new beginnings, random appreciation, and passage.

No two rituals can ever be the same. Rituals may be inspired by, not copied from, one culture to another. Inside our ritual space we create a place where our grief and our celebration can be given into the Other World, the Larger World. In ritual, we take the initiative to spark a process, knowing that the outcome is not in our hands, but in the hands of the kind of forces we invite into our circle. Powers are released in ritual space and given freedom to live and grow. When we leave ritual space, we carry the power of the ritual with us.

In our circles our authentic, natural selves are nurtured and appreciated. It is in community that we draw strength needed to effect changes inside of us as we grow. Community creates a

13

The leader who knows his or her own values and lives by them impeccably endows others with heart.

place to "return home." A true community is an open door to an open heart and an open mind. Within a true community, Spirit and love are the real guardians, the real police. Love latches onto us and will not let go. This is often our only salvation in times of real life challenges. Inside our circles we know that we must solve our current problems without creating new ones. Now is the time to nurture rather than fight, to support rather than to destroy.

In a family meeting held on January 1, 1990, at the base of Mt. Warning in Australia, Aunt Millie Boyd, aboriginal elder, said, "The Dream Time is over. Now is the Blend Time. The red culture brings us Spirit. The yellow culture brings us pure mind. The black culture brings us soul. The white culture brings us technology. This is divine planning. We all need each other. Blend."

Hold a candle close to reverence and you see fondness, deep appreciation, and gratitude. Together we must develop reverence for our mission, our products, our consumers, our children, our mates, our family, our team, our animals, and our Earth Mother. Great organizations and families have such reverence. The task of this "Now-Age" style of leadership is to uncover talent in the individual. We must not set goals as a carrot on a stick in front of others. We must *become* the goal. The old style of leadership reveled in performance problems. The leader of the twenty-first century is a scout and a tracker capable of noticing what is working and being very specific about nurturing it. We create ways to appreciate and acknowledge others. We strive to enhance their strengths and use them for the good of the whole.

The times we live in require the courage and self-discipline to live by our inner truths. The leader who knows his or her own values and lives by them impeccably endows others with *heart*. Others will emulate them to discover their own integrity.

True leaders of the twenty-first century take responsibility for the creation of oneness in the circle. We encourage, partake in, and invent new ways to bring people together. We know the power of the circle in all things. We know that inside the circle people feel contentment and "contentment" is the highest result of leadership. Contentment occurs when we are reflecting our deepest passion and potential, for our state of mind is more important than all our strategies. All true leaders are optimists. No exceptions!

As Jack Hawley (a precious friend) points out, leaders have vision, not "goals and objectives," are concerned with integrity, not status, are stewards of basic values, not "priorities," are givers, not "getters," deal in culture and a sense of community, not organizational form. Leaders acknowledge and appreciate contributions, rather than evaluate and correct performance. Leaders don't "make decisions," they establish a presence that makes their influence, guidance, and values felt throughout the community. They work with energy, heart, and spirit, rather than "effort." Above all else, leaders of the twenty-first century follow Spirit as far as they can. Then they simply vanish, leaving a legacy of love.

This book invites the same. This book embraces the Circle of Life with eternal respect and invites us to return to our roots: Mother Earth and all that is in Her.

May the Great, Great Spirit of Life bless each of you who labor daily to clean this world of the illusion of separation so we may all sing and dance and play together in peace. Bless each moment we are exiled to the wilderness and great outdoors. It is from these roots that we discover our own wildness and from this wilderness within we now know the Power that is Peace. Let us all bravely and lovingly pass it on.

May all the winds embrace you with the benefits of returning to the Circle.

Scout Cloud Lee

HONORING
THE CIRCLE

Today is a day when woman power, children power and earth power are needed.

—Alinta

Without question, the First Mother, the Mother Creator is finding Her way back into the Trinity where She has hidden as a "Holy Ghost" since the time of colonization. The smallest Circle, the circle of three, again has a Mother God to stand with Father God and Holy Child. The Circle, the Trinity, is sacred. This work honors the First Mother Spirit. The replacement of the feminine in the godhead is essential for wholeness as human beings and families together, shepherding our beautiful Earth. Let it be known that the Holy Spirit, Skan, That-Which-Moves-in-All-Things, is our Mother. She is Truth. It is our Blessed First Mother who holds us and nurtures our dreams, even as our own mothers held us to their breasts and fed us. It is our All-Father who champions and powers our dreams, in accordance with our Mother's truest wishes and our own desires. It is our Brother Jesus whose spirit lingers with us as a coach and friend. There are other spirits who journey among us as the circle of the Trinity enlarges to include the family of All-That-Is-and-Ever-Has-Been. Our ancestors who went before us serve us yet today. The spirit of life in each thing serves us yet today. The invisible and the visible serve us as we empty ourselves and make way for Spirit to move in us. Let our bones be hollow so as to allow Truth and Wisdom to use us. Let us take our place in the Circle for the Circle is sacred.

Ceremony, all ceremony, must begin with honoring the Circle. Elders have told us that "Christ" means "Circle." Jesus was a man of the Circle. The Circle is both the Center focal point from which all things flow, and the ever-embracing arms of the All-That-Is. When students begin studying the art of Karate, they receive a white belt. Most believe that the serious student of Karate strives to achieve the Black Belt. In fact, there are nine levels of Black Belts, the first of which is considered by some to be the least desirable, for this student knows enough to be dangerous. When one achieves the highest belt in Karate, it is not black, but white. They return again to the beginning, realizing that they actually know nothing. Similarly, the true sage has no devotees, and the true teacher is the finest student. The Circle is both the beginning and the end, the Alpha and the Omega. We live and breathe and have our being within the Circle. For those who prophesy the return of "the Christ," we know them to mean, "The Return of the Circle."

The circle is a feminine shape; a feminine sound. It is a protected and consecrated space, a space where all things and all people are equal. The circle is at the very root of equality. It is the symbol for equality. The circle is at the root to true humility where each is seen as important to the whole and none is more important than any other. God is a circle whose circumference is nowhere and whose center is everywhere.

Closed circles continue to be protective especially for workers of magic. A healer is a "Circle-drawer." The Circle is the symbol of universal deity and is invoked by the force of the full moon and the pupil of the All-Seeing Eye.

To this end, this book is offered as our gift to the Great Mystery.

Always we stand at the Center.

Collective energy is sufficient to draw water out of the desert. Come together. That is our only mission.

—Cloud

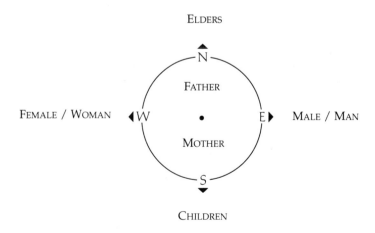

Seven Sacred Directions of the Circle

The term, "The Circle," is a way of expressing the relatedness of all things. A perspective that acknowledges one's experience of the physical world, the world of events, feelings, thoughts and relationships.

On this continent, Native Americans have called this circle of life "The Medicine Wheel." "Medicine" acknowledging the human being's journey around the circle results in a "whole"/complete human being and that this "human" lives in good and balanced relations in all aspects of life . . . physical, mental, emotional and finally, spiritual.

—Skye

From this place we send our voice up to acknowledge our All-Father as we see His manifest power in the Sun. The Sun sends energy downward to our Earth Mother, drawing life from her belly. We send our voice downward to acknowledge our First-Mother from which came all things material and necessary for our physical well-being. We bless Her spirit as She moves through all of life bringing fruit to our labors. We send our voice out four directions to ride the wind, and travel from tree to tree and rock to rock, and echo from the voice of all living things among their own kind.

We send our voice to the East where the Sun gets up each day. We bless all living things, visible and invisible, who live in the East. We do so remembering the birth of all things . . . new beginnings. In the East we celebrate the male principle and the seeding of new life.

We send our voice to the South, repeating our blessing of all things and remembering the days of our youth, our passion, our agility, our innocence and our trust. In the South we celebrate our children.

We send a voice to the West, blessing all the people of the West and all things visible and invisible. We welcome these energies into our circle, remembering the value of the sunset time when we cease our daily work and come home to the inner circle of family where we rest and rejoice in our togetherness. In this place we share the unknown and the dark places where we understand that all life comes, as a seed casts away its hull, expands its belly and burrows its feet into soil where it can gather the strength to push up into the light above the darkness of the earth. In the West we celebrate the female principle.

We send a voice to the North where wisdom lives in the hearts and minds of the old ones who wear white hairs; where the leaves fall away from the trees, leaving skeletons of life exposed to naked limbs wise enough to harbor new life to spring forth when the sun returns. In the North we celebrate our Elders.

Into our Circle we welcome All-That-Is from the four directions of the winds on earth.

Finally, we look WITHIN where resides our kinship with our Brother Jesus and all peoples of earth. Within resides the All-Knowing in touch with All-Knowing.

We stand at the center of the Circle, always. All ceremony begins with honoring the Circle. All ceremony, all prayer, all celebration, all rituals, all moments in time. We are related to all things, visible and invisible.

There are ways, great and small, to honor the Circle of Life. The following are a few.

A simple prayer bundle holds the throwing cloth of the Circle.

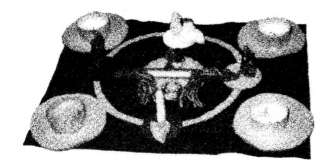

Skye's Prayer Bundle

The cloth is green to remember the Mother Holy Spirit that moves through all things on Earth. The circle is golden for this age in which we call together the Hoop of All Things as one family. The Eastern circle is yellow, like the sun and the yellow people in the east. The Southern circle is red, like the heart in love and the red people. The West is black, like the night time and the rich soil of the earth and the black people. The North circle is white, like the fallen snow, wisdom, the hairs of the old and the white people.

The center of the Circle is blue like the vast sky and the vastness of our All-Father's love. In the center of the blue circle is the golden cross where we stand with our Elder Brother Friend, The Man of the Circle. This simple cloth is thrown in private and acknowledges the Seven Directions of the Circle of All-That-Is. My private prayer bundle has special things that are put to the Circle. A small doll figure, carved and dressed to resemble me, is put to the Center. This placement is accompanied with breathing, centering and the making of music. Sage is burned to attract the sweetness of the invisibles. Each prayer is sent out with song and sweet smell. An old centering rock from my lineage is placed in the East. It belonged to an elder man of medicine. To the South is placed a clear quartz crystal with many triangles of the "Teacher Recorder." This crystal was given to me from my Grandmother

Woman holds, nurtures and powers the dream. Man champions and protects the dream. Child dreams the dream. This is the holy Trinity. This is the balance within.

—Cloud

19

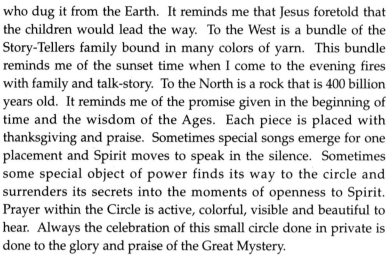

who dug it from the Earth. It reminds me that Jesus foretold that the children would lead the way. To the West is a bundle of the Story-Tellers family bound in many colors of yarn. This bundle reminds me of the sunset time when I come to the evening fires with family and talk-story. To the North is a rock that is 400 billion years old. It reminds me of the promise given in the beginning of time and the wisdom of the Ages. Each piece is placed with thanksgiving and praise. Sometimes special songs emerge for one placement and Spirit moves to speak in the silence. Sometimes some special object of power finds its way to the circle and surrenders its secrets into the moments of openness to Spirit. Prayer within the Circle is active, colorful, visible and beautiful to hear. Always the celebration of this small circle done in private is done to the glory and praise of the Great Mystery.

The Circle in the Village where the sacred dances and purification ceremonies are performed is a larger Circle.

Center Fire Circle at Village

In the center sits the Fire Circle, kept always sacred. (No cigarette remains and such are ever put into this fire.) The rocks surrounding this fire are arranged to celebrate the animals and energies of each direction. To the East is the Eagle Rock to celebrate illumination, vision and prophecy. To the South is the Turtle rock to celebrate the strength and endurance of youth and the back upon which the children of earth live and have their home. To the West is the Bear Rock who teaches us to dream, and sleep, and rest and bring forth dreams out of darkness. To the North is the Buffalo Rock that teaches us to use all things to the glory of Our Provider so there will be abundance for our Children out seven generations.

To the East of the Village stands a tall totem with the mighty Buck Rack. The golden colors of this shield remind us of the qualities manifest in the rising sun. This shield marks the East Gate of the Village.

Make our cause love . . . so the effect can be peace. Give love wherever you go.

—Grandmother Kitty

East Gate - Protection Shield

In the South is a Shield depicting our Aboriginal relations in the sun down-under, far to the South. This shield is child-like and reminds us to call all others "our relations." This is the South Gate of the Village.

To the West is a shield with 405 tobacco tied prayers for peace on earth. The female deer sits center, facing her partner in the East. She is mounted on the hide of the female cow given in ceremony to the elders. The hide comes from that part of the she-cow's heart. This shield is the West Gate to the Village and is called the Welcoming Shield.

South Gate of Village

West Gate - Welcoming Shield

North Gate of Village

To the North sits the Shield of Infinity, which is made to resemble a figure 8, and is from one continuous vine. Each circle is covered with the hide of the sacred cow, including her spine, top and bottom. The symbol painted on the two circles of the infinity sign say "Vision Us One People." This is the North Gate of the Village.

In the Village sits the Clan and the Tribal Sweat Lodges, used for purification.

The Star Lodge is a five-pointed pole house, which is for children.

The Star Lodge is screened and roofed with skylights. Children can be in the circle of ceremony with their own place to gather. The screen allows for them to see and hear all ceremony, while entertaining themselves quietly. They often fall asleep in the night celebrations and sleep in their own pole lodge.

The Polar Bear Lodge is a lodge for prayer and smoking the *chanupa* (pipe).

Clan and Tribal Sweat Lodges

The Sky Lodge resembles a basket and is a lodge of passage. It is often decorated with blankets and flowers appropriate to the type of passage, i.e. the marriage-makes-two ceremony, a rite of passage for the child-become-woman or man, the age-of-wisdom ceremony when the adult takes the place of elder, the celebration of harvest ceremony, and the one-who-owns-a-vision ceremony.

Star Lodge for Children at the Village

Polar Bear Lodge for Smoking

Sky Lodge for Passage

West Gate - Receiving Altar

*A*s long as I live, no matter
where I may be, this will be my
home.

—Grandmother
Princess Moon
Feathers
(Speaking about Open
Spoke Ranch)

The Receiving Altar in the West is the ask-to-receive altar place.

The Give-Away Altar is in the East. The Sun Lodge sits in the Southeast and is a gathering place for the men. The Moon Lodge sits in the Southwest and is a gathering place for the women. Each structure in the circle of life is a simple temple created to worship the Great Creator.

Celebration and ceremony begin with the drum mimicking the heartbeat of the Earth. This Mother Drum is joined by others creating a crescendo of drumming. The pace quickens, heightening the excitement of the moment. Rattles join the drums, alerting the ones-who-crawl that the Circle comes together for the celebration of All-That-Is. Flutes and other clap sticks, hand drums, bells, shells and sounds of music join the cadence, making it obvious that something of great importance happens here.

Amidst the symphony of sound is heard the deep, full call of the conch shell and the long hollow harmony of the digereedo. First to the East goes the duet calling for the East Gate to be opened. Little children carry food, drink and dessert to the altar at the East Gate and invite the invisibles of good will to join our celebration. The invisibles are offered refreshments (corn, rice, water, wine, cheese, berries, fruit, peanut butter sandwiches) and their influence is invited into the celebration. The duet of conch and digereedo proceed to the South where the little children repeat their offering and invitation. In this way, the invisibles living in the South are made welcome in the circle and the South Gate is opened. Again, the duo moves to the west and the children repeat their offering. Again, the invitation to the invisibles is made and the West Gate is opened. Finally, the duo proceeds to the north, where the invisibles of the North are welcomed and the elders remembered by the children and the Circle. The hostesses proceed to the center of the fire circle where the conch and digereedo duo call to the All-Father to hear our intentions and be present as promised when two or more gather in goodness. The duo calls to the Earth below requesting that the First Mother sit among us and witness our appreciation for Her great love. Finally, the hostesses call for the inward glance to see the Christ within and welcome the living Spirit of the Elder Brother to move within each heart. Tobacco is offered upward to the Spirit Above, then in each of the four directions of the wind. Beautiful blue corn is offered to the First Mother to re-seed Her for

Her gift. The drums begin again, joined by all music, while the sweet sage is burned and smoke is carried to each person, animal and sacred object. In this way all are purified, sweetened and made ready to participate in ceremony. In this simple way the Circle is honored.

HONORING
OUR ELDERS

I was a stranger in my own land; a widow that lived alone. Then I met Chief Cloud. She adopted me and gave me family. Now I will never be alone."

—Grandmother
Princess Moon
Feathers

Grandmother Princess Moon Feathers is our Elder. Over a century ago, a bolt of lightening struck a tree near where Grandmother's mother stood inspecting a birthing post she would use in a few months to press down her unborn child. That bolt of lightening, however, insisted that Princess come forth immediately. She was two months premature and weighed less than four pounds. Her eyes were glowing green and her hair was chrome white and three inches longer than her little body. She was left for dead. When the old Medicine Chief came the next day to offer condolences and rites, she kicked and squalled her defiance to the death angel. Her father filled two old whiskey jugs with water and heated rocks to keep them warm. For nearly one year this was Grandmother's primitive incubator. This all happened on a Cherokee reservation where Grandmother was born. Eventually her eyes turned soft brown to match her lineage, but her hair always remained fast growing, unusually long and very blonde.

Grandmother, a full-blooded Cherokee, is simply not an ordinary person. At age twelve, she had already taught herself to read and memorized the Bill of Rights of the United States and read the Bible from cover to cover. It was the last year she saw her people. All alone, she boarded a canoe and paddled down the coast to Key Largo where she hid out and became an original resident. There had been a $200 bounty on her head for being born a savage Indian.

In Grandmother's lifetime she has enjoyed fame as the Great Sabrina of the early Ringling Brothers' Circus. She was a card shark for Al Capone and a friend of Faulkner and Hemingway. She posed nude for well-known artists and strip- danced in posh clubs in Mexico. She single-handedly took on the mayor and city council of Charlotte, North Carolina, when the police department attempted to collect several hundred dollars of past due parking tickets from her. She uncovered an old existing law in the court house that granted any citizen access to all public roadways. She threatened to go to the media unless they retracted her tickets and granted her the right to park wherever she wanted.

Late in life, she found her once young sweetheart on "death row" of a V.A. hospital. She kidnapped the old man in a laundry basket and took him home to heal. They married and lived happily for fifteen years before he died.

Grandmother swears that she invented pantsuits for women and wore them to public gatherings where she rolled the first variety of condoms up and down her finger to demonstrate "modern birth control." Grandmother's 100 year old breasts stand full and erect to this day. She swears it's because she would never let any man suck on them.

Grandmother has been declared legally blind, but just completed writing her own autobiography entitled, "You Savage, You Lonely One." She has never taken any "Proctor & Gamble" medications. She occasionally indulges in a small glass of fine wine, but has never touched hard liquor or cigarettes. Her hair is still full and long and she can out-talk, -walk and -wit anyone we know. Grandmother Princess Moon Feathers is our Elder. She deserves to be honored.

We are blessed to be brought into a family circle who respects the Wisdom Years. The peach tree gives birth to a child; a peach. It is nothing like its parent the peach tree. However, when the seed within the peach falls to the ground and takes root, its offspring is a replica of its grandparent, the peach tree. So it is with our elders. We are like our grandparents, and intended to carry forth their dreams into our distant future. Our parents are but the bridge of passage to insure that the lineage of our elders is carried out seven generations.

It is good that an elder sits in every circle. It is good that they show approval of all that goes on. It is good that they hold the seat of honor. It is good that meeting their needs be equal with meeting the needs of our children. As productive adults, it is our great pleasure to serve our elders and our children. All that we do

I have worked on the messages from Grandmother Series for twelve years. When it first came to me, I thought of every reason why I couldn't do it. I couldn't bead, I couldn't sew— blah, blah, blah. But when I realized it was the old ones speaking to me, I said, "Yes."

—Mahisha

must cause our Elders' hearts to be glad and our children run happy as free spirits. It is good that an elder bless each phase of our comings and goings. When the elders choose to come to us and join our circle, it is the best of omens.

All ceremony begins with honoring the Circle of All Things. Next, it is good to present our Elders and seek their blessings. We once performed a Celebration of Peace at the World Expo in Vancouver. We invited Grandmother Caroline of the Hopi to come on stage and offer a blessing. She was escorted on stage by two young braves. The microphone was lowered to suit her small, delicate frame. The applause of the crowd died down and a soft silence settled over the audience. Grandmother Caroline waited in silence. She stood in stillness, her head high, her hands folded in front. She said nothing. After many minutes, the silence grew too uncomfortable for the expectant crowd. They began to shift and nudge each other.

Could it be that the old lady lost her tongue in front of this large civilized crowd? The dis-ease grew and swelled. The sound technician began to panic. "What are we going to do?" Grandmother remained undaunted in her silence.

After five or more uncomfortable minutes, the crowd and backstage crew settled into a simple stillness. Over the next many minutes, one-by-one each person present joined Grandmother in the Center of the Silence. When no thing existed in time and space except our unity, silence extended over many minutes of mass ecstasy, Grandmother Caroline leaned gently into the microphone prepared for her delivery and uttered "Amen!" Stunned and ecstatic, the crowd fell into applause unparalleled throughout the entire eleven-hour concert. They celebrated something beyond their ability to verbalize. Our Elder had brought us the Living Spirit of the Circle as a blessing. It is good to honor our elders.

In every circle our elders' chairs are comfortable. There is water, tea, coffee and drink to their satisfaction. Ashtrays are available for those who smoke and a strong escort is always available to them. Their meals are taken first and with special considerations for their likes. Their personal space is preserved to their liking. When they are praying, all things cease to matter around them. It is good to honor our elders.

When we perform, we offer our dance to our elders. We tease them and mock them and make them laugh and laugh. It is good to honor our elders. We long to see the old ones throw back their

I call this paradise. I wish all the world could see what I've seen in the last week. It has changed my life forever. I am no longer homeless. I am no longer without a family.

—Grandmother Princess Moon Feathers (*Speaking about Oklahoma*)

heads and laugh. When the old ones laugh, all is well among us. When their hearts turn to dust, the people perish.

One grand way to honor our elders is with the Give-away. Our elders have given their very lives that we might have a better way. What we give to our elders is likened to what we are willing to give to our Great Creator. In the flesh, our elders represent our First Mother and our All-Father. When respect is lacking for the elders, there is no respect for the Almighty. It is good to honor our elders. The following poem has been given to remind us about our elders. Its author is unknown:

✹

WHAT IS A GRANDMOTHER?
BY A THIRD GRADER

A grandmother is a lady who has no children of her own. She likes other people's little girls and boys. A grandfather is a man grandmother. He goes for walks with the boys, and they talk about fishing and stuff like that.

Grandmothers don't have to do anything except to be there. They're old so they shouldn't play hard or run. It is enough if they drive us to the market where the pretend horse is, and have a lot of dimes ready. Or if they take us for walks, they should slow down past things like pretty leaves and caterpillars. They should never say, "Hurry up."

Usually grandmothers are fat, but not too fat to tie your shoes. They wear glasses and funny underwear. They can take their teeth and gums off.

Grandmothers don't have to be smart, only answer questions like, "Why isn't God married?" and "How come dogs chase cats?"

Grandmothers don't talk baby talk like visitors do, because it is hard to understand. When they read to us they don't skip, or mind if it is the same story over again.

Grandmothers are very important. Grandmothers are the hub of the sacred hoop. They are beacons of light saying, "This is where you are going."

—Mahisha

Everybody should try to have a grandmother, especially if you don't have television, because they are the only grown-ups who have time.

❂

The Elders-Walk-Among-Us Staff is a part of our every ceremony. It is a walking stick. It was itself a horse and calls for the free spirit of all children. It is brought to a place of honor in the Circle and says to all who know, "The First Mother sits among us." She is the womb of all children, and she always sits among us. She reminds us to say "Thank You" to our ancestors before us. She reminds us to ask for their wisdom to dream us awake and sleeping. She reminds us that the way in which we treat our elders is the way in which we will be treated when we come into our age of wisdom. For those who patronize the old ones, there exists the sin of wasting hundreds and hundreds of years of wisdom. For those who honor our elders, there is the come-back of abundant living.

Among our lineage there is a hierarchy of respect that is never to be violated. Grandmother Alinta is our Elder. She is in her mid-fifties, a full-blooded Aboriginal. We call her "Grandmother" to respect her wisdom. When Grandmother Kitty came, Grandmother Alinta called her "Grandmother," for Kitty is in her sixties. Both Grandmother Kitty and Grandmother Alinta behaved like giggling teens when Grandmother Moon Feathers made an appearance. She is over 100 years old. If one is only one minute older, that one is the elder. It is an old tradition, that the buck stops with the eldest Elder. The final word is given by the eldest Elder (unless they defer to another). This line of respect preserves our basic principles, and curbs the unleashing of egos out-of-control. Among our elders, our women reign sovereign. Though the men and their medicine often take positions of leadership it is the choice of our women to have it be so. Always, the women have the final word. The decision of the men must support the well-being of the children and the tribal unity. In days of old, the old women could slit the throat of the chief who led the people into paths of sorrow. No one would bat an eye at the life taken in the night. Often the old women would sit stoically behind the old chiefs as they smoked their pipes and made deals with the white eyes. Their sobriety indicated their threat: "Decide

The final word is given by the eldest Elder (unless she defers to another). This line of respect preserves our basic principles and curbs the unleashing of egos out-of-control.

—Cloud

30

for our people's vision, or you will walk with the Death Angel." It is good to honor our elders.

During our week-long women's encampment, we honored our elders. Our first fire circle honored The Circle. Our second fire honored our elders. We gave gifts to each of them. Our gifts were songs we had written and recorded for them. We gave chants that honor their wisdom. We offered prayers that they travel long and in good health. The children gave gifts and one among us performed the old dance of the Macaw, known to be the medicine bird of one of the oldest societies of women elders. When the circle comes together, it is good to honor the elders.

HONORING OUR CHILDREN

*Children, do it as Spirit
divines to do it.*

—Grandmother Kitty

Most know that our elder Brother Jesus displayed His anger at the tables of the money changers who defiled His Provider's Temple. Few know that He was even more angry at His own disciples over their disrespect for children. His temple siege was a yelling type of anger. His anger at his own disciples boiled deep and leaked through His teeth. It happened in the presence of many people. The children had gathered very close to hear His wonderful stories. The pious disciples grumbled at the children and implied that they should stay away from the Great One. They blamed the mothers and wanted them to take charge of their offspring. Our Brother Friend spoke as if to say "READ MY LIPS." Then with the control that is known by one who flares his nostrils, He said, "The Circle that I speak of is known by the children. If you (adults) will join in their understanding, you will be as they are. You will surrender to their leadership, for they alone know the way." It is good to honor the children.

John Bradshaw, specialist on healing the inner child, tells us that ninety-six percent of the families in this country are dysfunctional. Within these families the children often bear the brunt of a wide range of wounding experiences — from the horror of physical or sexual abuse to the more insidious violations of emotional belittlement and the erosion of a child's sense of self. He states, "I believe that this neglected, wounded inner child of the past is the major source of human misery."*

---

*From *Homecoming: Reclaiming and Championing Your Inner Child*, Bantam Books, 1990.

Within the tribal hoop, children were held sacred. One would never think of interfering with the course of a child's natural curiosity and skills. Tribal roles were each considered important to the wholeness of the Circle and respect was given to each role. Chief, weather-maker, story-teller, scout, medicine sage, whip-carrier, drum-maker, drum-keeper, food-bearers, criers of news, hunters, warriors, lance-bearers, pipe-carriers, gathers — all were respected ranks in the Circle. There was much space for natural urges. It was known that humans must feel all of their feelings, and feelings are as diverse as the temperaments of the winds. It was known that disease was always a withholding of deep emotions.

When colonization crushed the matriarchal influence held in the Tribal Circles and replaced it with the smaller patriarchal units, natural urges were turned to dust. The people's hearts were deeply wounded. We have been systematically repressing our emotions for hundreds of years. Our emotions have been shamed.

When we express anger, we have been hit or abandoned or told, "What's the matter with you, talking like that?" Or, when we're sad, we have been punished and told, "Stop crying or I'll give you something to cry about." Or we have been shamed for feeling fear: "What's the matter with you, you big sissy." Or when we have been joyful, we have been shamed: "Don' get too excited. It won't last forever." As adults, we carry a shamed and wounded child around that is easily accessed with the look on the face of a lover or the tone of a boss' voice. Until we heal our wounded child, lost in the divided Circle, we will wander the straight road that leads from life to death. Within the Circle, we can walk the Red Road that leads us from life to life. It is good to honor the children.

A common message that runs through the testimony of those who walk the Red Road of Spirit is that childhood is a time of great receptivity to the Divine. It is also a time of grave vulnerability to family and other cultural influences. Alice Miller, psychoanalyst and author, suggests "we must regard our children not as creatures to manipulate or to change, but rather as messengers from a world we once deeply knew but which we have long since forgotten, who can reveal to us more about the true secrets of life, and also our own lives, than our parents were ever able to." We are beginning to believe children when they tell

I just wish every girl in the world would come and spend just one week here. It would make her stronger. She would find her self-esteem. She would find her courage. She would find the strength to live 100 years.

—Princess Moon
Feather
(Speaking about children and women's circles.)

My life is devoted to all children, I make playgrounds for the child in everyone.

—Cloud

us they have been abused. Let us also believe them when they tell us of their talks with the angels. It is good to honor the children.

Horse hair waved over the heads of little children is a demonstration of family affection for those little ones. When horse hair appears on sacred objects or is held in sacred bundles, it is a reminder of the Law of Seven Generations; a law that knows our current teenagers to be the children of our ancestors, back seven generations; a law that sees this new breed of children as those who will help us return to the Good Red Road of walking in balance upon our Mother Earth; a law that requires that in all things we plan for a better world for the children out seven generations in front of us. When a tree is cut down, it is told that its life will help make a better world for future generations. When the young willow sapling gives itself as a rib of the sweating lodge, it is told that children out seven generations will have a deep reverence and respect for tree spirits as a result of the many prayers and sacred teachings that will occur in the lodge. The little tree is given great reverence and respect for its willingness to give itself for the building of the sweating lodge. Its spirit is told of these intentions and given time to step outside the little tree before the hatchet comes to it. Its spirit is then invited to live in the little sweating lodge and hear the good prayers said there. In the building of the lodge, the little tree spirit is told of the special position of north, south, east or west and how that little tree will be a welcoming gate for all the invisibles from those directions. Little children are taught these things and so they learn to respect all of life.

Little children are made welcome at all manner of ceremony so that they might learn to reverence life. They are taught never to interrupt an elder or speak in a dishonoring way. They are taught to listen, both to the talk of the elders and to their own familiar-voice. At a very early age children are taught to recognize their own familiar-voice, knowing that the familiar-voice never forbids or compels. Children learn that their familiar-voice identifies truth, but never demands that one act on truth. The children learn to make choices and that choice-making is the most sacred act of all. The children come to learn that selective power is theirs alone and is for the purpose of spirit growth. The children come to learn that they must not only ask their own questions, but also answer those questions. The time between youth-seasons and the warrior passes quickly, but in the span of a lifetime, it is the most important. The Grandmothers say so. It is good to honor the children, for all generations in front depend on it.

Children are taught to go to the old people and hear the legends. "Make good use of what these old ones know," say the Grandmothers. "Guard your tongue as a child and in maturity you will think thoughts that will be useful to your people." "What puzzles you will drive you to mastery, and what is a mystery is only something natural that you do not yet understand. What you need to understand will come to you when you are ready to live the answer." All of these things, the Grandmothers say. "Find one with whom you dare to present your uncertainty and from whom you will receive advice. Confide in this person and call them 'Mother,' 'Father,' 'Grandmother,' 'Grandfather,' 'Uncle' or 'Aunt.' Respect these guides with your own good reputation so that they may feel pride in you." These things, also, the Grandmothers say. They say that children who cannot hold their tongues at home most likely will bring enemies into the Circle when they are older. Brave children are taught that whatever they fear in the dark, also fears them. They are taught not to fear the dark, the truth or the search for truth.

Early on the child is taught staying power; to endure pain, thirst, cold, mockery, and then the crowds would come to cheer them. But what crowd will cheer one who allows his morals to be defiled and her spirit to be corrupted?

Children are taught to be one with the trees and listen to the language of the sky. They are taught to view their possessions as something that they hold in readiness for the giving to those who are less fortunate. The child is taught that each one owns an important place in the Circle and that none will stand in the way of a different other. These things, the Grandmothers say, are important to teach our children.

Today it seems that very few children know where they came from. Their folklore is lost or at best shared in some simple holiday celebrations. Folklore is at the heart of self-expression and, therefore, at the very heart of self-acceptance. If our children do not know where they came from, how can they know where they are going?

Alice Walker, in "Living by the Word," writes of white children today who were raised by black people. These children knew their first all-accepting love from black women and then, at the age of twelve or so, were told to "forget" the deep levels of

Center life around children. All adults are responsible for children. [In our culture] children choose who they want to live with. First bring children up to respect themselves.

—Alinta

communication between themselves and the "Mammy" they came to love. Most of our Indian elders were educated out of their language and ways, leaving us to make the return journey to the Good Red Road in isolation from the teachings of our ancestors. Traditions have been tainted and changed so that nothing remains of the basic soul connection to Spirit, a connection that was well-known to most children before the age of shame.

For centuries the Native American fathers of our country lived on the land, making love to her through worship and praise, without raping and defiling this mother. Black Elk once said, "It is the story of all life that is holy and is good to tell, and of us two-leggeds sharing in it with the four-leggeds and the wings of the air and all green things; for these are children of one mother and their father is one Spirit." It is good to honor the children.

MAKING MUSIC

I, Cloud, am a professional songwriter, singer and entertainer. Skye has the voice of an angel. We both have had the opportunity to study with the famous Arthur Joseph of Los Angeles. Arthur is the voice coach of many great singers, actors and actresses in the industry. He is a gentle and genuine man. "In order for people to make music, they must be very clear in their emotions." Thus begins Arthur in our first vocal lesson; a lesson that left us both in tears. In the most sensitive of ways, Arthur begins his "vocal lessons" with a penetrating look into female abuse and how it has inhibited expression. Before the first session is over, we have seen our own vocal chords for the first time. Much to our amazement, our vocal cords look exactly like our own feminine genitals. Arthur made a particular point of saying that what goes into our mouth and down our throat passed by this very sensitive and beautiful instrument. This awareness, more than any other, called for my own cessation of smoking cigarettes and calling forth the spirit of my own music.

Barbara Walker points out that very old Eastern traditions make the female voice an important symbol of creation and the source of the original word of creation which the Greeks and Christians termed "Logos." It was a feminine voice that spoke into the void. It was the sweet voice of a mother who called forth life. It was a woman who uttered the first sound which collected light unto itself. It was First Mother who called us into form.

Each person prepares their own song . . . what song do you want to sing? Prepare a song that comes from spirit to you.

—Grandmother Kitty

In the beginning was thought, and her name was Woman. The Mother, the Grandmother, was recognized from earliest times into the present among those peoples of the Americas who kept to the eldest traditions. . . . . . . To her we owe our lives, and from her comes our ability to endure, regardless of the years of colonization. She is the Old Woman who tends the fires of life. She is the Old Woman Spider who weaves us together in a fabric of interconnection. She is the Eldest God, the one who Remembers and Re-members; and though the history of the past five hundred years has taught us bitterness and helpless rage so that we endure into the present, alive, certain of our significance, certain of her centrality, her identity as the Sacred Hoop of Be-ing. (Paula Gunn Allen, *The Sacred Hoop: Recovering the Feminine in American Indian Traditions*, Beacon Press, Boston, 1986)

As little children, we learn speech from our mother. It is her sweet voice that shapes the world of our mind. She is the Mother voice, likened to the wind, blowing from heaven and bringing the essence of soul to all things. From her voice we learn beauty above, beauty below and beauty all around. According to early Vedic sages, Vac was Her name. Vac was the First, the Queen, the greatest of all deities. The early Hebrew mythology has a type of Vac in the female deity Bath Kal or "Daughter of the Voice." In biblical times She was known as the divine afflatus, source of the prophets' inspiration; a precious voice of God, mysteriously female. (Barbara Walker, *The Woman's Dictionary of Symbols and Sacred Objects*, Harper, San Francisco, 1988)

In Gnostic literature, the female Logos said, "I am the Mother of the Voice, speaking in many ways, completing the ALL. It is in me that knowledge dwells, the knowledge of things everlasting. It is I who speak within every creature. . . . I am the womb that gives shape to the ALL by giving birth to the light that shines in splendor. I am the Aeon to come. I am the fulfillment of the ALL that is Meirothea, the glory of the Mother. I cast a Sound of voice into the ears of those who know me." (J. M. Robinson, *Pagan*

Christs, NYU Books, N.Y., 1967, pp. 466-467)

Each time I have heard the voice of God speak, separate from my own familiar voice, She has been feminine. It is with the voice of Creation, First Mother, that we begin the making of music. Our voice, molded in her image, is our first, and always our most significant instrument of music.

All of creation is given its own unique sound, for its very existence came from the well-spring of music. The musical sounds of the lyres are said to have initiated the very birth of the universe. It is said that the seven string lyres were directly connected to the heavens. The spheres produce seven distinct tones. This septenary number is the nucleus of all that exists. The seven harmonizing notes are given off by the turning spheres, and each note is correlated with a sung vowel sound. These harmonies are known as the Music of the Spheres, and were credited with the power to keep the universe in existence. (Barbara Walker, *The Women's Dictionary of Symbols and Sacred Objects*)

It is said that rattles were used in the process of creation. They represent the sound of the mingling of the elements in the birthing

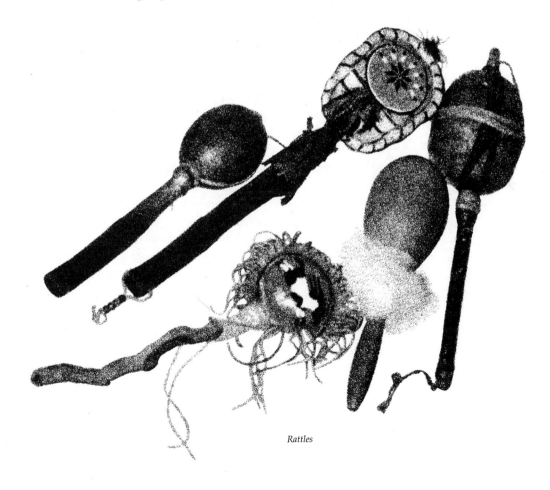

Rattles

Dance, for me, connects all things, all people, all time. By coming through the heart and movement of spirit, I experience boundlessness.

—Mahisha

of the world. Today rattles are used to dispel evil spirits and scare away meddlesome invisibles. Like the warning of the rattlesnake, the rattle sings out that only what is good for the whole shall gather. Rattles literally "shake down the energy." They chase away all that would disrupt. They are always found around the circle of ceremony and very often at the center of healing.

Our Uncle Bear Heart first taught us about the making of a singing gourd. When he first went to his grandfather and asked for a "singing gourd," he expected to be given a rattle immediately. However, the process took more than a year. First his grandfather had him pick out that type of gourd he liked best. Then they gathered the seeds of that gourd and readied them for the planting season. Together he and his grandfather tilled and made the ground ready to receive the seed. When the moon was right, they made their prayers and gave their offering unto the Mother Earth. They prayed for the sun and rain to come to nurture their little seed. Each day after the planting they returned to sing to the little seed and send it a voice to comfort and call forth. Together they watched as the ground cracked and the little plant began to peek through into the light. Each day his grandfather spoke of growth and love and tenderness. He showed Bear Heart how brave the little plant was to push through the ground towards the light when it was so small. He told him how the little plant felt vulnerable to the rabbits that came to eat in the garden and showed him how to protect the little plant until it was big enough to fend for itself. Bear Heart and his grandfather watched over the little plant every day, observing each new growth. He remembers how exciting it was when his gourd plant began to sprout little blossoms and then tiny little gourds began to form. As each gourd grew, it took on its own unique shape and Bear Heart and his grandfather would make a game of guessing which gourd would be the special "singing gourd."

When at last that day came to pick the most special gourd, Bear Heart knew exactly which gourd wanted to "sing for him." Together they made a prayer telling the spirit of the gourd that this little gourd would sing around many circles and asking the spirit of the gourd to guide them in bringing its song to life. It seemed like an eternity before the little gourd was dry enough to make into a rattle. Little Bear Heart dreamed night and day about the design he would paint onto his rattle. At last the day came to make the first holes in the gourd, the holes that would receive the handle. His grandfather explained how the seeds of his gourd would be saved to make more gourds for others.

After the gourd was opened and the seeds removed, Bear Heart's grandfather took him to collect 100 singing grasshoppers to give song to his gourd. Very carefully they poured water into the grasshoppers' holes in the earth, tricking them into believing that it was raining. When they came up to sing in the storm, Bear Heart and his grandfather would catch them and bring them to the gourd. One by one they put the singing grasshoppers into the little gourd and let them sing out their song. After 100 grasshoppers had visited the little gourd with their song, the gourd was ready to be painted and receive its own singing stones. These were gathered from the mounds of large ants. Bear Heart and his grandfather spoke to the ant people and told them about the making of music. After they had explained exactly how each little ant rock would be used in ceremony, they carefully selected 100 of the finest ant rocks they could find. They left food for the ants, in exchange for the stones. Bear Heart then spent days painting his little gourd. At last, the ant rocks were carefully placed inside the gourd, where they waited for the handle to be carved.

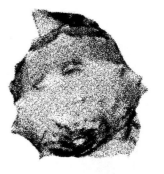

Calling Conches

Finding just the right stick for the handle provided Bear Heart and his grandfather several days of fun walking in the woods. Since this was Bear Heart's first carving, it took several more days before Bear Heart had successfully carved and polished his gourd handle. It was such an exciting moment when the handle was perfectly fitted into its receiving holes and laced to his beautiful gourd.

When, at long last, Bear Heart took his little rattle in hand and began to tap out his favorite "thank you" song, he knew the truth of music. All things sing, and together they make the music of creation. He now, for the first time, knew himself to be Creator. Here at the center he stood with his rattle, giving his strength to the rhythm and song of his heart. From the center of his heart, out through the gourd, out onto the wind, and back again to his ears and into his heart, he created music. So it is with all things.

No ceremony or ritual is complete without music. From the call of the conch to the final beat of the drum, music is the energy that moves the circle.

It is said that the drum was once the very center of the Catholic Church until it became associated with pagan rites and was banned from worship. In this way, the very heart beat of spirit was removed from religion. Today, more and more groups are picking up the drum of spirit and giving music to the beating of our own hearts and the heartbeat of our blessed Mother Earth. Beautiful flutes are singing the sounds of the elements and the birds, while horns and bells speak to the waters, the wind and the creatures of nature. In the way of our childhood, we may now say, "Sticks and stones may break my bones or else they'll sing my song." We envision the day when little children, teens and adults alike carry some musical instrument in their pockets so that they can spontaneously praise nature or join in a rock concert to celebrate life on our Good Mother. May all the sticks and stones that have broken bones and hearts become rhythm instruments to praise our Maker. May all the metals of the war mongers be honored by becoming bell gardens for children to play their music. Let us see our children dancing on earth drums built like trampolines on the earth. Let them run gleefully through bell gardens making music with their sticks and the remolded remains of bomb casings. Let the sounds of the city air sing out in praise of life. Let the music begin. Let every ceremony be conscious of the power of sound in creation. In the beginning there was a Tone, and the Tone became Light, and the Light became All-That-Is. Let the music play in all ceremony until all hearts beat as One.

Just as First Born emerged from quivering mud to the rhythm of her own heart, so each person knows the true rhythm. Some discover the true power in song, the power for making spiritual contact. However, before any become true seers, they shall recognize themselves as fit controlling powers, as people who own the earth with their love. Then the true song will render up its power and with music we shall re-create our Paradise on Earth.

Sing to renew weary hands at work. Sing to keep safe the many as they move together to new heights. Sing to blend One heart with the many. Sing out that we might be One. Sing as you make something. Sing to quiet the spirits and attract what you want. Sing as the sacred object is being made that will hold the people together. Sing when the people's food is being prepared. Sing into all things the great love of God flowing through heart, hands and voice. Make music. In all things, make music.

THE MAKING
OF PRAYERS AND
PRAYER BUNDLES

"Great Mystery! Hear me! I am Cloud. I send out my voice gratefully in four directions. Hear me! You are my Mother and my Father. Hear me! I am relative to all who swim, fly, walk or crawl. From the very beginning of my being, all of me relates to each different creature on earth and beyond. My heart, my head, my hands, my arms, legs and feet, all serve all-my-relations. I and they recognize One Great Mystery. You are in all things. *Taku skanskan*! You are spiritual vitality. You are love! I am Cloud and I will speak!

"I clasp hands with all of creation. My words travel to the ears of the All-That-Is from my heart. I speak with gratitude for your great love that brings me into direct relationship with all things. I show my obedience to your divine law by my deep respect for each thing on earth.

"I stand with the Great One, Jesus, and acknowledge his act of love that profits me this audience at your throne. I follow His example and His heed: 'Believe as a little child. Become again as a little child.' I come to this place at the Center as a little child. See my good intentions and know of my devotion for our children out seven generations.

"When I am off the mark, forgive me and align me again on the path of the sacred arrow to the heart of truth. Do this for me as I am willing to do it for myself and others. Let my head be small enough to wear the many hats that are passed to me each day. Let my feet fit easily into the moccasins of all my relations that walk on this earthly star path.

Talk from the heart is sacred wherever it happens...

—Mahisha

"Stand me tall in the presence of both friends and enemies. Hold back my tongue when my words would bring imbalance. Let me speak always to spin the sacred spiral that brings together all things in perfect harmony.

"Keep strong the sweet aroma of my heart's fire burning, until that day when I am finished with your work on earth and you call me home. And, when that great day comes, bring me home singing.

"I stand center in your presence, which is far more precious than all of your many names. Let the giving of our gifts be the vehicle for your miracles here in this land of many gifts. Spirit Divine, flow through me unhampered by confusions and indecision.

"I seek my own power, not the power of a spirit helper. Recognize me as woman. Recognize me as a reasoning power. Recognize me as a healing power. Let me renew those who come seeking my touch. Recognize me as a generating power, creating in your own image. I shall keep my spirit in readiness and know my own spirit to be my greatest ally . . . the only reliable ally I shall ever know. I will expand my heart to let your Great Spirit in, and thus be the example of Oneness on earth. Let me know the power that is Peace . . . and share it in every breath. Grandmother! Grandfather! I send you my voice. Hear me! From this earth, with your breath, I send a voice. I live! I live! I am Cloud. In deep gratitude, I have spoken! Ho!"

Such is my prayer today as I write, having outlived doctors predictions of imminent death due to terminal cancer . . . cancer they can no longer find. God answers prayers! Not until the tears from the very depths of my soul had warmed my cheeks and soaked my breast did I regain balance. Not until I had wept all of my tears did I understand their quickening power, a power that shuts off the twisted thoughts that create dis-ease in the first place. Just as a lifeguard is able to distinguish the cry of anguish from all the sounds of surf and sunny beach play, so God is able to hear the cries of one who calls for help.

On January 7, 1991, I discovered a "growth" the size of a half-dollar inside my right arm pit. It seemed to appear out of nowhere. Warned that it could be cancerous, I instantly changed my diet, climate, activity schedule and work orientation. I moved to Florida to run on the beach for awhile. I wanted time to "be with this unusual growth." It seemed to shrink over the months, as I prayed and asked my Dream Walker to direct me toward healing. One night I dreamed a red-headed surgeon who was to remove the "growth." A few days later I happened by the clinic of a country surgeon who welcomed walk-ins. The surgeon was, of course, red-readed.

On the morning of July 3rd I entered a Daytona hospital to have the growth removed with day surgery. That morning I had run four miles on the beach. That afternoon the surgeon was telling my family that I had two months to live. "Make my day, Doc!" Something certainly seemed wrong with this picture. I was the picture of health and felt fine. However, "denial" is not a river in Egypt! I had to consider the possibility of walking the Spirit Trail soon. I let the possibility sink in. . . . all the way in to the depth of my being. It was then that I knew that it wasn't the truth. However, my family would not be satisfied without medical proof. I endured the dehumanizing tests to find the "mother node." Nothing! Two months later the Cancer Center in Oklahoma discovered that I had been mis-diagnosed. Instead of Cancer A (which is fatal) I had Cancer B (which is not only fatal, but untreatable). That's been three years ago. To the medical community, I'm one of those miracles. To me, I am Cloud, a child of the Great Provider, in touch with All Knowing. In Dream Time, my recently deceased uncle came to me, escorted by an angel, and told me, "Your departure date has been extended indefinitely." To this day I believe the "growth" to be the result of a leech bite I received in Australia almost exactly two years earlier. Above all else, my "growth" helped me do just that—grow. It is easy in life to capitalize on one's gains. However, it takes something very special to profit from one's losses. I have touched humility and learned forgiveness. It was during this time that I learned the "other half of praying"—listening.

J. Edgar Hoover once said, "The spectacle of a nation praying is more awe-inspiring that the explosion of an atomic bomb. The force of prayer is greater than any possible combination of man-made or man-controlled powers, because prayer is man's greatest means of tapping the infinite resources of God." Isaac Newton, one the greatest scientists who ever lived, said, "I can take my telescope and look millions and millions of miles into space; but I can lay my telescope aside, go to my room and shut the door, get down on my knees in earnest prayer, and see more of heaven and get closer to God than I can when assisted by all the telescopes

When I sit in one place repeating thanks, I deny myself expansion. Once is enough.

—Cloud

and material agencies on earth." Dr. T. Bulkley once addressed the British Medical Association in these words. "As a doctor and one whose whole life has been concerned with sufferings of the mind, I would state that of all the hygienic measures to counteract disturbed sleep, depression of the spirits and all the miserable sequels of the disturbed mind, I would undoubtedly give first place to the simple habit of prayer." Dr. Joseph Parker once said, "You can tell when a person ceases to pray. A face grows in vulgarity that does not commune with God day by day. It loses beauty. A person's countenance witnesses against them. There is an invisible sculptor that chisels the face into the attitude of the soul."

A simple Mr. Rogers once said, "Prayer is the greatest unused power in the world, and faith is the greatest undiscovered resource." The quickest way to get people on their feet is to first get them on their knees. A preacher once complained to a stone mason, "I wish I could deal such changing blows on the stoney hearts of my sheep." The simple stone mason replied, "Maybe you could if you worked like me . . . on your knees."

The Bible proclaims, "Before they call, I will answer; and while they are yet speaking, I will hear." So, how is it that prayer is so often the last resort when all else fails? A story is told about Alexander the Great. It seems that a simple courtier dared to approach him and ask for financial aid. The great leader told him to go to the treasurer and ask for whatever amount he wanted. A short time later, the treasurer appeared and told Alexander the man had asked for an enormous sum. He, of course, hesitated to give out so much money. "Give him what he asks for," replied the great conqueror. "He has treated me like a king in his asking and I shall be like a king in my giving!" The greatness of our Provider is such that no request is too much. How grieved must be our Provider in the face of the smallness of our requests.

When we pray holding the good of the Tribe in our hands, we tap into a well-spring of resources. "Owning the camp" is owning in spirit, love and intention to care for the needs of the whole. That which is in harmony with the whole and in synchronicity with what benefits the Hoop of the All-That-Is is an easy order to fill from Control Room Central. What difference if one person's truth walks them tall and another person's truth bows their heads and bends their knees, as long as none interfere with the course of another. We are each a single mystery inside the Great Mystery.

Pray always that spirit will hold the rope for you.

—Kactus

We are each a knowing in touch with All-Knowing. We are each a body living within a soul that touches all things. This is where the truth lies. Let us throw away harsh thoughts of one another and pray for peace on earth.

Peoples everywhere pray with different rituals. The Native Americans often pray with the pipe, allowing the pipe to soothe and bring a person's thoughts back to the people . . . the people as a whole. In passing the pipe, it is possible to regain calm and wait for all hearts present to beat as one heart. The sweet tobacco blend is the horse that rides the breath of our thoughts spiralling up and out to touch the ears of the Provider. The sweet smoke makes visible the breath that owns the soul of the prayer. The sweet smell attracts the invisible spirits of the assisting ancestors and calls attention to the one who prays. The sweet tobacco blends with the All-That-Is and enjoins the support of the universe. We buy with our attention, exactly what we pay attention to. The ritual of prayer through sweet smoke holds the attention of the one who prays, and attracts many others to turn their attention to the One. A good question to ask as we pray is, "What will I buy with my attention today?" This is a good question to ask ourselves throughout the day and night. A prayer is money in the universe. "Ask and you will receive," whether that asking be conscious or unconscious.

The Aboriginal elders pray with the sweet smell of eucalyptus leaves on a fire. This smell of the sweet fire awakens the breath within and the elder without. The island peoples pray with the sweet smell of flowers. Three times they will join their breath with that of the fragrant island flowers. Three times they will send their floral scented voice to the Great Spirit. Then, they will hold their prayers secret in their hearts until they are answered. The sweet fragrance has the effect of glorifying God with sweetness and catching the attention of the Great One, amidst all the other prayers sent.

Catholics pray with frankincense and myrrh and the Baptists line their churches with pretty flowers.

The world over, ritual and prayer are formalized to entrain the hearts of people and attract the consensus attention of the spirits.

Sometimes the Universe must rearrange many things before fulfilling an order. Several years ago I traveled to Ohaua to learn from an emcee named Johnny. He blended a multi-cultural show at a Hilton Hotel in Hawaii. He was the first person I ever saw play a nose flute. Not since have I heard a sweeter or purer sound. I instantly sent forth a prayer for a nose flute. Some three years later I returned to the Big Island to host a week-long seminar. As usual, I invited some of the "locals" to share their sacred ecology with us. A beautiful Hawaiian dancer came with her troop. It is traditional among native peoples to honor any elder and a holy person with a gift of tobacco. It is a way of saying: "Your prayers are for the good of the people and I wish to see your prayers made solid with smoke and sweet smells. Your breath is God's breath." Not knowing the tradition of the islands, I decided to gift my guest in a similar fashion. The difference was that I chose to give something from a place far from the Islands; something that could not easily be obtained by the "locals." My gift was a beautiful little box of pure amber. My new friend was so deeply moved by my act that she shed tears of joy. During her sacred ceremony she played a most beautiful nose flute. I remembered my prayer of years back; however, I held it secret in my heart. As our guests were leaving to board the boat that brought them into our remote location, my guest hesitated in the sand. She seemed to listen for a brief moment. Then she reached into her bag, turned and presented me with her own nose flute! "This is for you, Cloud!" she gleefully announced. We both embraced with tears of joy, for we had both heard the voice of God speak. God answers prayers in a way far more beautiful than we can imagine. Often I think of some Divine Commander-in-Chief perched at a Control Center in the sky. When our prayers are registered at Control Room Central, a specific scout is sent to purview the entire galactic kingdom to find the most perfect fit to our prayer. Sometimes it takes longer than is comfortable for us, but always the result is worth the wait. Whatever one needs or wants to know, the Unknowable Mystery sooner or later reveals, and that which we call "mystery" is only natural when, at last, we come to understand.

Almost all medicine togs, tools and toys are made of prayers. A medicine bag to some is like rosary prayer beads to a Catholic. The love, intention and attention of the creator is put into any medicine bundle, making the object a living prayer. Each time the object is used in ceremony or worn, the prayer and the attention it sends is re-activated. My own specific Prayer Bundle was inspired by the late Grandfather Frank Fools Crow and his life of powerful prayer and devotion.

Cloud's Prayer Bundle

The throwing cloth is green like the Mother Earth. A golden circle is sewn onto the green cloth to remember the great hoop of the All-That-Is. A blue circle with a golden plus mark sits in the center. The blue remembers Sky Father, as the green remembers Earth Mother. The golden plus remembers the life of devotion lived by the Morning Star, Jesus. A golden circle sits in the east of the golden hoop, to remember the gateway of the east and the people of the east. God bless the yellow people. A red circle sets on the south of the golden hoop to remember the gateway of the south and the people of the south. God bless the red people. A black circle sits on the west of the golden hoop to remember the gateway of the west and the people of the west. God bless the black people. A white circle sits on the north of the golden hoop to remember the gateway of the north and the people of the north. God bless the white people. On the backside of the throwing cloth is a white cloud smiling — to remember myself as the Center, woman, made in the image of God.

When I pray, sweet grass and sage are burned around the circle. Soft chanting and flute playing still my spirit and the spirits of those invisibles who gather to witness my calling. I begin by placing a small doll made in my own childhood image in the center of the golden hoop. In this way I remember myself to be a child of the Creator. I remember myself to stand always at the Center. At the east gate I place a centering stone passed on to me from my Grandmother. It once belonged to an elder man of medicine. I think of the east gate as having strong male energy. To the south I place a recorder crystal given to me by my Grandmother. It reminds me that the greatest wisdom is held in the hearts of our children, and to our children goes much honor. I think of the south as the place of the child. To the west I place a "story-telling family of carved rocks." A Jewish grandmother gifted me these story-telling rocks. I think of the west as the place of the feminine. These rocks remind me of family. To the north I place a small rock that is 400 million years old. It reminds me of the wisdom of the grandmothers and the grandfathers. I think of the north as the place of the grandparents. When I look around the hoop, I see all of life, male and female. I see perfect balance. It is within this point of balance that I place my attention. From this place of balance, I buy my life.

Sometimes I pray with a black blindfold on so that I can see the Creator's images for me more clearly. I sit quietly and watch on the blank screen of my Strong Eye. Sometimes I pray with my eyes open, looking from object to object. Sometimes I wear a clown mask made of soft, white deer skin. When I wear this mask to pray, I usually want something very special and I wish to attract the Creator as a seductive little child. These are times of having fun with God. Sometimes I turn the image that is me to one of the directions in search of some specific learning. Sometimes I lay the image of my face down on the Mother. In times like these, I come mostly to listen and feel. Sometimes I place the image that is me looking up. On these occasions I come mostly to watch. Always, I am taken back to my childhood when everything was possible. By the time I get my bundle all laid out, sweetened and sung to, I am a child again. Then talking with God is as intimate as it was when I was a child in the swamp.

Most of my medicine togs, tools and toys have their own beautiful medicine bag to live in. I am careful to return each thing to its place so that each thing has a living experience of my respect and appreciation. This is good training for how to treat all things. My Prayer Bundle is the only sacred tool that lives in an ordinary fanny pack. I like to take my Prayer Bundle with me many places, and my orange and black fanny pack can "pass as white" anywhere! Once I thought to make a beautiful sacred bag for this Bundle, but my Bundle enjoys our masquerade as much as I do. Having fun with prayer is powerful, enjoyable and exciting.

Always I am met. Always my heart enlarges to embrace any situation with love. Each time I spread my Bundle to pray, I recall our Brother's advice: "become again as a little child and thus inherit the kingdom of heaven."

RITUAL CLEANSING

The Lodge of the Sun Dog is the name of our newest sweating lodge. This Stone People Lodge is built in the Cheatham Wildlife Reserve in Tennessee. When the final rib was fastened into place, a Sun Dog* appeared in the sky. There had been no rain for days and none in the forecast. The sky was totally clear, holding no clouds. The Sun Dog appeared toward dusk, the sun already tree high on the horizon. The circular rainbow window of light came out of nowhere and lingered for a full five minutes over our lodge. A large shaft of white light shot from the north gate of the rainbow window, reminding us of the prophecy regarding our ancestors. The Sun Dog is a rare, but natural, phenomenon, which is visible to those who will see in these last days of old forms falling away. It has been told that when we see the Sun Dogs appear with the sun we know that our ancestors have returned in white bodies and red hearts to teach the old ways. It is a time to share medicine with all who come to learn. Our Stone People's Sweating Lodge named itself with this strong omen: The Lodge of the Sun Dog.

The sweat lodge, or Stone People's Lodge, is a very old form of purification. It is a global tradition among indigenous peoples. A dome structure is built with a pit inside. After the structure is adequately covered to hold heat, hot rocks are brought into the lodge, where they become the source of steam. Water is put to the hot rocks, creating a simple but highly effective sweating house. In virtually all illness, sweating is prescribed as a means of purification.

*A sun dog is a full-rainbow circle around the sun that has bright white lights at the Four Directions.

The degree of ritual brought to the sweating lodge varies. To the plains Indians, the sweating lodge ceremony, or *inipi*, is basic to almost all types of passage ceremonies. Before the dances-with-the-sun ceremony one enters the *inipi* and clears away the old before entering the sacred sun-dancing circle. Marriage, visioning, naming, adoption (*hunkayapi*), warring, deciding, creating, planting, traveling, harvesting and countless other life activities are cause for ritual purification.

It is good to clear and clean the past before stepping with intention into the future. Is is good to pause with all past experiences, recognize their value, appreciate their value and let them go with blessings. In this way, no thing from the past is presented as an obstacle to forward movement. Ritual cleansing is a very old and accepted way of dealing with the past.

There are as many types of ritual cleansing as there are types of ceremonies. Even the baptism by water performed by the fundamentalists of the Christian faith is a type of cleansing from "sin" (which literally means "off the mark"). "Sin" is derived from the archer's sport of shooting for a bulls eye. The degree of "sin" is the degree that one's arrow is removed from the mark (bulls eye). Though we will share our preferred types of ritual

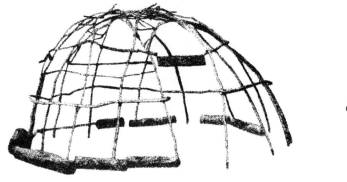

Clan Sweat Lodge

Tribal Sweat Lodge

*So, everybody, every night,
look into that mirror and say,
"I love me. I am precious."
Even to the point of saying,
"I'm the only person in the
world." That's the best
healing emotion of all. Then
you can get up in the morning
feeling ten feet tall and you can
do it and remain that small . . .
because humility comes with it
. . . humbleness comes with it
and that's the greatest weapon
too. If you're not humble and
your "I love me" goes to your
head . . . well, you'll come
down.*

*When you're humble, Mother
Earth will give you all.*

—Alinta

cleansing, it is important to note that the intention behind the action is what makes the ritual a cleansing. In these days of Spirit, each of us must attune with our own desires and reasonings to create meaningful cleansing. The simple act of washing one's clothes in a prayerful attitude may well be the most powerful of all ritual cleansing.

The sweating lodge ceremony is called by some the Stone People's Ceremony or the *Inipi*. Most who engage in the sweating lodge ceremony simply refer to their practice as a "sweat." It is a literal meaning, for that is exactly what happens in the ceremony. People sweat. Then they sweat some more. And, then they sweat some more. I have heard elders say that a couple of hours in a sweat lodge is worth ten days of fasting. I most certainly prefer sweating to fasting! To those who either smoke or drink, the sweat lodge is a bittersweet friend. It is painful to experience the alcohol and nicotine rising to the surface of the skin, and it is deeply cleansing to the system. Any illness that needs to be sweated out is so done in the sweat lodge. However, there are infinitely more valuable lessons to be gained from sweating.

Those who sweat have come together with a common purpose and agree to endure something beyond the normal comfort zone. They do so together. There is an intimacy in the lodge of circle sitters that may not exist outside. Some perform the sweat in scant or no clothes in order to truly experience rebirth. While newcomers to the ceremony (and especially those who think like whites) display concerns about having sexual feelings in the lodge, it is certain this will not happen. They quickly learn that sex is the farthermost thing from their minds. Survival is more the issue for the newcomer!

It can get very hot in the sweat lodge. That's the point: To sweat out the old and make room for the new. The host controls the degree of heat in the lodge. The host "pours water."

Sweating is particularly difficult for those who use alcohol. The alcohol tends to increase the body temperature and feels like deep burning in the skin. It is also very purifying to clear out the toxins of alcohol. The same is true for nicotine. The nicotine collects on the tongue during the sweat and is best scraped off immediately after coming out of the lodge. There is an old belief that one owes one year of service to the Great One as directed by the sweat leader, should one lack the endurance to stay for the traditional four "rounds" of rocks. Thus, if one is a drinker, it is best to be advised that much endurance is required to complete the sweat.

Entering a sweat lodge is very much a part of the ritual purification. When we pause at the door of the lodge . . . an opening that requires entry on hands and knees . . . it is good to have an open heart to the All-That-Is. We should not enter the lodge with grudges against anyone. The energy comes back on us in the sweat lodge and, if what is unsettled is put out in our energy field, we are bound to experience its maximum rebound. We usually pause at the door of the lodge, announce our names and make a statement that declares relatedness of all things. "*A Ho, Mitakuye Iyasin!*" is a widely used greeting and pronouncement for entering the sweating lodge. It is a Sioux phrase meaning "Greetings, All My Relations . . . I come in good relations." Entering the sweating lodge is akin to entering the womb of the Mother Earth, our true Mother. It is good to enter with a pure heart and a clear intention to live in the Truth.

The ritual that occurs in the lodge is highly individual and specific to the needs of the participants. However, it is fairly common to bring in four rounds of hot rocks. What is said and prayed in each of the four rounds is released with the opening of the door at the end of each round. The participants can easily see their prayers and what is released leave the lodge in the steam that rushes for the sky at the opening of the lodge cover.

To emerge from the sweating lodge clean, clear and renewed is akin to rebirth. Perhaps the ritual cleansing of the sweating

Learn from heart, not eyes.

—Alinta

Tribal Sweating Lodge

The greatest teacher is our own self, our own mind, heart and path. The greatest block is fear.

—Alinta

lodge is, in some ways, like the baptism by immersion of some Christians. It marks a renewal and beginning again, a time to change directions and turn towards the light.

There are many other forms of ritual cleansing. Even taking a shower or bath is considered a form of ritual cleansing that has been embraced by the New Age. However, bathing as ritual cleansing is as old as life itself. Ritual bathing is still widely used as a form of renewal. Very often, fresh, flowing water is preferred. Just as the pipe is smoked with definite attention to The Great Mystery, Mother Earth, all creatures, family, friends and self, so it is with ritual bathing. Water is thrown in response to each specific request or one submerges for each thing that is remembered in the ritual.

A beautiful form of ritual cleansing is one in which a bowl of scented water is passed around the circle. Each person has the opportunity to "wash their hands of the past" or wash their neighbor's feet to rid them of the "dust of weary travel" in life. This is a tender and sensitive way to welcome a group together and to prepare for the new experience of One-Heart-Beating in the circle. It is common to float flowers in the bowl of scented water so that all can see that beauty is truly everywhere.

Smoking or smudging is another common form of ritual cleansing. Sacred grasses and herbs are burned while the smoke is pulled or pushed with a feather around the person or object. It is common to wash one's hands in smoke after a day's "hunt," be it literal or figuratively. Sage, cedar, juniper and sweet grass are common grasses and foliage used to smoke or smudge. It is good to begin ceremony with a simple smudging of each participant, so they may release all that they have brought with them and become fully present in the moment. All objects to be used in ceremony are also smudged to clear them and awaken them to the function at hand. The sweet smell of smudging attracts the invisibles and reminds the visibles that something of importance is happening.

Other forms of ritual purification include a vast array of fasting rituals. One may fast from food, certain types of food, certain types of drink, thoughts of a specific nature, behaviors that are limiting, associations with persons heretofore associated with, activities that are too comfortable, sex or any other form that interferes with the specific purity that is desired.

Perhaps the most unique ritual purification in which I have participated was one we co-created to cleanse and clear old reactions and responses. Skye and I were completely alone in our ritual until the most outrageous moment.

We had spent the day making paper bag masks of our most repressed and unexpressed emotions. We each made five masks. When we were satisfied that our masks represented our true inner selves . . . we costumed, flooded our outdoor arena with night light, cranked our music to the max and began to dance awake our feelings. We danced separately and we danced together. We laughed and we cried. We moaned and we groaned. We screamed and yelled and we fell into silent stupors. We exhausted ourselves with our self-divined ritual, all the while thinking we were somewhat insulated from our behavior because our faces were hidden in our masks. Then, as fate would have it, some unsuspecting person wandered into our ritual space. To this day we do not know who it was, but we are certain that she left convinced that we were a lost cause.

We have laughed many times about this ritual and never have we had the guts to repeat it with others. However, this one act allowed us to open the door to some place heretofore untouched by another. The journey down that beautiful corridor continues to be one of life's most amazing dances.

Although there must be infinite ways of ritual purification, we have mentioned those most common, and an unusual one, so that our readers will feel free to commune directly with Spirit and receive rituals directly from the Source. These rituals are only for stimulating creation. One final form of ritual purification bears sharing: sound as a ritual purification.

If you have ever sat in a drumming circle for more than thirty minutes, and hopefully for hours, you know how cleansing it can be. All thoughts leave and all hearts begin to beat as One. It is common to use rattles to clear and clean one's etheric and emotional bodies. The finger cymbal or Tibetan bells are another form of clearing the larger body and bringing focus to thought and action. Today there are many types of bells, gongs, chimes, etc. available that clear the energy fields of the chakras. These "shamanic" tools are available through most New Age stores and many mail order catalogs. Some are even advertised in the tabloids at the market. It is said that first there was sound. Then there was light. Then there was form. "In the beginning there was Tone . . . and the Tone became . . . All-That-Is!"

The common qualities of people of greatness are:

the quiet knowingness of . . .

. . . I know who I am.

. . . I know where I'm going.

. . . I'm here to share.

—Colonel Lyn

CHAPTER 7

DANCING THE DANCE:
Life As a Ritual Performance

Tina Turner has an old song, "What you see is what you get. What you can't see is better yet." We'd like to expand this concept to say, "What you see is what you get. What you *do* is stronger yet." In fact, so often, what one is doing is often that person's "undoing." Actions speak louder than words. A thought thought a thousand times becomes a word. Word spoken repeatedly becomes a deed. A deed defines our very existence. Life is a ritual performance. We get exactly what we pay attention to. We buy, each day, what we spend our focus of attention on. We are what we do. An old Apache-trained acquaintance of mine used to throw his head back, laugh into the sky, and say, "What will you buy with your attention today?" Our every action is an ingredient in the recipe for our lives. We will get more of what we do each day. So, what will you buy with your attention today?

We keep an old iron pot of stew or chili cooking over an open campfire outside our mountain cabin in Tennessee. Friends can drop over anytime and have something hot to eat. I don't remember when last the pot was washed, but it never really needs cleaning. As a pot of venison chili nears the bottom, we add several more helpings of soaked beans, onions, tomato sauce, venison and spices. Poof! More chili, slowly cooking over the open fire. Sometimes when we tire of chili, we add vegetable broth, fresh vegetables, spices, and poof! Stew! We are always adding and taking away. Every day the ingredients change with the flow of traffic to the fire and our attention to taste. Life is very much like our pot of stew. With our every breath we are adding to and changing our lot in life.

This morning I awakened at 6:30 a.m. with my alarm kitten named Wildflower. When the sun gets up, so does she. She comes to purr me awake so I can feed her and begin my chores. After attending to our kittens, puppy and sprouts, I conduct a brief morning ritual of scrubbing my face, hands and teeth. Then Gaby and I hit the woods trail for our morning run. Gaby is my schnauzer. She's my strongest support towards health through outdoor exercise. If I should attempt to skip a morning run for a few extra minutes at my typewriter, Gaby pesters me until I give it up and go for a run. Always, I am grateful for our close encounter with Mother Nature, the sweat and the sweet laughs I get from watching Gaby leap and bound through the woods.

Our morning ritual always ends with prayer time in the village. Gaby and I cuddle up on a big bale of hay and breathe our way into a blissful Oneness of the breath of our Great Provider that flows through all things. The gentle reminders and the great ideas that flow into this space are duly noted and we hit the showers to clean up for the day. Next is one of my favorite rituals. Breakfast!

My singing started in the woods, followed me to the showers and now always accompanies my artful dicing and slicing of fruit and nuts for my morning cereal. We approach contact with Spirit through song . . . our own voice singing. Usually, I know my mood by the songs that come to mind. Usually, I find myself singing my own power song in Apache, which translated means, "I am not afraid. I have come to do wonderful things. I am visiting this place. Make a way for me. I will come again until my work is done." This morning I was singing a repeated pattern of a song I am in the process of writing. The current lyrics go something like this: "Old friend of mine . . . I wouldn't take a million, billion, zillion dollars for our time . . . together." It did not surprise me to hear a knock on my door an hour later and find an old friend standing there.

During my eating ritual, I read something uplifting. I've just finished the Book of Solomon in the Bible. I started Isaiah, but it wasn't nearly as inspiring, so I laid it aside and picked up *In the*

I am the dance and it is boundless, connected to every-thing, everytime, everywhere. This happens because I'm coming from spirit and as spirit I've known there is no time, no space, no boundaries. It's all happening at one time.

—Mahisha

I contact the sacred through dance, by creating a space deep inside. There I experience a sense of no boundaries. It is timeless there. A lot of times when I'm dancing, the room changes, depending on the dance I'm doing. I return to a time when I did the essence of the dance in another place in time.

—Mahisha

Spirit of Crazy Horse. This informative documentary on the atrocities done to our Native peoples is both educational and in line with my current work with a Time-Warner project. Everything that I do is directly molding my life and being aware of the dance makes choice so very much fun.

Choice is our most sacred act. Our every thought is made by choice. We must enter into a wakeful dance and choose a life in balance. We must bring back our race of people who recognize each person as owner of the earth; a race of people who recognize nothing more sacred than choice; a race of people who have no spiritual elders save their own reasoning. When we are unable to choose, it is good to ride far from camp where no one can hear our pitiful cries of indecision. Indecision, the neither-here-nor-there attitude, is responsible for more abuse and aggression than any other thing. It is annoying to be in the midst of indecision. When one lacks choice, one lacks contact with Source. It is rare that I will persist in the company of one who is constantly saying, "Oh, I don't know. It really doesn't matter to me." I enjoy the company of those to whom life really matters. I enjoy the opinion of others. All people do have an opinion about most things. It is good to choose and act accordingly. Only in this way can we feel the truth of choice.

My friend, Melvin, doesn't understand and, therefore, doesn't like people of a different race. I don't agree or disagree with his opinions. Color simply is not an issue with me as it is with him. What I appreciate about Melvin is that he is so strongly choosing and taking full responsibility for his actions. He even attributes his regular attendance at church to his dislike for these people. He knows that his attitude is unholy and it keeps him returning to the prayer pews. My church is just these woods, which Melvin says is fine for me. He says church is for people like him. He declares that he needs to go to church 'cuz he . . . well, he's just so ornery that he needs to go to church. It makes him feel better about being so bad. When Melvin arrived at the door this morning and wanted to go chop wood, it was easy to leave this old typewriter and haul his wood for him. You see, Melvin owns all the land around this neck of the woods and he's mighty particular about who sets foot on his land. He's right to feel this way, because folks have lost the respect for others' property. I help him keep poachers off the land, and I pick up the litter that the "maggots" around here mindlessly pitch out their windows. The most beautiful woods chapel one could ever hope to see is on Melvin's land, and he grants us permission to go there any time we want. I'm always happy to help my friend, Melvin. We visit while we cut wood and today he told me what songs he thinks I should sing at the Palace tonight. One of my morning prayers was for direction about my program tonight. Melvin came as God's messenger. Melvin's also the kind of guy who takes his skill with a chainsaw right to the limit of safety. Today we pulled down an old dead tree with his truck. I'd say we had two or three close calls with danger. He gets his mind set on completing a task and, come hell or high water, he completes the task. I'm the same way. That's one of the things I like about Melvin. Another message from Melvin was, take it to the limit! We quit about noon, stacked wood and he left. I had a bowl of chili and here I am, back at this typewriter.

So, what have I bought with my attention thus far today? Health, wisdom, knowledge, friendship, companionship and a few good laughs along the way. This one thing I know: life is bound to bring me more of the same, and I'll gladly take it. Today, for a few hours, Melvin and I became two that acted as one heart. Our friendship is bonded in sweat and laughter, and when we were all done working, he gave me all the wood. He only wanted the exercise and the opportunity to suck some fresh air in the woods on a beautiful day. Perhaps he also wanted the joy of my friendship as much as I his. My life is about this one thing: that all hearts will beat as one. Already today, I have come a step closer to this thing.

I got a letter today from an old sorority sister from years ago. She is completing a Master's Degree in Education. She has a singing voice as beautiful as Streisand and much more charisma than Barbra. She decrees that she wants a career singing. However, she hasn't really spent time with her music for four years. We get more of what we pay attention to. I want a recording contract. Therefore, I sing everywhere I go: In the grocery store, in the car, in the shower, in the woods. I sing. I practice music in the afternoon and perform my music at night. I want a recording contract, so I sing. I also want my books to be published in paperback and available to folks at the grocery stores and news stands. Therefore, I write every morning. I share my manuscripts with the neighbors and mail copies to friends to read. We get what we pay attention to. Life is a ritual dance. We must

For my Macaw Dance costume, I used feathers that were to go on my wedding dress last year. Things changed and, as it happened, the feathers are representative of a marriage that happpened within myself.

—Mahisha

We step to a time now where women must lead the way. One woman, with peace in her heart, can part the waters of an angry crowd of men.

—Cloud

keep our Spirit in readiness for there shall never be a truer friend than our very own Spirit.

Tonight I perform at the Nashville Palace. I came from a Palace. I am a child of The King and The Queen. I have always known of my royal lineage. Once I even saw the beautiful palace that is my home. It floated down from the sky on a pink cloud one morning at sunrise. It sat on the horizon for about thirty seconds before it disappeared. I am a spiritual Blue Blood. I love to perform at palaces. When Harmonic Convergence rolled around, I headed for Los Angeles. The origin of the celebration was centered at Palenque in Mexico. The natives called Palenque, "the Palace." I wanted to welcome the beginning of this new time by performing at the Palance. Judy Garland once wrote and performed a song in which she sang, "You ain't played Hollywood, if you ain't played the Palace." Prince wanted to have a performance at the Palace to his credit, so he arranged a concert there. I also decided to play the Palace. Today, the once proud Palace Theater is home to heavy metal, rap and drugs. However, once a month the owner allows a New Age act to come in . . . kind of like a community service.

On August 17, 1987, Cloud and troop performed at the Palace. All the spokespeople for Harmonic Convergence had fled from Los Angeles and headed to Mt. Shasta, Stonehenge and Machu Picchu. Consequently, I ended up with the microphone for CNN, CBS, NBC and ABC news in Los Angeles. Mind you, I actually knew nothing about Harmonic Convergence, except that some 200,000 people were celebrating life together on planet earth. They were coming from all over the planet to points of power and praying together. They sang and danced and celebrated our good Mother Earth. It really didn't matter to me if the Mayan calendar was ending and a new age beginning. What did matter was that many hearts were beating as One. Into this space I divined to perform a ritual celebration and call for a world reunion . . . a world party.

With $300 in our pockets and a road map to Los Angeles, we left Oklahoma bound for California. Klint sent his station wagon out front. It was packed to the gills with our stage props. We followed close behind in our little Phoenix. It was our mission that drove us across the desert, over the mountains and down into the valley of Los Angeles. We felt like the Little Train that Could, bringing "good things for all the girls and boys." Our mission was to create a stage for entertainment that exalted life in harmony on our planet. We went against all sound advice from galactic psychics who vowed that "Orion's Bandits" would attack and destroy us. Since we had no earthly notion of who or what "Orion's Bandits" represented, we gallantly drove forth. With no small miracle, we were able to secure the Palace Theater, locate twenty-four New Age performers to join our ritual celebration, hire the services of a sound crew and join forces with the famed Ron Hay to help produce and direct our show. All this transpired in less than three weeks. We attracted full network coverage for our event and even *People* magazine. In this space we decreed the entire earth as sacred and called for a world-wide party. I stood in full costume on the corner of Hollywood and Vine, blew my conch horn gratefully in four directions, called to Spirit to send my voice to the four corners of the earth, and then declared this spot sacred, and all other spots on earth. The media, of course, could not grasp such a concept, but they kindly reported our celebration with only edges of sarcasm. The full page spread in the *L.A. Times* did not fully grasp what our ritual performance meant, but they were impressed with the celebrities who attended. Little did they know that our act was felt around the world. I believe it seeded the current trend in inter-global sharing of music, as seen in recent Paul Simon concerts.

It is said that a single leaf falling in Oklahoma is felt around the world. With this simple understanding, we have dared to center ourselves on our land at the very center of the United States, and there we have prayed for a world reunion. We have created world shields and global music. We have gifted the art of life as a ritual performance with all who came to share. We have made ourselves solid. Before a star explodes into the galaxies, it first implodes and becomes very solid. At its most solid point, it explodes into the universe. Let us make each action one of choice. Let us put away indecision. Let us become solid.

When I first met Linda Gray from the television series, "Dallas," she was making a shift out of the role of J.R. Ewing's bitchy wife. Needless to say, when one portrays a certain character on the screen, that action ripples out into real life. Linda was uncertain in her passage. I suggested she make a conscious and definite walk through every doorway in her life, as she coached herself regarding the quality and strength of her passage. I modeled how that might look, as we practiced on back doors and garden gates. As I strolled, tall-walking, through the gate, I affirmed, "I choose to make my transition with grace, poise, ease, confidence and control. I bless that which I leave behind and look with anticipation into the truth of my ever-abundant present." We practiced and she went on her way. A few weeks later she arrived on our ranch in Oklahoma to experience "The Challenge of Excellence." Here she had the opportunity to walk logs and beams suspended fifty feet in the air. She jumped from a six story high pole and successfully grabbed a trapeze eight and one-half feet away. She chanted repeatedly, "I Love You, Linda!" "I Love You, Linda!" and found joy and confidence to choose her retirement from "Dallas." Within a short period of time she began to receive other, more uplifting, roles on television. Life is a ritual performance. Begin to do what you want to do more of, and you will attract it to you. What we do is what we get.

Be literal in this concept. Once it is understood, life can be exhilarating. If you are crossing over a bridge, go to a bridge and cross over to the other side. If your desires require that you cross over a certain "line," draw a line and then ceremoniously cross over it. If you are passing through a portal of life, make a portal of branches or have your friends make a portal of their arms, and then walk through the portal. If you are in a period of darkness that exists before the light, walk in darkness into light.

In all such cases, it is important to take the time to value what is left behind. Acknowledgement and appreciation is all that is required to feed the appetite of that which tends to haunt us. Some choose to attempt starving the ghosts of our past. However, there is truly beauty in all things. When we take the time to find this beauty and acknowledge it, it can rest from its hampering ways of seeking attention. Attempting to starve anything will result in a ravenous response of over-indulgence and gorging. Addicts are made of starvation and perceived need. Feed all things with appreciation and acknowledgement and they will go to the light. For some energies, this means growing and flourishing. For others, it means fading away. First, however, acknowledgement and appreciation are required.

Repetition is important in ritual performance. Remember that you get more of what you do. So, do more of what you want to be doing more of. If you wish to sing as a way of life, then sing as a way of life; even if your current job is different from music, sing in the halls and bathrooms. Sing at your desk. Sing on the way to work. Sing as a you prepare a meal. Sing in the streets and stores. Let others begin to expect your happy voice singing. Become addicted to your own voice singing. Sing! If you want to sing, you don't just listen to others sing on the radio. You only attract more of listening to others sing! If YOU want to sing, then sing!

If you want to be in love with someone special, then behave as though you're in love with someone special (and let that someone be you). Treat everyone you meet just like you would if you had just had your breath taken away by the most beautiful person in the world. Treat each situation in the day as though you are head-over-heels-in-love. If you want to be "in love," then just "be in love." If you mope around feeling sorry for yourself, then you will attract more of feeling sorry for yourself. Life will bring you all sorts of experiences which will reinforce your actions. Then others will begin to feel sorry for you and then life will bring you even more "stuff" to feel sorry about. What you do is what you get more of. Smile and the whole world smiles with you. Cry and the world avoids you. Then you'll have something to cry about. Dance the dance! Life is a ritual performance!

We are rainbow children. I am Seminole, Dutch, Irish, French, German and English. Skye is Norwegian and Iroquois. We create, with our lives, a bridge across a gulf; something to bring together the races of entirely different natures. Each time we cross a bridge we affirm, "I am a bridge. Because of me people may pass freely from shore to shore." We are eagles. We fly in pairs. We seek high places. We love the wind and the sun. We are spirit and approach Spirit with our own voice singing. We are co-creators with Spirit and recognize ourselves as fit controlling powers, as people who own the earth. We have learned that regret never brings comfort . . . only more regret. We know that distrust begets distrust. We know that weeping in regret comes after our actions have betrayed us. We realize that weeping as release warms our cheeks and our hearts and helps us regain our balance. We know the quickening power of feeling our feelings as they arise. We know the power of a tear understood that shuts out twisted thoughts and prevents unreasonable acts. We weep when we see something we love die, for we know that there is no more powerful influence in heaven than the tears of a child.

Our Brother Friend said, "Become again as a little child," and, we know to do so calls forth a world acceptable for children. Let us dance a dance that returns our beautiful planet to a friendly environment for children and animals. When we do so, all other things will find a paradise waiting to be appreciated.

Practice makes perfect. The Law of Attraction is a universal law. We get more of what we do! The concept is simple. If you want to dance, dance! If you want to sing, sing! If you want to take a leap into the unknown, leap into the unknown all day long! Eat something you've never eaten before. Behave in a way you have never before dared. Talk to a stranger. Try things that are new. Try you hair in a different style. If you want to be a star, act like one . . . the one you want to be. Prepare for notoriety in every act. Make your phone unlisted. Dress in ways that draw attention and learn to handle the attention. Improve your public image. Abandon behaviors that would bring bad press, poor health or disapproval from your adoring public. If you want to travel, travel! If you want to be a homemaker, make home wherever you are.

If you want a promotion to boss, begin by being your own boss! Instruct yourself and elicit the type of support from yourself that you would want from your underlings. If you want to play sports, condition yourself and play sports! If you want to write, write! Write a journal. Write letters. Write poems. Write! If you want to be beautiful, act beautiful! If you want to be healthy, think healthy, talk healthy, be healthy! If you want to understand something, then stand under it! Become the underling, the fledgling. Listen, watch and learn. If you want to bike across Canada, then begin by biking to work. If you want to bring balance to a situation, take every opportunity to balance yourself . . . on curbs, logs, fallen trees, bricks, stones, river rocks, etc. If you want to get on top of a situation, then get on top of things! Climb a mountain or a tree. Sit on the roof. Visit the fire tower or the Empire State Building. If you want to climb the corporate ladder, then climb ladders! If you want to "get even," then measure out portions of everything for awhile and learn about "even!" Draw your lines with a straight, even ruler.

Do literally what you want to do and you will attract more of the same. In the process you will awaken some part of yourself yet sleeping and moment-by-moment you will begin to enjoy the dance. Above all else, have fun! Remember, you will get what you put your attention to. So tell us, what will you buy with your attention today?

CHAPTER 8

PHYSICAL PROWESS:
A Sacred Act

Our Grandmother Moon Feathers lived to be a hundred years old. She attributes her good health through those many years to the fact that she never smoked, drank, took Proctor and Gamble products or let a man suck on her nipples! Until the day she died, she proudly displayed a full and perky bustline. She said breasts droop when spirits droop and women's spirits will droop if they spend their lives trying to suckle people. Grandmother practiced natural healing and she swore like a sailor. She said it's natural to express yourself however you please, and she wasn't about to spend one minute of her life trying to please anyone else. I believe that she was the most open and accepting person I have ever known. She truly practiced "live and let live." She had an opinion about everything — and an educated one at that. She taught herself to read when she was twelve years old and read the Bible to prove it. She was physically fit until the day she died, which she did in the simplest way. She had dinner with her friends, went to bed and passed before the sun got up. Her cat was purring on her chest when she left. When I think of physical prowess, I think of Grandmother Moon Feathers and I aspire to be very much like her when I reach my hundredth year.

When Grandmother died, she dropped away her robe (her physical body). All that she was still is, except for her shell, which she left on a beach in the Keys. As a child I thought the physical

I have always been a leader and a teacher and I really enjoy instilling confidence, individuality, knowledge of competence and independence in young women. All my life I have seen passive, unhappy women who stay in a place out of a sense of duty in order to pleasure another. They do this rather than pleasure themselves. I have great respect for women who step out and know who they are and where they're going. I respect women who take their power.

—Colonel Lyn

body was the whole of a person, and when their physical bodies died, so did they. During this time of my life I was extremely proud of my body and wanted it to be healthy and active. Then I became interested in my spirit body, and spent many years feeding my spirit body, sometimes to the dismay of my physical body. I would take my physical body to many limits of fatigue, indulgence and neglect. I was often conscious that my physical body was struggling to maintain in the face of my spiritual journeys. Now, some years later, I recognize the truth and the beauty of my body as the Temple of my own Holy Spirit. Just as I would want my own home to be clean, well kept, in good repair and embellished with that which enhanced its comfort, so would I want my spirit's home to be clean, happy, well kept and in good repair. While my Spirit walks this place, I will have it abide in a residence of good repute! So it is that a warrior learns to feed in balance both the physical and spiritual bodies.

Our physical bodies are, in essence, our own mind's experience of itself. Our thoughts produce neuro-chemical responses in our bodies. When we think a pleasurable thought, our bodies produce chemistry that supports our pleasurable mood. When we think a sad thought, our bodies produce chemistry to support sadness. When we think a scared thought, our bodies produce chemistry to support fear. And, when we think an excited thought, our bodies produce chemistry to support our excitement. Our physical bodies are the willing servants of our thoughts. As a man thinks, so he is! And, as a woman thinks, so she is. There is a specific and direct physiology behind each thought, word and action. Likewise, each action produces a particular type of thinking. For example, if I am sitting hunched over with arms crossed over my chest, it is not likely that I will be talking about expanding my horizons. Likewise, if I am standing erect with my arms expanded, it is not likely that I will talk about closing off or shutting up. The physical body is a good barometer of the spirit body. It is likely that what is going on in the physical body has been going on in the spirit body for some time. What is happening spiritually is eventually going to manifest itself on the physical plane.

The task of our tenure on earth is to learn to manifest ideas into form. Thus, we are given this physical plane on which to play. It is as if we are given a lump of clay and asked to create the world. We begin by creating our own physical bodies in the way that we see the world. It is ever so difficult for me to hear a fat preacher talk about abstinence of any sort. If he is talking about abundance and giving and growing, I can tolerate his obesity.

Our bodies and what we create with our bodies is the experience of thought itself. We perceive all things with our physical senses. Reality is only as we perceive it. What is considered to be real and what is considered to be imagined are both perceived the same by the body. When we dream that we are being chased, our body believes that we are and we awaken in a cold sweat. If we imagine something horrible is going to happen to us, our bodies respond with all the appropriate signals and tensions. Although it is possible to be very specific about the physiology of physical prowess, it is most important to note that physical prowess is the result of spiritual and mental prowess. We are what we think. By tracking people's movement in life, it is possible to know much about their spirits.

If they stomp around like elephants, they are heavy in their spirits. Perhaps they are tentative in their movement, choosing neither here nor there. So it is with their spirits. Perhaps they are light and graceful on their feet and touch lightly all with whom they come into contact. So it is with their spirits. It is impossible to be a spiritual warrior without also being a warrior with much physical prowess. A spirit contained within a body that has little flexibility and movement is constrained in its expression. Physical prowess is a vital and central part of the walk of the warrior.

There is a poem that I heard as a child that impressed me greatly. It said something like this: "I'd rather see a sermon than hear one any day. I'd rather watch the way you act than hear what you say." When observing behavior, a simple rule of thumb is in order. Believe what you see above what you hear. Actions speak louder than words. This simple truth has led me to study the art of "tracking" the human experience. That is to say, I have developed the art of observing human behavior as one might track a deer or coyote in the woods. After years of tracking the human animal through the jungles of life, I've made a few simple observations which might be of interest.

First and foremost, people perform better when they are having fun. I'm certain that the Goddess' favorite behavior is play! Certain things happen when people are having fun: Their blood sugar is up, the fatty acids are high, their adrenaline flows, endorphines and enkephalins are released, which are endogenous

I am a laughing grandmother. I have been gifted with a natural comedian sense of laughter. I knew I didn't need to be a serious grandmother. I am a laughing grandmother. The world needs laughter.

—Grandmother
Princess Moon
Feathers

Women, stop being victims and step forward, recognizing your own power. It is nobody's fault about where you are. Take personal responsibility for life and what it is bringing you. Your circle of women will provide support and information to make this journey.

—Colonel Lyn

We must remember that we are Spirit, here to experience a physical-human experience.

—Grandmother Kitty

opiates. The liver manufactures more glucose, adding fuel to the tissues, and the pupils dilate to increase the peripheral vision. Their breathing is stimulated and epinephrine dilates the respiratory system and heart. People feel better, move better, see better, think better and hear better when they are having fun. They are more flexible in their movements and much more expansive. Physical prowess requires that one be able to enjoy life, laugh and have fun. Conversely, one who has more fun is more physically fit. The bottom line is this: It is a warrior's discipline to truly enjoy life, play, dance, move, jump, leap, laugh, sing and stretch. Anything that prohibits or inhibits these behaviors should be avoided. Very simply, the physiology of excellence requires that a warrior be always sworn to fun. To choose pleasure over aversion is a sacred act that benefits the one and the whole.

A second observation is this: What you see is what you get. Perhaps what you don't see could be better yet . . . but don't count on it. Trust what you see a person being. She will never disappoint you. If she moves away from you while telling you that she cares about you, trust the movement. She will move away in the face of love. If she always seems to be opposite you in a room, she will likely have the opposite point of view about most things. If she stands behind you at a cocktail party, she will very well stand behind you with your political party. If she whines and complains that the world is full of jerks, she has only to stand in front of her mirror to see the leader of the pack.

Some time ago I began playing a creation game that is still in process. I began to understand that we are always on stage; that someone is always watching. Thus, even in my private places, I practiced being on stage. Perhaps this has reduced my stage fright a bit, and it has certainly allowed me to practice excellence in my life. My desire to be on stage has become a present reality. I am always on stage and every performance is a key performance. Each action is a set-up for the next opportunity. Each opportunity taken is an action that sets up yet another opportunity. Just like building a house, each block of the foundation must be firmly set for the entire structure to be solidly and beautifully built. Each action is a building stone in the temple of my life. It is with sacred choice that we act on each moment of life.

THE PLAYING
OF GAMES

There was a time when warriors did not kill for glory. They merely "couped" or touched their enemy. This was the game of life. To always be in readiness for the coup. One's physical prowess was required to be constantly alert for the enemy's touch. There was no concept for theft. What people took care of and kept in close attention and affection, they owned. When they no longer guarded it with love, or regarded it with attention, it could easily be "couped" or taken by the enemy. This was not cause for anger, but for embarrassment. It was considered slothful to allow another person to sneak undetected into camp and take your wife or horse. This was cause for stories of laughter to be repeated at the winter fires. A warrior kept himself in peak condition and attention to avoid being the object of a winter campfire story in the enemy camp. The game of life was a game of physical prowess, alertness and cunning. Coup was a game that sustained health of the tribes. Then something happened to change the game. Encroachment into the lands pushed tribes into smaller and smaller gaming territories until they were forced to kill each other to survive. The game took on more serious consequences.

Today, life is still a game with serious consequences. How we play the game determines the degree of success and happiness that we are awarded. When we play the game with less than our best, we diminish the game for everyone. And, the more our lives touch others, the greater the repercussions to ourselves, be they good or bad. It is useful to see ourselves as a gamesperson and a team player in life. To heighten this awareness we created "High

There is excitement and inpiration in acknowledging your own self-worth. Be creatively competitive.

—Mahisha

Games." A High Game is a game whose design, logistics and outcome make major strides towards mastering the act of creating. That is to say, a "High Game" awakens us to the fact that we are, indeed, the Creator's hands, heart and mind. It is up to us to re-create heaven on earth. The very first "High Game" that we created is called Indian Coup.

Indian Coup is a game of tribal unity and survival. Each clan is equipped with headbands and feathers. Each clan member holds a feather that symbolizes their own power walk in life. They each also wear a headband distinguishing their clan. A large gaming field is selected, usually one to two miles square. The clan members are encouraged to become familiar with the territory by the light of day, since Indian Coup is played under the cover of darkness.

Drums play throughout the day as clan members prepare their clan totems, songs and dress. As darkness falls, the clans gather to designate their clan leaders. These leaders include: War chief, peace chief, scout, crier, pipe carrier, medicine leader, song maker, story teller, warriors and braves. The clans gather by the council fires to pronounce their leaders and their clan names. Much time is allowed for each of the clans to gather for strategizing, giving power songs and painting for commitment on the journey.

Each clan has become familiar with the animal call of their crier as they will be led by that sound across the vast territory at night. The criers are led onto the gaming field first. With the criers in position at the opposite ends of the gaming territory, the clans embark on their trek to the safety of their designated sanctuaries, within reach of the criers. They must cross the gaming field undetected and reach their crier without being "couped" by opposing clans. The pipe carrier is worth the entire clan and is thus very well protected. It is believed that the pipe must be safe. "Where there is one who walks in balance, there exists the possibility of others walking in balance."

Real and imposed handicaps are always present in the game of coup. Some are old and blind. Others are physically impaired and must be carried. Still others are young and frightened. The game requires that all these variables be considered in the design of the strategy to get the clan into safe territory. If one is "couped" or touched by another clan's member, that one must relinquish her personal power feather. When the drum sounds to end the game, the power feathers are collected from the clans and the clan with the most wins. Indian Coup usually lasts into the early morning, as clan members leap, crawl and run in the night. Sometimes the creatures participate in the play by joining the criers in the night. An owl may join in with the crier who is imitating an owl call. This, of course, adds to the complexity of the play, as clanspeople must distinguish between what is really an owl and the clan crier. It is not uncommon to lose a clan member in the woods for awhile.

Indian Coup allows each clan member to act on circumstances. What we see in this game is how we are. What we do is who we are! When we gather around the late night fires to debrief our journeys through the gaming fields, we are often surprised to find that our style of "playing the game" is exactly our style of playing life's game. Sometimes this style is embellished and appreciated. Sometimes it is a startling mirror of actions we then choose to change. Once I lay in wait for one who stalked me. When she came so close as to step on me, I instantly became a snake in my mind and struck out at her. My imagining was so strong as to frighten the opponent into stepping away from me, and I continued to remain undetected in the night. This awareness has allowed me many moments of repeated loans of power through my imagination. Truly, what I imagine to be true, is! Conversely, I once played the game of Coup in hot pursuit of only one other opposing clan member, to the exclusion of all other players. I realized that I had actually done this in my life and, in so doing, missed numerous opportunities at success in areas I did not turn to see. My focus was so solidly on one thing as to miss many others. At this level, focus is abused.

Indian Coup is a powerful game for trying on new roles and bringing understanding to others. It is common for us to assign the duty of "scout" to anyone in our group who tends to be critical of others. A scout must travel twice the distance of any other player. It is their duty to travel the gaming territory and report back to the clan about what lies ahead. They must also lead the clan across the field with accurate information. Having been scouts, they discover how important it is to listen to the insights of others who have seen differently.

Those who hesitate to "speak out" are often given the job of "crier," a job that requires that they call out for hours to guide their clan to safety. For one who is always giving away power, they may find the job of medicine person to be powerful. In this position they must empower each clan member with some strong

I am amazed at the honesty of the communication and the blending of one and everything. I've never found it in 100 years in the white man's world. But, I found it here among the women.

—Grandmother
Princess Moon
Feathers

My Crow relative calls me "Red Tail Hawk Flying On the Sunlit Wind." The children of our tribe call me "Crazy Hawk Flying On Every Wind." Being "crazy" is the most fun. It grants the freeedom to be myself.

—Cloud

reminder of strength or agility required to traverse the gaming field. Likewise, the pipe carrier may well be someone who tends to shirk responsibility. Warring personalities are asked to become peace chiefs and peaceful personalities are given the task of becoming a war council. The more opportunities that we each have to view life from all its many angles, the more we can see of the whole. We are each a part of the whole. We are each a knowing in touch with All Knowing. We are each a mystery inside the Great Mystery. As we relax and see truly that life is a grand game and we each play our part, we begin to enjoy life more and more.

It is always amusing to hear some serious adultish person proclaim about playing, "Oh well, it's just a game." Just a game is all that life is and we dare to be excellent players. Many other games are valuable in awakening teammates to the Game of Life.

Dream Walker-Dream Stalker is a "high game" to prepare us to carry forth our dreams. Those who know their dreams spend days making their own dream shields. Those who do not yet have such clarity make stalking sticks to coup their dreams. Both are taken into ceremony, cleansed and blessed. Both dream walkers and dream stalkers go into the sweating lodge and prepare to play the game with no attachments to the past. When the time comes for the journey "to the drum," a small fire is built at some distant place in the gaming field. A simple heartbeat on the drum starts the game. The dream stalkers have gone ahead and prepared to ambush the dream walkers. The dream walkers have the awesome task of carrying their dreams all the way to the council fire on the gaming field without being touched by the stalking stick of a dream stalker. How one carries her dream is direct feedback about the potential success of the dream walker. Most people who carry a dream seem to give up along the way. The ones who succeed are the ones who stay with their dreams and keep coming. Patterns of demise are easy to see on the gaming field. Those who stalk a dream are also surprised to find out the depth of their commitment to identifying a dream. Others are surprised to find out how satisfying it is to actually help others carry their dreams to the council fire.

Other games are designed to hone our skills as players of the life game. Meet Me At The Mountain challenges leaders to devise ways to move large numbers of people over rough grounds while overcoming all the urges to give up and give in. Ambush is played on horseback and allows clan members to deal with issues of discrimination, as one clan attempts to ambush the other. Family Fusion challenges techniques of competition to contribute to unity versus division. It also encourages flexibility and creativity. Hunter-Hunted allows participants to reframe their feelings about persecution into techniques of stalking the hunter. Fighting Fair is a Fair of Fighting Events in which participants learn to fight fair and square in a way that is fun. Tying the Knot is an event to allow participants to discover where they stand with commitment. The possibility of High Games is infinite. Any game we play with the understanding that "what I do here is actually what I do!" can be considered a high game. We are always on stage. There is no dress rehearsal for life. This is it. This is life. Play it to the fullest!

CHAPTER 10

THE MAKING
OF ALTARS

This morning we walked a half-mile through the Tennessee foothills to what we fondly call the Cliffs. High above the winding Harpeth River sits a ledge of flat rocks. Growing out of these amazing rocks are four very old cedar trees that have taken the shape of the bonsai trees of Japan. A simple deer trail leads to this cathedral in the woods. Everyone knows that this place is special, even the deer. From this vantage point we can gaze across the green, plush valley below. We sit so high that the birds fly below us. Sometimes a cloud touches our heads. Mother Nature built this particular altar and, without sign or definition, everyone who goes there knows that this is an altar.

An altar is an obviously special place where one's attention is drawn to attitudes of gratitude and appreciation. An altar marks out both a place and a time for worship. It is common in our journeys to stop along the trail of life and build a little altar or shrine to the beauty of a place. In so doing, some others come along and linger awhile to appreciate and say a special "thank you" to the Mother Earth and Father Sky. Children are famous for innocently building altars to beauty. Remember our own sand castles on the beach that caused some adult to linger and appreciate beauty? Remember the beautiful rooms of a castle we imagined and built with rock markers in the woods of our playgrounds? Remember the innocent piles of rocks we put along a path in the woods to mark a turn or direction? For children, it is natural to build altars to celebrate life.

As I began to recover my childhood, I began to recover my joy in building altars. Now I live inside an altar. Each nook and cranny of our home is an altar to honor beauty. There is a center altar which takes up a quarter of the floor space. Outside our sweat lodge sits an altar. There are two central altars in the village. Council Rock is a natural altar in the gaming fields. I even carry a small portable medicine wheel altar with me to set up at places I stay on the road. I suppose I might be possessed with "altarmania" and would certainly not recommend my lifestyle as a necessary example to follow. I simply enjoy spending my every "waiting" minute serving Spirit in some way, and building an altar and expressing appreciation gives me great satisfaction and provides my creative kid with lots of fun. My friend, Kactus, is also an altar freak. She has travelled the world taking pictures of shrines and altars and she has become famous for making amazing altars. It is with delight that we feature several of Kactus' creations in this work. We also share our own. We do so not as models to be copied, but as ideas for inspiration.

Altar

World Altar at Eagle's Nest

As long as I live, no matter where I may be, this will be my home.

—Grandmother
Princess Moon
Feathers

Altar

Altars begin with a central foundation. The energy of the foundation is important. My current cabin altar in Tennessee is built on "pony" skin. I once wrote a song in which the lyrics say, "This ole pony don't ride double anymore." This was another way to say, "I am exploring a monogamous relationship." Where I currently live is a cabin built for two, a peaceful place to explore monogamy. Pony is a good foundation for the altar. To either side of the pony is a simple prayer cloth, one for each of us. Onto these hand-woven prayer cloths we can put objects that help us focus our intentions of the day or week.

An altar also has a centering piece or place of central focus. Our altar in the Eagle's Nest in Oklahoma includes one whole wall of our Grand Room and extends into the floor. The centering piece on the floor is a large turtle shell sitting on a log table. Under it is a soft rabbit skin. The turtle represents "Turtle Island" or specifically, the Mother Earth, as represented by our own continent. We are reminded of our commitment to care for our earth. The rabbit is soft, cuddly and prolific. We pray that the Mother Earth is cared for in easy ways and that she will continue to be abundant. On the wall behind the turtle hangs a World Family Shield with arrows crossed in partnership with an Apache pipe. It is backed with a beaver skin to denote the building of dreams. The shield displays twelve eagle feathers for the twelve tribes of All-That-Is. Below the shield sits a picture of the Christ. On either side of the shield hang pictures of our women and children. We are reminded that the tribes flourish as long as a woman's heart is held up high. When her heart turns to dust, the people perish. Circled around the Family Shield are my own shields. The shields I choose to display here are my Victory Shield, Eagle Shield, Mystery Shield and my Heart Shield. Around these shields are pictures of children. We are reminded to always honor "the child within."

The Bible sits open on the floor in front of the turtle. It is opened to Psalms 23 and reminds us that our Shepherd Chief is ever present. Our staffs stand as a gateway to the altar and our handmade musical instruments surround the turtle on the prayer cloth. Today, Grandmother Moon Feathers' picture sits in the center of the altar. She is currently making her passage into the Spirit Camp on the Other Side. We have lighted candles and made prayers to help her on her journey. Our smudging fans, ceremonial feathers, drums and corn pouches also find their places on our altar. Favorite rocks and crystals have a place as well. Our central altar of our home is our place of prayer and worship. When others come to join us, we circle around this central altar. It is the focus of our home.

Every other display in our home is also a small altar. One honors our Indian heritage. Another honors our western influence. Still another honors our feminine aspects and another our masculine. Yet another honors our work and another provides protection. Those in our private spaces honor our parents and

There is one living God for all living things. What color is God? No color. What color is the tear falling out of the black man's eyes or the white man's or any race? It's clear. Now, when you sport a smile, we do the same thing no matter what color we are. When we use the gifts of a tear and a smile, there is no prejudice.

—Grandmother
Princess Moon
Feathers

Vision Us Altars

My spiritual quest is my own and I see God as both male and female. As a woman, I love the gentler aspect of female teachings and leadership.

—Colonel Lyn

Altar to a Son

each other. The turtle outside our sweat lodge honors the Mother Earth and all that she gives to us. The altar in my prayer bundle honors the four directions of the wind and the four peoples of the earth. Each aspect of an altar carries an energy like unto itself. A bear fetish is shaped like a bear and calls the bear energy to itself. A bear claw contains the energy of the whole bear and brings that particular energy to a bundle. Each thing carries the medicine or energy of that thing and becomes like an ingredient in stew when combined into an altar. All things can become an altar when consciously put together. Even when something is not consciously put together, it attracts itself unto itself. This attraction principle is very important to understanding the making of an altar.

What we sow is what we reap. What we build on our altar and in the altar of our lives is what we will surely get. Those that allow others to decorate their home are people whose destinies are not of their own design. They give the power of direction away to others. Those that simply fill the walls of their homes with stuff to cover over the holes, ask that whatever they put there be multiplied. If our attics are filled with junk, so are our minds. When we leave the past behind in a move to another place, we truly change our lives. When we wish for a new beginning, let us clean out our attics and put away things of the past. Let us make room for what is new and different. Let us also realize that the difference will come as we consciously choose what we want in our environment. What we focus on is what we will get. What we appreciate with our attention is what we will grow. May the altars of our lives be filled with beauty all around us.

The following altars are illustrations of what is possible in the building of an altar.

Finally, the time spent in building an altar is time spent in purchasing what we pay attention to. The process of building requires our attention. Once the altar is built, it is a visible and constant reminder of what we put our attention to. For every second that we have our attention to that thing, it is in the process of manifesting. Our attention calls into form that which we imagine. An altar serves to focus our attention long enough for creation to occur. Truly, an altar alters our destinies just as obviously as it alters our attention. The most magnetic and attractive energy in the universe is that attention of appreciation. When we recognize beauty, we tap into the universal pool of favorite feelings and speed up the process of manifestation. Let us build altars along every roadway and every moment of our lives, so that we may assist in the healing of our Mother Earth. Let our appreciation restore Her health and beauty. Let us all, again, live inside the altar of Heaven on Earth.

Altar to Grandmothers

The Eagle's Nest is an Octagon Altar to World Peace

CREATING SACRED SPACE

It is a good daily practice to SIT WITH YOURSELF. Hear yourself say, "I trust myself and am genuinely true to myself. I have a pure intent. I work not for others, but I sit with myself and know in my heart that my intent is aligned with whatever I want."

—Mahisha

On August 17, 1987, we stood at the corner of Hollywood and Vine in Hollywood, California. At 2:00 p.m. we blew the sea's Queen conch in four directions. Our drums summoned hundreds of on-lookers to gather around us and the group of network television crews who had been called to this moment. It was the culmination of Harmonic Convergence and the news media was frantic to document some small part of the celebration that sent hundreds of thousands of people scurrying to mountain tops, caves, sea shores and beautiful valleys. To the media, who had arrived at the day with little or no information about its significance, the entire happening was some weird New Age event that had something to do with the ending of an era.

Most well informed persons in the Los Angeles area had gone to Washington to Mt. Rainier or to California's own Mt. Shasta. Many celebrities who could have informed the media of the significance of "Harmonic Convergence" had joined the throngs on the mountain tops. We were all that the media had to depend on for information. We were, perhaps, as well informed as most and could have offered some scientific explanation for the spontaneous gathering of the Tribes of Abraham. Certainly, we could have offered some insight to prophecies foretelling the gathering of 144,000 souls to usher an old era out and a new era in. Perhaps we could have offered some of this type of information. However, the moment was prime to utilize national media to decree that which is most certainly the truth. Into that moment in time, with full network television and radio coverage, we formally declared the entire earth sacred, (including this prostitute and drunk infested corner of Hollywood), and we called for "A World Celebration . . . A World Family Reunion."

On August 17, 1987, the invitation went out to our planet: "Let us come together for one day of feasting, singing, dancing, playing and praying together. Let us beat the drums together, light candles together, breathe together, sing together. And, let our reunion be televised via satellite to the entire world." Such was our invitation. "Let this time of the coming together of the 144,000 be the seed of such a world event. Let our celebration at the Palace Theater this evening be the ritual to cement our invitation into the annals of history." That evening we celebrated the ending of the Mayan calendar and the beginning of the Golden Age of Peace. Over twenty-seven New Age performers participated in our celebration, into which we sang our prayers for world peace and harmony. The Palace Theater, now known for its heavy metal drug culture, was transformed into a sacred altar to draw the curtains on a new age.

We visioned together a world in which war materials were converted into bell gardens for children. We saw global exchange of food for all and cultural exchange among all peoples. We visioned the faces of thousands of children blending into one global family. We visioned one global community. We visioned this together and then we danced and sang our gratitude. By our strong intention we created sacred space at the Palace Theater and we claimed the entire planet as our altar.

It is true that the entire earth is sacred, and all that lies on, within and above her. However, for most, this level of consciousness is not yet a reality. Thus, in all that we do, we create sacred space through our rituals and ceremonies. This means of "reminder" is our simple way of continuing to help our planet awaken to the dream of One World-One Family. The means to create sacred space are endless. We mention only a few to stimulate the imagination and unlock possibilities that are yet unknown. We begin with the simplest and most obvious way: Notice, acknowledge, appreciate, sing out to the world around us, "Hello! You are beautiful! I love you!" The trees and the animals hear our voices and sense our great love and appreciation. They come alive with excitement and good feelings for our simple acknowledgement. They begin to breathe their good skan into us and open to receive our breath of skan. We exchange life-giving essences and consciously blend with the All-That-Is. Through our

What is special about dawn? Well, early this morning, while the world was sleeping, I got up and I saw what is the most magnificent miracle. God took his big hands and rolled back the darkness so quietly. In comes the glorious beauty of the sun, changing the color of everything. The sky brings warmth and clouds for rain for the little flowers. I never miss the first call of a bird. I'm outside looking for what God has given me.

—Grandmother
Princess Moon
Feathers

I came here on a red clay road with beautiful trees on either side and just enough hills. There were no signs of civilization. I thought I was dreaming. You know, at 100 years you always wonder if you're hallucinating. Well, I said, "It's okay if I am. It's a nice dream. It's nature." This place lives with nature. Flows with nature. Doesn't fight with nature. It is the most refreshing place of my life.

—Grandmother
Princess Moon
Feathers
(Speaking about our Oklahoma Ceremonial Grounds)

simple "seeing," the earth beneath our feet and the sky above our heads become sacred and lend us the power that only comes from that which is truly "sacred."

The simple act of grooming, fertilizing and caring for our planet is an act of sacred respect. For the time being, I have adopted a two-mile stretch of road to keep clear of litter. Each time I lift trash from my Mother's belly, I feel Her appreciation. She lends me strength and good will in exchange. Often times She shares special ideas with me. In a time when our world seems so very sad, She cheers me and gives me the hope and trust required to rise yet another day with laughter on my lips.

Another common practice is to carry corn meal, tobacco, corn seeds or any other type of seed for planting on the earth. It is good to think of the seed pouch or tobacco pouch as a wallet for the Mother Earth. When we walk on Her and enjoy Her bounty, it is good to pay Her with something that helps Her grow more.

Always it is important to recognize Her sacredness when we take from Her bounty. A simple prayer thanking the plants, or the scenery, or the trees or the water that we partake of is common courtesy. When we are picking, it is good to ask the largest plant if it is okay to take some of the harvest, and then listen to the answer. Plants love us very much and will share their secrets when we acknowledge that they are sacred. When we acknowledge that all of life is sacred and that each act is an act of choice and is therefore sacred, then life is a sacred dance lived consciously each moment. Each act is a sacred act; each place a sacred place; each moment a sacred moment; each thought a sacred thought. When we live at this level, we fully participate in creation of a better world.

There are certain ceremonies that are meant to create sacred space. One of the simplest is performed when a group first comes together. Perhaps each one present has travelled some distance to be present. Others have made a journey of thought and preparation. All have brought with them the experience of their individual journeys. Before all hearts may begin to beat as one, it is useful to establish the time and space together as sacred. Ceremony is strengthening because we have the opportunity to remember that we are not alone in our struggles and triumphs. We remember that we are part of a greater plan and a larger community of humanity. Our individual loads in life become lighter as we come together. In the case of community, one and one makes eleven. Our cares are shared and our joys multiplied. We are part of the whole and ceremony is a reminder of this oneness. Before putting aside our individual concerns to join the circle, it is respectful to acknowledge each person's journey and capacity for success. The new group assembles in a circle, seated for comfort. Simple drumming and shaking rattles can begin to entrain hearts and souls. A bowl of floral scented water is placed in the center of the circle. When possible, fresh flowers float in the warm, scented water. While soothing music is played and all center inside themselves, the bowl of water is passed and each person in turn washes their hands of any cares that were brought to the circle. This refreshing act allows each person to make ready to serve the circle.

A simple adaptation of this theme involves partners washing each other's hands and massaging them with a nice oil. This anointment is a powerful nurturing act to acknowledge our life's work. Another variation is to wash the dust from each other's feet. A foot cleansing and massage is another way to acknowledge each other as sacred, and the time to be spent together also as sacred. It is good to pass a simple form of nourishment such as buffalo meat or orange plugs as a symbol of nurturing and caring for each other. When one person is being prepared for passage such as marriage or adulthood, grooming the entire body is a powerful anchor for creating sacred space both without and within.

We must understand the need for privacy and respect of sacred space for each person.

—Skye

Smudging or smoking is yet another way to create sacred space. The sweet smoke of cedar, sage, sweetgrass and pinon drifts into the ceremonial space and calls for sacred attention. The person or object that is smudged is called to service. This is a form of awakening. Likewise, the broadcasting of cornmeal, tobacco or sweet fertilizer is a way to create a specific boundary for ceremony. Pathways may be created in the same manner. Even flower petals create a sacred pathway upon which to walk.

I am reminded of a story involving a little girl, a crystal globe, grandmothers from around the world and Mikhail Gorbachev. During an anti-nuclear demonstration in California, a grandmother passed through the line of media and signed herself in as "a grandmother for peace." She, unlike others present, did not represent any organization other than her own grandmother heart's desire to see a world of peace. When the media read her "title," they interviewed her on television. The response was

*What is sacred? All heart
communication is sacred.*

—Mahisha

astounding. Grandmothers from across America wrote her asking
to join her "Grandmothers For Peace" organization. She was
forced to formalize the group that responded to her plea for peace.
Within a year, she and her "Grandmothers for Peace" had
scheduled a trip to Moscow to meet with Raisa Gorbachev and
Russian Grandmothers for Peace. During a large gathering of
grandmothers, Mikhail Gorbachev himself entered and seated
himself among the grandmothers. A small child, holding a crystal
globe, wove her way through the mass of grandmothers. She was
preceded by other little girls throwing flower petals on the floor to
create a pathway through the grandmothers. Ultimately, their
snake-like trail ended in front of Mr. Mikhail Gorbachev. When
the child held the globe out to Mr. Gorbachev for him to accept on
behalf of the "Grandmothers for Peace," he lifted the child onto
his lap and wept like a baby. The dance of a child and the
pathway of flowers created a sacred space and a sacred moment in
time. Shortly after this event the Soviet Union ceased to exist. The
creation of sacred space is a powerful act and is always recognized
by the All-That-Is.

RITUALS
OF PROPHECY

My Kahuna medicine sister, Kahilia O' Pua, brought me to my first Awa Pua ceremony. It was her gift to me when I shared my own personal vision of world peace. This ancient Hawaiian ritual is used to see into the future. It reminded me very much of my first tea leaf reading. The Awa Pua plant was specially prepared to just the right consistency. Pua sponsored me in my first ritual of prophesy, making prayers, offering incantations and then passing me the coconut bowl containing the Awa Pua. I was to see into the swirling, silvery forms in the bowl three times. First, I was to see into the Great Mystery. Next, I was to see into the lives of my friends and family. Lastly, I was to see into my own life. Each time the bowl was passed, I was instructed to center my attention into the dark liquid abyss and pay attention to the forms that would communicate with me. After seeing I was to drink from the liquid, thus taking the vision into myself. It took me several trips to this particular ceremony before I began to actually see the forms in the bowl. When my seeing began, it was so simple as to embarrass me. The seeing was literal. The Awa Pua plant created a type of liquid that did, indeed, create shapes in the bowl. In this way, this ritual of prophecy was likened unto a tea leaf reading where tea is steeped, drunk, and then the leaves are poured into a saucer to be read by the tea leaf reader. When I learned more about tea leaves, they too could be read quite literally. Perhaps the same is true for Tarot readings as well as Rune and Medicine Card readings. All of these rituals are rituals of prophecy.

Before discussing the value and form of rituals of prophecy, it is important to mention the most obvious rituals: those of vision questing, or crying for a vision, and sun gazing. Both rituals are deeply rooted traditions for seeking guidance for the future.

Crying for a vision may begin with youth and be repeated at various turning points in one's life. Often, a single vision quest will be so revealing as to divine one's entire life. Vision questing is most often sponsored and supervised by an elder of experience and personal vision. Preparation for a vision quest may vary, but often requires purification both in the sweating lodge and preparatory fasting. The one who calls for vision may also be asked to attend any number of ceremonies as a way of focusing and preparing to seek a vision. In our modern society, it is common to read, meditate and pray in order to acquire the attitude of humility required to open to Spirit. Reading materials may vary, if they are used at all. The outcome of reading would be to acquire an academic appreciation of the process of seeking vision. If the sacred pipe is used in the vision quest, its meaning should also be well understood. Obviously, experience in ceremony and direct contact with Spirit best prepares one to seek vision. In some cases, extraordinary visions come without any preparation or self-denial. However, in most cases, voluntarily placing oneself in solitary confinement with the elements for a period of several days brings one into the submission required to serve Spirit.

When possible, one can go with blanket, pipe and ceremonial offering into the hills and find help under the cover of God's great sky. Most importantly, it is essential to know one's heart in solitude where others cannot reflect. In truth, crying for vision is a call to the inner most reaches of our own souls in search of ourselves. Those things created from inside our deepest yearnings will surely manifest themselves in our lives. As in all things, we will see what we want to see, whether that "wanting" be of conscious or unconscious origin. What we see in visioning is a reflection of our souls. To be without food and water for an extended period of time enhances our inner search and lightens our body's work. With little digestion to attend to, our body surrenders to our search, and somewhere within and without we see . . . usually what we want to see. We attract to ourselves that which is congruent with our own source. When we cry for a

This is what I saw on the mountain top. The men will come together in brotherhoods. The old women will laugh and be joyful. The lions will lay down with lambs; wolves with rabbits. A child will lead the way. That time is now.

—Cloud

vision in isolation, we can trust what we find, for no other divined it for us.

The same may well be said for sun gazing, another form of visioning the future. Fatigue and self-deprivation bring one in contact with Source and, in that moment of coming to the Center, we become one with All-That-Is. In that moment, we realize that we are the very center of all that we recognize. We realize that all things flow from us and return to us.

My old friend, John Grinder, once stated that he and his friend Judy did their best work when they were delirious with fever. Somehow they would work themselves into exhaustion and, in the exhaustion, they would relax all controls and surrender to some deeper knowing. From these beyond-exhaustion states would come works of genius. Perhaps workaholism is just a modern form of crying for vision. At the very root of it is exhaustion, fatigue and self-deprivation. It seems extraordinary that we seem to need suffering to see. My own aversion to suffering explains why we will spend more time in this book discussing fun and easy ways to engage in rituals of prophecy.

My own personal experience with visioning the future came unsolicited and unexpected. I was concluding an eighteen-day training program for Canada's psychiatric professionals. Their final exam required that they costume as their favorite childhood hero. The exam was set in a day of fun. During the course of the activities, I was spontaneously pulled to my knees, where I raced, on my knees, as a child. I was being dragged along by my own twin sister. As children growing up, it was I who dragged her along most of the time. I was four minutes older than Jan, which meant that I was the elder. The experience of having my sister pull me across the floor on my knees instantly accessed my inner child at such a deep level as to "become again as a child." My heart, and therefore my soul, opened wider than I ever knew possible. For fifteen days a window opened into the future. Perhaps the information that I saw and heard was always very close by. However, the absolute state of childhood lifted a veil, an experience so powerful it still staggers my mind.

I neither ate, drank nor slept for fifteen days. My brain acted like that of a dolphin. One side rested while the other side saw. Then, they would switch. My inner hearing was so greatly enhanced as to hear earth shifts around me. The angels sang for

I am at the stage as an Elder where I decide if I'm here for the new world. I had a little peek into the new world and it looked pretty good.

—Alinta

me and, while it was brand new, it was also very familiar. I could feel my body being fed by the flowers, air and water around me. To eat was totally unnecessary and not even a conscious thought. I felt totally nourished all the time. My body lost all normal odors and only the strong scent of roses could be noticed coming from my skin. My breath was the sweetest of all. I experienced a presence at my shoulder. A deep knowing directed my seeing and my thoughts were those of acknowledging what I heard being said to me. The voice was familiar as no other. Miracles were the norm. I travelled eighty miles on a totally empty tank of gas knowing that there was more than enough. I reached into my own injured knee and "popped" free movement that had been inhibited for years. I completely understood things that even today I have difficulty in repeating. I understood the process of creation and how very important language was in creation. A curtain was pulled and I saw clearly into the future. I saw myself appearing even younger than I then looked. The entire direction of my life turned at the end of that fifteen days of visioning. And, my own prophetic experience came without a moment of fasting and crying for vision.

Today I call this time of seeing a great loan of power. With it I know that we are truly the source of creation as we open and allow the greatness of Spirit to flow through us and use us in the Divine Plan. The extent of our power is in direct proportion to our openness and willingness to be utilized. For those who need to starve and suffer to surrender, let them seek tradition. All that is ultimately required is surrender, open child-like surrender. Whatever one must do to overcome fear is what is required to receive prophecies.

My beautiful Aboriginal medicine sister, Alinta, told me that alcohol was very good for the short vision. She said that it created a type of relaxation that allowed spirit freedom to act. I confess to experimenting with this theory. I missed the freedom of complete surrender; there is truly no sweeter experience. I sought to return to this state with my beloved wine. For a time, I was able to relax with wine and see it as an ally. However, there came a time when I pushed the edges of excess and the spirits that came to use my states of relaxation were not the Great Spirit. Like Alinta, I no longer use alcohol for anything other than teasing meddlesome spirits at the gates of a ceremonial ground. I leave small goblets filled with fine wine or tequila at each gate. I also leave rich pastries. With these I invite meddlesome spirits to linger at the gates of ceremony, eat, drink and be filled. They can then go on their way having done no mischief. My days of experimenting with alcohol allowed me to meet my own demons and make friends with that which could and would destroy. I have come to see that all things in moderation have their place. I see that there is a place for all manner of disposition and mood. Finding that place is the key to peace and harmony in every environment.

Recently I have cultivated a habit of talking to myself in the mirror each day. After doing so, I find that I can sit and listen to my deepest Self more easily. I picture myself looking into my face. I look, with my strong eye, into my own face and there I place all my questions and responses. Then I listen to what comes back to me through my own reflection. I am taking full responsibility for my own beautiful part in creation by performing this ritual with myself. I see clearly that I must truly respect each choice that I make. I could spend long hours imagining how others might respond to my actions. However, in the final analysis, it is I who must truly approve or disapprove of my actions. This daily ritual of facing myself, asking and listening, is the simplest and purest form of prophecy that I know. We will surely grow what sits at the core of our being. If we are to see into our future, we have only to see into our own souls. All that awaits us out there, lives in here.

Sometimes it is fun to play with my own energy. I like to do so with a new deck of Voyager Tarot cards. I rarely follow the rules. Every type of divination has a formal way to shuffle, spread, ask and receive information. I'm a rebel by nature. If someone tells me that it "must" be done a certain way, I know that it surely doesn't have to be. I often find myself listening to the very best advice of the experts and then doing the exact opposite. Therefore, do indeed take your own kind of liberties with rituals of prophecy, and with all rituals for that matter.

Writing music has become a definite form of ritualized prophecy for me. I count my musical abilities as a gift. While most other talents I exercise have a fair amount of ego attached to my years of work, writing music is basically free of such encumbrances. This is because I did nothing specific to cultivate an ability to write music. I simply noticed a song hanging around in my energy field and decided to sit down and allow it to form

My elders said, "Go teach the white people, because we are entering into a new world where we are one."

I said no to the request to teach the white people. I changed after I saw children killed at Nimbin. Then I saw a vision of the new world where we're going and the new way we will be living.

So, I began to teach white people. The elders said that no white person could have the right to say, "We were not told."

—Alinta

91

Twice is a pattern. There is an old saying, "If you see something come twice, it is a pattern; three times a habit; four times an obsession; and five times a compulsion." When we use this knowledge well, we create the alchemy of change.

—Cloud

on paper. This has been a consistent occurrence for the past few years, so I'm certain that my music is ladened with messages about my life. So very many of my songs have directed my movement through time and space that I sometimes feel like the singing prophet. This was particularly noticeable recently when I wrote a song entitled, "Gone With The Wind." I felt the presence of a very dear soul lifting me into the shuttle seat of a space craft and then flying me around the world for a bird's eye view of humanity. The soul seemed so very free and able to move between dimensions. Intuitively I knew it was a passing song. When I arrived home from the trip to Florida that had given birth to this song, the phone was ringing. It was a messenger informing me that my hundred-year-old Cherokee Grandmother had passed sometime in the last two days. She was found dead in her bed. The song, "Gone With The Wind" is most certainly Grandmother's song.

When I sang this song to an old friend, he felt led to give me his new deck of Voyager Tarot Cards. I've thoroughly enjoyed shuffling them to my heart's desire and then, while holding a thought in mind, drawing the middle card. (I like being in the center and "centered," so I always draw the middle card.) I ask my energy to interact with the cards and inspire me to shuffle until the card that wants to speak to me is in the center. Of course, the card that I draw is always "right on." This type of ritual of prophecy is fun and enlightening and provides a focus for my conscious thoughts. Truly, what we focus on is exactly what we will buy with our attention. Thus, what we focus on is, indeed, our future.

I like the Medicine Cards, too. However, I rarely do a reading. I run to them when I've seen some animal in nature throw itself into my path. I figure the animal has a message that I might do well to heed.

Always, no matter the form of our choosing, whenever we come seeking, we will find what is ours to find. What we find is attached to our own essence and is attracted to us for a reason that has no logic except to us. Whether our questing be formal and depriving or whether it be fun and exciting, it will always tap into our own deep well of understanding. We are each a knowing, in touch with all knowing. Whatever ritual we use to see into our future, we are certain to see our own selves reflected back to us. Just like my mirror shows me myself reflected back to me, so does each thing, place or person that holds my attention. I am always being shown myself as I am and as I will become. If we can find each breath to be sacred and each act to be a ritual, we will discover that we are always engaged in a ritual of prophecy.

DREAMING:
Awake and Sleeping

I am emerging from a time of sorrow. Yesterday I blamed it on "the change." Today I claimed a certain kinship with death and saw that life in The Other Side Camp must be a viable choice. For the past many days I have had to consciously get myself up, dressed and out for a run through the woods. I know that once I return from my time alone with the woods, life will take on a different perspective. Over the past year, we have lost three very dear friends. Each one left unexpectedly. All were healthy at the time of their deaths. All were global workers and dreamers. The sadness that I face is some sadness that their dreams were never fulfilled. Grandmother wanted to travel the world. Cliff wanted to see our ranch grow into a beautiful village. Claire wanted to create a center that would network with centers all over the world. And I imagined in my own mind what each of their dreams would look like. My dream is to see their dreams fulfilled. Somehow, when they passed, I felt a loss of their dreams.

Today a hawk braved the rain and snow with me. She flew directly across my path as I ran. I knew that she brought a message. The step that my friends have made from this side of dreaming to the other is a simple step. That is all. Nothing is gone from their dream. Grandmother will travel the world freely now. Cliff will have a grandstand view of our ranch transforming into a village and Claire is now watching her daughter mold her ranch into a magnificent center to network with our globe. We are the dream, awake or sleeping. While we weep our losses on the front pews of the church, the choir is filled with rejoicing of the spirit ones who have gone before. On this side of the dream we weep at a funeral. On the other side of the dream they rejoice at a homecoming. The dream lives on!

Last night I traveled back to my hometown with my father. He was very warm and friendly with the blacks there. My father is a bigot of the worst variety. He simply never understood blacks. He did last night though. He laughed and teased and played along with black and white alike. I was dreaming. My body did not know that what I saw was only a dream. I awakened with more energy than I have had in several days. The beaches were clean in Ft. Myers and the buildings were beautiful in design. People were playing together in peace and harmony. I am certain that what I saw exists in some dimension.

Some say that when we sleep we return to the real world. They say that our day-to-day existence is more like the sleeping dream. They say that when we relax our conscious minds, which are so limited, our unconscious minds, or spirit minds, take charge and journey into the real world. I like to think this way, with a major adaptation. I believe that all of life, awake and sleeping, is the same dream and our warrior journey is to dream consciously. Thus, my first thought upon awakening is, "How did I dream?" I spend quiet time each morning reflecting on my Dream Walker and my journey. I write my dreams down so that I can remember them and use them to prophecy. My Aboriginal sister, Alinta, does the same.

We spent January 1, 1990, on the top of Mt. Warning in Australia. The true name of the Mountain is "Cloud Catcher" and I am her spirit keeper. My Aboriginal Elder, Aunt Millie Boyd, passed the mountain into my keeping. The ceremony was performed by Lorraine Mafi-Williams within the witness of some thirty people. Lorraine told us that "The Dream Time" as we once knew it was over. She said that it is now "Blend Time." The Dream is now awakening on every level of experience and it is our duty to bring together all facets of the Great Dream. I call this decade "The Decade of Promise." The promise given in the beginning of time is now awakening. This is the Dream. We are the Dream. I first knew this time had come when I joined my Uncles in a peyote ceremony in the Native American Church.

My Uncles are leaders in the Native American Church. I personally have never felt called to peyote as a medicine. Therefore, I have only joined their worship service in the morning when the women provide the food. Prior to going to Australia, I felt a strong call to attend service. My Uncles were also quite

All of us women borne have more dreams and visions and desires than any one of us can achieve. This is the nature of dreams and visions. Learn to recognize the true forward sight and use all your skillful directed power to bring these futures into reality. Some of the future visions are for inspirational energy and some are for bringing into reality. Use the inspiration and information to fuel your determination. As you practice and live with your dreams and visions, you will learn more effectively to work with their energy. It sometimes seems easier to close down on our dreams and visions and to live in numb hopelessness than it is to work with hope, for change and joy. Go gently and slowly and be loving to your own self.

—Spider Redgold

95

Do not get caught in crisis, anxiety or anger for those who are not yet changing, or who are not moving in a way that you believe to be best. Know that true change occurs when the choice is made to spin different energy. Be calm enough to see the truth that where you are, at the present moment, can be the beginning of change. By naming the accurate, true name of the present moment, it is possible to "be here now." When you are fully in the present moment, it is possible to move on, bringing change into each present moment with you.

—Spider Redgold

insistent. I laughingly tell people that I didn't feel anything strange or unusual happen as a result of partaking of the Christ energy held in the peyote. The only thing that happened was that a large elephant appeared on the floor of our tipi. Other than that, everything seemed quite normal! Of course, a large elephant is nothing to ignore. It simply said to me, NOW! The time of the promise has returned! We wait no more! This is it! Now is the time to come together. The Dream has been heard. It is now manifesting. So it is! I now view my dreams differently. Our ancestors before us have spent their lives insuring that we might be the benefactors of the Dream, not just the American Dream, but the Global Dream of one world. What appears to some to be global disaster is, in fact, the very thing that is causing governments to come together. Even the simplest person knows that ecology is a global issue and that we must create global legislation for our planet. We are truly one people. This is the Dream.

On July 3, 1991, I returned from dreaming asleep just in time to see a sign hanging mid-air in my bedroom. The sign read, "The Angels Walk With You." The sign came as a clear affirmation that the outcome of my scheduled surgery would be good. I reported to the local hospital at 7:00 a.m. for a day surgery. I had found an egg-sized lump under my right arm on January 7th. By three o'clock in the afternoon, I was being driven home with a very glum group of friends. The doctor had decreed that the lump was malignant and I had two to six months to live. The next seven weeks proved to be the most amazing time of my life. Overnight, people began to treat me differently. Many immediately bought into the illusion of my impending death because a "doctor" decreed it. Try as I might to convince them otherwise, most were programmed to see truth as medical science. I knew that the diagnosis was not my truth and my Dream Walker clearly showed me that angels were with me. After seven weeks of undergoing thorough medical invasion of my personal space, even the doctors had to admit a "misdiagnosis." The night before the final revelation was presented to my family, my recently deceased uncle and an angel came to me in dream time and told me that my "departure date had been delayed indefinitely." Again, my dreamer foretold my future. Additionally, my Dream Walker took me on a journey to a ceremonial fire within the belly of the earth. In this place I placed my own bones on a fire and was given a brand new body. However, I knew that I was still on earth because I was left waiting on a curb for a movie to begin. I'm certain that waiting is a function of the earth plane.

I am amazed that so many people place their lives and their destinies in the hands of a medical profession that doesn't even know the patient's name, when within each person resides a Dream Walker with simple and accurate information. As we think, so we are. What is truly important for people to know will sooner or later be revealed to them, if they but seek and listen. No other person has more information about us than we have about ourselves. None. This morning a young man with a publishing company discovered that I was a doctor of "something." "How can you help me?" he asked. "Only to remind you that you are the only one that can truly help you." was my reply. "You are your own dream. All that you do, say and think speaks to the dream that you are." We are IT! There is nothing more! In the words of my co-creator and playmate, Skye . . . "WAKE UP!"

There are numerous ceremonial and ritual ways to "wake up" and discover the dream that we are. We will mention a few of the ones that have empowered us. Skye and I first met at a dream dance in Oklahoma. In order to honor the vision I called forth, I summoned fifty Excellence Players to Oklahoma to dance awake the Dream. We called our dance, "Super Bowl." With the exception of Skye, all the players had experienced the Challenge of Excellence and were ready to take the next step. For us, the next step was to truly give form, song and dance to what we could imagine. In the days of our ancestors, it was common for many tribes to come together and re-enact the vision of one of their leaders. In this way the people held the dream solidly in their own beings. They had a common experience of the victory that was foretold. They spoke of it around their winter fires and passed down legends of the re-enactment to their grandchildren. Their hearts beat as one heart when they thought of the future. The Super Bowl Camp was to become like this tribal tradition.

We began our week of re-enactment with a Grand Parade honoring the Mother Earth. We costumed in our finest warrior regalia, painted our horses, decorated our tractor and wagons, gathered our rattles, bells, shields and drums and circled the land with singing. We stood at Her center and offered Her our prayers. It is still humorous to recall how surprised Skye was to learn that our Mother's Day Parade was not to be down the main street of

I dreamt I was in a cave with other Medicine Women. I took the top of my head off and the universe spilled out. Around the cave were women painting on the walls, dancing, singing and drumming. I heard in my ears, "When we remember the ancient arts of divination by throwing sticks and stones and bone (entertainment . . . singing, dancing, drumming), we will know how to lead our people to safety through the coming earth changes."

—Virginia Davis

town! She had brought a costume that would suit such an occasion.

During the week we successfully walked on fire together. We danced in the gaming field with representatives of many Indian nations present. We did so to honor the part of the vision that saw all the Indian nations coming together to dance in the old way. We took a cottonwood tree in the old way with warriors "cornering" the tree and young "virgins" chopping it down. (My nine year old niece was the only virgin in camp, so we pretended!)

We erected our Dream Pole and danced gazing at the sun and our beautiful Dream Shields. For days we had cut willow, racked shields, painted and embellished our Dream Shields. Each of us made a Dream Shield to represent our own individual Dreams. When the sunrise ceremony that lifted the shields into place came, we cried with silent pride in the beauty of our composite Dream. All day and night we danced to and fro, chanting and singing to our Dreams. Late in the night we went into the sweating lodge and there we prayed for our dreams. The next day we cut our shields from the Dream Pole and then we danced with our Dream Shields.

For one solid week, we focused on our Dreams. We made Dream Shields; we carried our shields across the gaming fields in wild games of Dream Walker/Dream Stalker; we sweated for our Dreams; we prayed for our Dreams; we walked across fire for our Dreams; we jumped from six story poles for our Dreams; we costumed for our Dreams; we painted for our Dreams; and we performed dramas and skits for our Dreams. We dreamed together for a week. Awake and sleeping, we focused on our Dreams. It is now seven years later and for those of us who dream of world peace, we can see that our dream is coming into form. We have watched the Berlin Wall fall and the Soviet Union disappear. We have watched major corporations take stands in behalf of our rain forests. We have seen entertainers from across the globe take the microphone in behalf of the Mother Earth. And we watch peacefully as our Indian peoples come together to celebrate 500 years of survival against the influence of the white people. We praise them for celebrating the peace and dignity of all peoples.

Truly the Dream is wakening in this time in which we live. Each sign is an omen of something to come. Each dream is advance information about the shape of the Dream. We have only to pay attention. Pay attention to our dreams, awake and sleeping. Pay attention to our day dreams. Pay attention to the forms of books and movies to which we are drawn or which we are given to examine. Pay attention to the responses of those around us. Pay attention to those who choose to contact us or to remain out of contact. Pay attention to spatial relationships. Pay attention to colors of the season and of our own clothes. Pay attention to the music and the dance. We are the Dream. The Dream is here, now. This is it! WAKE UP!

RITUALS OF RESPECT:
Honoring All Our Relations

In the beginning of time, an old friend spoke with me about power. She said, "Do you see that beautiful bush? In a moment you could drop away your definitions of what you are looking at and find yourself in the moment . . . recognizing the life before you. In that moment of being truly recognized, that little bush would open and flow its power to you." I'm sure I nodded and uttered the all-knowing, "Aha" and walked on.

Later she shared with me the notion of respect for our elders, whether they were one minute or one hundred years older. I considered myself equal to all, young or old. It was more a matter of who had the best idea; not how old you are.

I have come to know that respect has little to do with ideas and everything to do with "seeing."

In the beginning of each moment there is someone to recognize. It begins with the source of our being, filters through our body, mind and soul, ripples out to everyone we see, feel, hear and touch and all those invisible to our senses. It goes to all around; the universe within and without.

Wouldn't it be wonderful to meet each moment and all within it as though it were the first time? We are the creators of this beautiful, blue planet.

A true warrior is equal to all things. No greater and no less. A warrior is equal to an elephant and an ant, as great as the greatest king and as simple as the most flea-infested dog. A warrior recognizes kinship with each living thing. A warrior looks around and sees mirrored everything that exists within his or her very own soul. This is easy to do when one stands gazing on a beautiful spring vista. It is just as easy for the warrior when staring at the smelliest pile of refuse. Each thing on earth deserves respect. The warrior respects herself and all things equally.

I recently adopted two miles of country road in Tennessee as my own personal act of beauty. The litter laws in Tennessee are not enforced, leaving the roadsides to become deplorable collections of human waste. Looking at the mess I felt that the human animal must be the most vile of all God's creations. This is the attitude that began my "act of beauty." I first vowed to clean up all of my road . . . some five miles. However, after cleaning bottles and cans and paper waste from the lawns of neighbors, I began to feel as though I was somehow invading their personal space. What right did I have to walk onto their land and take their trash? None. Thus, I clean only the part of our country road where no one lives. It's the most beautiful section of the road and some are beginning to notice that it is free of litter. It is easier for me to create ritual to respect mosquitoes than it is to respect people who litter! It is easier for me to crawl into a sweat lodge with a good heart towards a tick than it is to feel in "good relations" with the man who throws his Lite beer cans on my lawn! And yet, rituals of respect expect us to find the point of respect for all things. This includes our human brothers and sisters.

Ceremony at our ranch begins with much focus and preparation. Shields are cleaned and repaired. Food is prepared. Instruments are collected and taken to the Village. We bathe and costume for our own ball. When the drums begin their steady, incessant beat, people begin to gather . . . people and dogs and cats and insects and horses and birds and critters unseen and all the world of invisibles. From four directions the participants arrive to celebrate and show respect. As participants begin to arrive, they join in with their own rattles, bells, flutes, sticks and stones. The hill of the Village comes alive with rhythm. It is obvious that something is happening. Seers squeal at the hundreds of invisibles who clamor at the edges of the Village to watch the festivities. Their presence is definitely known. Even unsuspecting corporate executives comment that they feel as

There are always spirits around . . . good spirits and bad spirits. Honor both.

—Alinta

I live in the Florida keys in a humble conch shack that is full of spiders, scorpions and termites. People say, "Why don't you kill them?" I say, "They aren't hurting me." I don't own the world. I will share it with them. We got a little agreement. I will share with them and they won't eat me.

—Grandmother Princess
Moon Feathers

though they are being watched. The ranch animals take their places as people arrive, reminding everyone that ceremony is always at its very best when ALL things are respected.

Once the assemblage is together, the drums come to a sudden halt and the Queen Conch bellows her voice in four directions. Always we call out to each of the directions, welcoming the energies and people of the East, South, West and North. To show our knowledge and respect for what is inherent in the winds, we call out those things that we learn from each of the directions. Children carry food and drink to each of the four "Gates" of the Village and tell the invisibles that they are welcomed. A runner circles the Village with sweet burning sage to bless all who come to the circle. A prayer of "Thanksgiving" is offered to the Great Mystery for all things. As many as come to mind are mentioned individually to show respect —even the minerals, rocks, wind, trees and tall grasses. A speech is offered in which we acknowledge our part in the whole and our Oneness as creation. We are asked to think of any one thing that we would not want present and we bring even that thing or person to the circle in our hearts and minds.

A space is made in ceremony for those wishing to speak of their own appreciation to step forward and offer their "thanks." Before any other aspect of ceremony is performed, this honoring of All Things is done. If any one thing is so abhorred as to limit oneness, it is offered up to the circle, for always there is one in the circle who can bless each thing and understand its value. This is what is important. That each thing be held in the light for all to see. This is all there really is to do in life . . . to hold each thing in the light for all to see. I have often been quoted saying, "If just one person can hold a light for you, you will surely succeed." In learning to respect each thing, it is thought that each one of us will come to hold a light for ourselves for all to see. In the words of the song of our childhood, we sing, "This little light of mine, I'm going to let it shine." This is at the very root of rituals of respect.

Grandmother Alinta tells us that she has a common practice with children. When they do something great, and when they do something hurtful, she stands them in front of a mirror and has them look into the mirror as she says, "You are precious." Then she has them say, while looking at themselves, "I am precious." If you think that this is simple, just stop this instant, go to the mirror, look yourself in the face and say, "I am precious!" If our every action can be one that we ourselves respect, we will know true happiness. (Excuse me while I run to the mirror to "precious" myself!)

In the making of personal medicine bundles, it is good to place some representation of a life of respect for all things. A seed may represent that which grows in the earth. A feather may represent that which flies. A discarded shell may represent that which is called insect. Hair may represent the animals. Soil may represent the earth and a small rock or rock sliver, the rock people. Medicine that shows respect is strong medicine, because the more that our desires touch the well-being of all things, the more likely the power to all things is to participate in our dream. When our desire for Oneness is so strong as to cast a shadow on "individualism," the forces of power within the individual will rise up and obstruct our dream. Always when opposition exists, there is lack of respect for something or someone.

Respect is what grants free passage in life. Where it is lacking, there is conflict. When we hold ourselves above others, we invite conflict. Rituals of respect seek to teach this principle. I have learned this one the hard way. We were raised in an environment of high competition. The adjectives "better," "best," "greater," "higher," etc. were common forms of expression. My own belief that my values were "better" than others, or that my own training technology was "the best" have often landed me in hot water. It is a fine line to hold regard for one's own gifts while acknowledging others simultaneously. Now it is more comfortable to think of my gifts as having a place that is useful in the scheme of things. It is sometimes not as comfortable to believe that others' gifts also have a place in the scheme of things. However, "I am precious" even in the face of my irritating regard for my own beliefs above others. This gives me something to work toward.

An associate of mine is younger than me and not as schooled. I even like to think that my life experience gives me some leverage in our relationship. I say, "I like to think this," when, in truth, I actually like to think of myself as a person who doesn't think this way . . . although, I do. I'm the elder. That gives me some degree of leverage. It allows me to rest when I want to and feel extra prideful when I excel in some physical feat. Beyond that, it really has little to do with respect. Kat, however, is forty years old and still says, "yes, ma'am" and "yes, sir." She was raised to respect her elders: the priest, your mother, the boss and the teacher. I, on the other hand, was raised by a father who told me to tell anyone who tried to boss me around to "Kiss my a_ _." Kat regards our seven year age difference with respect. She calls me her teacher and, as any good student of the martial arts (which she is), she knows that her service to me leaves more time in the day for me to "teach." She religiously waxes the wooden floors and cooks delicious soups for me. She lights up like a little child when she speaks of my abilities and she is as happy as a pig in mud when she is building a fire or chopping wood for our council circle. She serves me like I serve "the world." While my focus is on respect for the "All-That Is," hers is on me. Needless to say, I find this disconcerting at times. However, I am precious, and my discomfort shows me how others must feel uncomfortable when I am busy lending my assistance to the planet.

The other day, Kat extended her hand to help me step off a rock in the woods. I declined her help and grumbled something about being made to feel like an old lady. I had to laugh at myself and see that Kat's training as a Disney employee and a police officer taught her to help everyone up and down the curbs of life. I also had to see that perhaps my youthful fervor of years past to save the planet must have made both visibles and invisibles uncomfortable. As my croning party comes closer and closer, my fervor to save anything has diminished. I have come to respect all life's right to life or death. Choice is a sacred act, and who am I to spoil someone's party? Now I only hope to live happy and prosper along the way! If the sharing of my gifts can bring happiness to others, I am happy and I love being paid for it.

Yes, I've come to respect myself enough to get paid. Before I gave one damn about rituals of respect, I made lots of money. I made a lot of money and I spent a lot of money. I had no regard for money. Then I went through a very pious (and I might add, stupid) period of my life when I actually hated money. I, quite naturally, didn't have much of it then. Now, I LOVE MONEY! And, loving money attracts it. I have come to respect money for what it can do and my growing wisdom allows me to make different choices about it than I used to. Now I know that money is fertilizer and I respect how quickly it makes things grow. I am a bit more conscious of what I spread it on.

I run several days a week. Sometimes I really enjoy it. Most often, I have to motivate myself to get all suited up for the chilling winter weather and step out into the cold to pound the pavement. What could possibly motivate me to do such a thing? Respect. Respect for my body. I know that the way to get things moving in life is to get things moving in my body and one way to do that is to move my body. When we wiggle, we squirt. Sitting slumped in a chair is a slight wiggle that renders a type of slight squirt of that which inhibits. When we run free, we squirt elevating chemicals that heighten our awareness. It is not possible for the brain to squirt inhibitors and elevators at the same time. It's either one or the other. I run to respect my body's means of lifting my spirits. Running can be viewed as a ritual of respect.

Approximately 50-60 percent of my diet is living food (fruits and fresh, uncooked vegetables). Another 20% of my diet is whole grains and rice. About 10% is liquid, mostly water, carrot juice, orange juice and skim milk. And about 10% of my diet is "happy food." "Happy food" feeds my spirit and the CHILD in me. These foods include chocolate, ice cream, biscuits and peanut butter and jelly. Basically, I eat a healthy diet. Occasionally I eat fish, chicken and venison. I'll also eat buffalo when I can get it.

I've learned to eat to honor both my body and my spirit. Eating can be considered a very sacred ritual. As a child I heard my Grandfather say (at least a million times), "Bless this food to the nourishment of our bodies and us to Thy service." Only now can I truly appreciate what he was saying. The way in which we nourish our bodies is perhaps one of the most sacred of all rituals of respect. It has taken me many years to learn the value of "respecting" the temple of my body. As far as foods go, I know through experience that we can absolutely live without food. For fifteen days I neither ate or drank and was completely fed by the energy of all that surrounded me. I breathed water from the air and drew food from the breath of the plants. However, I love to eat. Food is fun! Now I am truly thankful to all food for the sheer pleasure it affords me. I am truly grateful to the birds that sing to my tomatoes and the wind that is held in my beans. I love the bees that pollinate my flowers and make my honey. I love the rain for watering my plants and the sun for pulling them towards the sky. I fervently maintain that the most important ingredient in food is love. What is prepared in love will nourish. What is sung to will carry that vibration into our bodies. Both eating and the preparation of food is a ritual of respect.

Bathing and personal grooming is a ritual of respect. Soaking in salt, minerals, bubbles, vinegar, and even bleach is a ritual of respect. Filing my fingernails and polishing them is a ritual of respect. Brushing my hair until it shines is a ritual of respect. Polishing my boots is a ritual of respect. Making beautiful medicine objects to wear is a ritual of respect. Costuming in bright colors is a ritual of respect. Keeping my home clean and orderly is a ritual of respect. Grooming the lawn is a ritual of respect. Keeping my animals clean, fed and groomed is a ritual of respect. Keeping my car in good repair is a ritual of respect. Living, truly living each moment to the fullest, is a ritual of respect. It is easy to see when people lack respect. It shows in all that surrounds them.

For several years we struggled to pay for our land and keep it from those who would take it from us. During those days, we made beautiful shields of protection and hung them in the Village. We painted our cement Indian and stood her as a lookout in each of the four directions. We brought vulture feathers from the fields and tacked them above the doors to scare away meddlesome spirits. We planted cedar trees around the property to send out a scent of "protection." When our beloved horse friend, Chivas Regal, died, we buried him in his orchard and knew that his strong energy would claim this land for the family. Each of these seemingly "desperate" acts was actually a ritual of respect. We held the land as our family's sacred ceremonial ground and we respected Her enough to create focus for Her survival. She survived.

When our Elders and Grandmothers came to our Women's Gathering, we employed the services of a wonderful gourmet cook to serve them at every meal. We lit candles and played beautiful music for them. We created an atmosphere of respect for our Elders. Each breath of this service was a ritual of respect. We declared the main lodge house off limits to any who did not have a personal invitation from the Elders. In this act, we created a ritual of respect.

We periodically and regularly invite friends and family to the ranch for a day of clean-up and grooming. The hours spent in the peach orchard trimming and pruning is a ritual of respect. Mohawk spends hours grooming and training the horses. This is a ritual of respect. Skye mops the ceilings of the store rooms and carries off anything that is not used in a three-month period. She is a living, breathing ritual of respect. From the formal to the daily acts of caring for properties and the environment, we are constantly afforded the opportunity to perform rituals of respect. The degree to which we do this is most certainly evidence of the degree of respect that we command from our world. Respect, like love, manifests in action. Let us roll up our sleeves and mop. There is much respect to be manifested in our world.

RITUALS
OF PASSAGE

At fourteen I first looked upon my Mother from eyes that said to her, "On this day, and evermore, I shall act as I see fit." It was many years later before my twin sister did the same. Growth into adulthood is not a thing of counting winters or standing tall. It is a matter of orderly and well-intended advancement. Tradition has called a girl a "woman" when she first begins to bleed. At fourteen I was still flat-chested and bloodless. I was then, and remained, a virgin until I married at age twenty. Something beyond tradition called me to adulthood. Perhaps it was my own sense of adventure or my resolute knowing that choice was mine and mine alone. I was not a defiant child. I sought to bring honor to my family. From the age of fourteen forward my Mother expressed her views regarding my choices, but always she left the making of choice in my hands. By choice, I honored her wishes— all but twice. I am nearing the half-century mark and still, by choice, I notify mother about my comings and goings.

Though mother is of native descent, we were raised without knowledge of traditional ceremonies. What I knew, I knew instinctively. I was "visited" at age four by a Spirit Being who counseled me to "become impeccable." I was informed that I would "be guided" and to take the opportunities that life offered to me. From that moment forward I understood that I was not, in truth, only my mother's child. I belonged to a larger family and my own will was the one I must learn to respect above all others. For as many years as I can remember, I have been saying, "Here we are, alone in life with no adult supervision. Let's play!" At age 46 I participated in my first "passage" ceremony for young women. I was chosen as "auntie" by Christina. As I sat sweating with her in the Lodge of the Stone People, I wondered about the magic that causes one to "feel and behave as an adult."

Children belong to their mothers and their grandparents. Youths belong to their teachers. Warriors belong to themselves alone. A quick glimpse into the lives of most couples of adult age lets one discern that very few true warriors exist in the adult world. The barbaric practice of "belonging" to another is the root of deep soul remorse and divorce. Passage rituals are designed to create awareness of the freedom and responsibility that comes with maturity. Perhaps the first passage ceremony is that of birth.

Recently a team of doctors and nurses were amazed to hear a newborn baby boy speak quite audibly as he cleared the birthing tunnels, "Oh no! Not again!" He then closed his eyes and went into the normal coma that awaits a foot tickle or pat on the bottom. When a soul passes from spirit into form, it is definitely a time for great compassion and understanding. The courage required to take on flesh is unspeakable. Can you imagine leaving the beautiful celestial realms where we danced and sang as children of the harmonies and then coming into the cold, sterile world of an operating room? Further imagine arriving home to the sounds of the six o'clock news!

The old practice among our Native American ancestors of spending the nine months of "in uterine" time walking among the trees, smelling flowers and listening to the sounds of babbling brooks would be most respectful to our children-en-route. Let our first passage ritual be that of blending our children's essence with the very finest that our earth has to offer. And when the soul returns at birth, let it be into warm ocean water among the loving dolphin, or at the very least, let it be in a nature-filled environment with the sweetest of all music available. Let the communication be sounds of satisfaction as in the *hmmms* and *ahhhs* and *cooos*. Let the touch be gentle and the smells sweet. Provide for the mother in such a way that all her needs are met and she feels the most nurtured of all. Let the introduction of family and relatives be gradual and easy. Let the step into sunlight be after many days of close cuddling and nurturing in a warm and protective environment. Let the naming come from the child-soul as spoken into the ears of the one relation that is prone to truly "listen." Let the umbilical cord be placed at the root of a young tree planted for the child, or dried and placed into the infant's first medicine

Wisdom is not something that is crammed down your throat. It is something that happens to you and you draw upon it like a well. It's a reservoir of experience that crystalized into spiritual meaning.

—Colonel Lyn

bundle. Let our children swim in warm, clean, clear waters as early as possible so that their physical forms record maximum freedom and support into every cell of their bodies. Let this ritual alone be sufficient to clean up our rivers and streams. Let the air that each soul breathes be filled with the loving skan of the breath of trees and plants that are happy and well fed. Let the air be filled with the joyous singing of birds and bees. Let the wind that rides the skies, viewing peaceful and harmonious living, be inhaled by our infants so that at their time of passage from spirit into form, they feel joy and exultation. Let this be our first ritual of passage.

Let us remember that all newborns come recently from the place of the Grandmothers and Grandfathers. They come recently from the place where they know everything. They bring to us the wisdom of the Grandmothers and Grandfathers from the beginning. Know our parentselves as the force that blends to make a body for a soul that lived long before we even knew each other. Know that the newborn lives in the everlasting seed and knows everything from the very beginning. Let the newborns listen to the sounds of wind and rain, earth sounds and sky sounds. Let them relate these sounds to the sounds that their spirits already know. Let them do so at this extended time of passage into form so that one day their young eyes and ears will perceive as their spirit intends, and, in each unique perception of color and shape, contribute to the act of creation on earth. Birth is the most fundamental ritual of passage.

All young children are moved by their own spirits in a direction that they will come to recognize, if they are granted passage into their own way. The Catholic Church says that children brought up in the ways of the church until the age of six will return to those ways when they are older. There is much truth in this statement. The patterns that are coded into the nervous system, flesh and blood of any being program that being for a lifetime. To change that programming is an art form understood and practiced by few masters.

By the age of ten, the tribe can see the place a child will take in the hoop. Each child is unique and brings a knowing from the pool of All-Knowing that is intended to make a specific contribution to creation. There is a place for each disposition. There is a proper place for each act. To avoid the danger of a father or mother trying to make their off-spring into themselves, the custom of our ancestors allows the youth to choose a second father and mother, a *hunka* parent, or parent-by-choice. This one of different blood is not personally ambitious for the child. This one respects the sentient being that his soul is and grows the child according to the child's own disposition. Before reason drives any youth forward, it is important to avoid knocking mischief into them. When allowed to blossom naturally, each child is extraordinary. A child who is not ordinary will not live life as an ordinary adult. The youth seasons that pass between child and warrior are regarded by the Grandfathers and Grandmothers as the most important in all of life.

It is good when the children are allowed to go to the old people and hear the legends. Let the youth sit with their grandparents and listen to these old ones. Let the young make use of what the old ones know. Let the young learn to guard their tongues so that in time they will mature a thought that will be of use to the people. Let the young be encouraged to hear their own familiar voices which never forbid nor compel. Let each one learn that the familiar voice within speaks the truth, but never demands that the young act on the truth. Let them see around them an example of "choice" being made by each one alone. Let there be cultivated an environment in which respect is given for the power in each person that is a selective power, a power that always results in spiritual growth. Let the child see an example where caution rather than fear is taken as a life companion. Let the adults with easy hearts surround the young. Let the child know that always someone watches. To bring honor to the tribe means to live in a good way in thought, word and deed. Let the entire family assume responsibility for influencing the youth through the youth-to-warrior years. Let all adults know that their every breath is providing movement to a child who is "passing" into the warrior years. Let all adults understand that their example will be multiplied and expanded in the youth. Let the example of the adults be that of honoring each individual's earth walk. These years of teaching through example are the most enduring ritual of passage.

The formal ceremonies to celebrate passage into warrior years are many and varied. The Jewish tradition celebrates manhood at the age of twelve. Apache tradition celebrates womanhood at the time of bleeding. Other traditions require displays of physical prowess and warring feats. Sororities and fraternities require

Take it in, welcome it in, let it do its work, let it out.

Through the testing times is a quiet resolve held softly in your heart. What do I want for myself today?

Stand tall.

Listen in your body, brain and heart.

Make a space to receive and let spirit guides help.

—Colonel Lyn
(Speaking about cancer)

Grandparents whisper early learnings into the child's ear before speech. At three years, boys go off with grandfathers and girls with grandmothers.

At age three, stand the child in front of the mirror and have them say, "I love me. I am precious." If children can love and respect themselves, they can love and respect everyone.

—Alinta

degrees of humiliation. Some traditions see marriage as the stepping stone into the age of the warrior. Some traditions see getting a job or leaving home as the formal ritual of adulthood. Still others grant adult status on youths when they can drive a car.

Our experience with designing passage ceremonies is that most adults currently have no idea if or when they passed into adulthood. When the men are left to their own devices for designing a passage ceremony, they correlate manhood with getting drunk and "getting a piece." Their all-night vigils result in drinking parties, loud singing, wild and dirty jokes and games of smashing beer cans on each other's heads.

The women, on the other hand, spend their time bathing each other, braiding each other's hair, embellishing each other with flowers and sweet scents, drumming, chanting, sharing a pipe, sweating together, massaging each other and dancing through archways covered with beautiful flowers. We have found sweetness lacking in the men's ceremonies and outrageous fun lacking in the women's ceremonies. We now prefer to attempt to bring a more androgynous blend to all passage celebrations. The recent "Men's Movement" forwarded by Robert Bly's material has done much to bring passage-into-manhood back into our culture.

On a vision quest in 1989, I saw clearly that the "brotherhood" would come together.

The image I was shown was a valley filled with children and young women playing. The elder women cloistered together to enjoy the family gathering. The old ladies were laughing, with their heads thrown back towards the sun. I don't recall seeing the old men. The young men were perched like cats on rocks along the cliffs surrounding the valley. Though they were some hundred yards or more apart, they maintained a very intimate communication. The simple nod of the head or flip of the hand would cause great laughter along the rim of the cliff. It was obvious that these "brothers" had spent long hours together and had many secrets and inside jokes. A child appeared at the head of the canyon and the voice of a grandfather said softly, "The child will lead the way."

This vision calls me forward through litter and smog and political chaos into a new day when the direction of the children is truly in the hands of loving family. I see a day when a child no longer need be subjected to the tyranny of modern schools in which each individual is expected to achieve the same thing. I call for a day when children are reintegrated into our families where they live and learn with family all day long. I see a day when neighborhoods and boroughs form hoops for sharing knowledge with the children; where each nature of skill is respected and the children all have the opportunity to learn from the craftsperson of choice. I see a day when children and their growth to warrior status is the single most important focus of society and the economics prove it. The experience of the passage years from childhood to warrior status is the most enduring of all. Let us find ever more colorful ways to celebrate this time of coming to the age of reason — and may the reason that each child achieves be one founded on choice that honors peace and dignity for all.

Before leaving this age of ritual passage, we must embrace Grandmother Kitty for her shining example of love and respect for the children. For hours and hours, Grandmother Kitty sits with the young girls and answers their questions about bleeding, boys, questions of authority and visions of destiny. Each child is given special attention and a special gift to remind them of all Grandmother has to share. An aunt sits with the circle and the girls laugh together and share their own experiences of growing up. The mother is viewed as a woman whose relationship to her daughter is passing from mother to friend and confidante. The mothers sit with other mothers and consort about letting their little girls go. Aunts and mothers scheme to provide the young women with beautiful dresses or other forms of ceremonial garb.

Fresh flowers are cut for hair and pathways. Food is ceremonially prepared with conscious selection of foods that bear seeds within for the young woman who carries the egg of her future children. Tomatoes and okra and apples and peaches are used to show the young woman the truth of her womb. The sweating lodge ceremony, the feasting and the dancing all conspire to mark out the truth of girl-becoming-woman. The ceremony lasts for days. Whatever is required to create focus and memory is included in the ceremony. Whatever is required to summon total family support for the new young woman is acceptable ceremonial practice.

The result of the ceremony is that a young woman be looked upon as a reflection of the Earth-Mother during a growing season when the winds smell their sweetest and the air tastes the best; a time when the sun pledges to warm and ripen all living things. It

We pass on our Aboriginal name to girls here in America so that our culture and our names spread. It is a great honor that the great women of my culture will be living in little girls here.

—Alinta

A human comes to life as a child, excited, curious, trusting; aided by her own will and commitment from her family . . . she retains these qualities her entire life.

—Grandmother Kitty

is meant to remind the young woman and all who attend her that she is a physical manifestation of the Earth and from her will spring forth life for all future generations.

Passages for young men are to leave the youthman seeing himself as the sky that brings movement, warmth and rain to the earth. When this level of respect is the center of ritual, and the earth and sky are embraced in ceremony, all things around, above and below resound the truth of youth-becoming-warrior. With the passage rituals of manhood and womanhood, as with all others, come freedom and responsibility. The freedom comes with the lessening of adult supervision. The responsibility comes with reason and choice.

During the warrior years of adulthood we experience the effects and consequences of our choices. We will choose our families, our life vocations, our dwelling places, our friends, our fun and fancy, our challenges and our spiritual proclivities. Our spirit selves will seek expression in our bodies, enriching us when free and abandoning us when imprisoned. Truly, disease is a withholding of our wildest spirit dreams.

Marriage is the expected next passage, followed by parenthood, grandparenthood, retirement or the age of wisdom and death. At some point, divorce may become a time of passage.

It is common, in older traditions, to see a person acquire two or more names in the course of a lifetime. A child is given a child's name and that name molds the character for the formative years. When the child becomes an adult or a warrior, he or she is given a man or woman name. Again, at various points of success or failure, the adult can acquire a name remembering an event or a strong characteristic that emerges. Sometimes in old age, a naming occurs where an elder gives his name to another and assumes yet another name. Each naming is a time of great passage. We are shaped by what we are called. We hear our names more than any other sound. It is important that the sound of our names empower us along our journey. As a child I was named Janet Lee, after a movie star. Soon after the age of reason, I was named after the character "Scout" in the book *To Kill A Mockingbird*. According to English tradition, I took my father's last name until I married, at which point I took my husband's last name. After divorce and leaving the government system, I dropped both my father's and my husband's last names. When I stepped onto my spirit's path, I took the name brought to me by a child and the Great Spirit. I am now Dr. Scout Cloud Two-Children Lee.

When I carried my husband's name, I was a wife. I experienced being seen as an extension of another person. I was Mrs. Louis Carroll Gunn, III. You can imagine how a little girl taught to say, "Kiss my a_ _" to those who assumed superiority would like being "the Third" of anything! When we divorced, I kept Gunn as a last name and became Dr. Scout Lee Gunn. For these years I got the experience of being "under the Gunn." These were fiercely competitive years in the university system of "publish or perish." When I stepped from the ivory towers onto my own corporate pedestal, I dropped my Gunn. Overnight I became an unknown. Dr. Scout Lee had no following or history. In essence, this passage forced me to begin again. Along the way a new challenge presented itself. I was named Cloud in a set of circumstances so unusual as to let me know that this "naming" came straight from the Throne. The same was true of "Two-Children." The all-too-familiar "Scout" became "Cloud" and I got to make another major passage. "Scout" is a tribal position of truth-bearer. It is also a command to act in a certain way in behalf of the whole. "Cloud" on the other hand is formless, constantly changing, ever-moving, here-today-gone-tomorrow, and capable of both great beauty and great storms. The ceremonies accompanying each naming passage marked a moment in time, but could have, in no way, foretold the extent of the change wrought in the naming ceremony. Perhaps every young bride, about one year down the road past becoming "Mrs. Somebody" can appreciate the extent to which a naming changes things.

Rituals of passage regarding naming ceremonies can vary from weddings or fraternity initiations to give-aways, painting and sweat lodge ceremonies. I now enjoy "sweating" away the footprints of a walk with one name before accepting another. I also enjoy using red paint on the crown, strong-eye, throat, hands, heart and feet of the person receiving a new name. Any change of costume or gifting that reinforces a new name is appropriate in ceremony. Perhaps a party or a feasting is in order. Even a trip to another part of the country may create awareness of the impact of being called who you are on a changing path of life. Today I am simply called "Cloud" and the statement, "Cloud's here!" usually engenders squeals of delight from those who have come to know that Cloud is sworn to fun!

Do not go to sleep unless you have made right first. Keep everything right in order to be sure nothing is left undone if you should die.

—Alinta

Perhaps the most festive of all rituals of passage is marriage. David and Annie's wedding lasted for one week and consumed the energies of all 80 persons who gathered to celebrate 8/8/88, the date they chose to formalize their bond. The week was filled with games of tug-for-peace, horsemanship, climbing the ropes, sweating, fire-walking and great feasting. For one whole day the women of our clan nurtured Annie by bathing her, braiding her hair with flowers, passing the pipe, massaging her, decorating her tipi and readying her wedding garb. The men spent equal time with David doing the things that men do together, which from all reports included much laughter. The men also assisted David in gathering his finest warrior's garb and writing his statement. Blankets were gifted to David so that he could wrap one around the shoulders of his new bride. A "Share Pouch" of corn was gifted to Annie to present to their bond as a sign of nurturing the dream. The grounds were lined with luminaries, flowers and beautiful crystals. David's steed was painted and saddled for ceremony.

We all rehearsed our entry dance to the magnificent outdoor sanctuary, the children leading the way. The women danced like woods fairies into the circle and the men stampeded down the hill like warriors on a hunt. David galloped into the ceremonial grounds on a massive paint horse, with his feathers and cape flying in the wind. He was truly a warrior in search of his woman. When he found her hiding in her tipi, he rushed in to capture her and bring her to the council of warrior friends and family that sat assembled to approve this mating. Sweet music was offered by those with musical talent. Words of wisdom were shared by the elders. The children made their own special presentations and called for a vow from the couple and the circle to "hold the children high." David spoke his intentions to serve humanity and thus make his woman live with comfort and pride. Both affirmed their connection to the Great Mystery. Then, rather than speaking words, each performed a ritual of song and dance to express their marriage vows. David played his flute and Annie danced. When David wrapped the rainbow blanket around Annie's shoulders and Annie presented David the marriage pouch, the bond was sealed in the hearts and minds of the circle. The marriage was followed with great feasting and dancing around the fire until the dawning hours of the next day.

Other marriage rituals have acknowledged each of the four

directions in the following manner. First the couple goes at sunset to the ocean or mountain stream and there they bathe each other, carefully washing away each year of life up to the moment. They cast to the sea any representation that leaves them bound to another time or space. Brooke cast an old wedding band into the mountain stream. Tarzanne poured away drink no longer used. The Captain took off a chain of a deceased wife of fourteen years past and gave it away. This time of reflection is a time to look within and "thank" each life experience for its learning, and then "let it go." This is a time spent together in the West place. The night time and the next morning are spent separate from each other. The men advise the man of wisdoms about marriage. The women do the same for the woman. This is a time of seeking wisdom from the North. When the bonding ceremony comes, the sun is high. It is a time for new beginnings and is thus considered an act for the East place. Finally, feasting and celebration follow as the afternoon winds fly kites and children play in the fields with their dogs. This celebration is a thing of the South place where passion and youthfulness are relived.

Other bonding ceremonies involve the use of the bonding stick. Quite obviously, a bonding stick is used in marriage ceremonies. It is also used in adoption ceremonies (Relatives-by-Choice), business agreements and team commitments.

The bonding stick is different from the marriage stick. The marriage stick is a beautiful stick into which a couple carves, paints, sews or otherwise symbolizes major events in the relationship. The stick is a form of history-keeping and follows the couple to their resting place. The bonding stick can become the marriage stick after the ceremony. A bonding stick is similar to a "promise stick" or a covenant. It is used when the bond is made in the presence of witnesses to the Great Provider. The formal term for the bonding is called "Coming-to-the-Stick." It is an act that requires maximum commitment. When one comes to the stick, that person recognizes that there is no chance for divorce. To turn from the stick engenders the wrath of Spirit and all who witness the bonding. The ceremony is simple. A circle of people, who agree to witness the coming-to-the-stick, gather. The couple who performs the ritual sits center and takes the stick together. They face each other and place their right hands palms down on the stick. Then they each place their left hands palms up in their partner's left hand. This forms an unending circle of giving and

You were told when you were born that you were going to die and that every day is precious and every day is a celebration. You don't really hang onto the idea that "I've got to stay alive to get this done." You hang onto the idea that you are preparing your death song, so you can sing all the way along (across).

—Grandmother Kitty

In the old way when two desired to come together in a marriage bond, the tribe took three days.

On the first day, the woman's family all gathered and told the man and his family all they knew of the woman . . . both good and bad.

On the second day, the man's family gathered and told the woman and her family all they knew of him . . . both good and bad.

On the third day, the Medicine Person asked again if this bond was one they yet wanted. If it be so, the only recourse of disputes remained in the partnership. All others would turn a deaf ear. All had been told. They could only look at the past, make the adjustments and create the next step.

—Grandmother Kitty

receiving. Each is saying to the other, "Into your receiving, I give my best, and from your giving, I open to receive. We both give and receive always."

Those who witness the ceremony agree to "turn-face" should either or both turn from the stick. Friends and family who are invited to witness the ceremony may choose whether or not to attend the ceremony. If, in their hearts, some feel the bonding is not "right" for both persons, they will decline to witness the ceremony. This serves as a barometer for the bonding couple . . . for the truth is the truth and everyone knows it! As one of my friends told me when I was considering stepping to the stick with someone, "There is nothing that could stop my loving you. I would never turn-face on you. Therefore, I will not be at the ceremony if you step to the stick." To turn-face is to place someone in the world of the living dead. You neither speak to nor about them. They are ostracized from the circle. Those who sit in the inner circles of all who sit in the circle also turn-face. In smaller communities, this is a powerful form of peer pressure and a strong reminder to be very certain about commitments before making them.

In 1990 we adopted Grandmother Moon Feathers into our circle, thus returning her to the circle of relations that she had been without most of her long adult life. This adoption was a major point of "passage" for all of us. For Moon Feathers, it meant family that she had for so long been without. She delighted in telling others that she had all the benefits of children without ever having to change our diapers! Princess Moon Feathers has passed from this plane, but she is strongly our Grandmother in The Other Side Camp and God help anyone who attempts to impede our progress on earth! She is a mighty force with which to contend.

Another passing that we mention is that of death. Claire knew of her passing and asked to "lay in state" among her dearest friends for three days prior to her cremation. She further instructed Jeffery to have her ashes flown over her land in California along with those of her father, who had died only months before. Jeffery bathed her in ginger, massaged her and held her in those last moments of passing. For three days he sat vigil with her: singing, laughing and playing her favorite music. He was joined by dear friends. Each time a phone call came from some place around the world, he would hold the phone to her ear and offer her spirit the message of farewell sent by a friend.

Without autopsy or embalming, she was cremated in the simplest wooden box. Her ashes were immediately flown to California to be cast on the wind over her Hill-of-The-Hawk. This was Claire's choice about her simple passage ceremony from body back into spirit.

Grandmother Princess Moon Feathers wished that all symbols of the white man's world, in which she was forced to live, be removed from her body. Family washed her body, removed all fingernail polish and gold jewelry, braided her hair and wrapped her in her woolen Indian blanket. With her small canoe and her personal medicine bag, she was laid into the Mother Earth at Pine Key, Florida. She also asked for little pomp and circumstance and most certainly no embalming and autopsy. Grandmother was never very big on birthdays or funerals. This was Grandmother's choice about her simple passage ceremony from body back into spirit. During the days of passing, the family played my music, which Grandmother so loved. A funeral is the final passage ritual. It is good to have it done your way.

Being reminded that Grandmother despised birthdays reminds us that birthdays are yet another form of "passage rituals." When we achieve the age of one, we have already lived one year and are beginning our second year. Certain birthdays are held as special throughout many cultures and should be mentioned as times for ritual passage celebrations. Age six marks the end of a deeply impressionable time and the beginning of developing reason. Twelve marks the age of social expansion. Sixteen marks the age of being able to drive. It may also mark the age of sexual exploration. Eighteen and twenty-one mark the age of legal adulthood as denoted in the right to vote and drink. Either age may also coincide with the age of reason. Let it be noted that some people never really grow up and come to the age of reason. Twenty-seven marks the end of preparation for our life's work. Forty marks the beginning of the good life and fifty marks the legal age of the crone. Sixty-five marks the legal age for retirement and perhaps coincides with the age of wisdom. This final age is the time when one puts aside all other responsibilities and teaches the young. This is the true age of the elder, although "elder" status is conferred at fifty or when enough gray hairs crown the head. Our passage from and into spirit is borne on the wings of innocence, beginning with its freshness and ending with its wisdom.

Here's a little experiment. Think back to a time when some relations said you looked like "so-and-so." That's the reincarnated spirit to carry on and on and on . . . that eternal life. So, reincarnation is no big deal.

—Alinta

On January 29, 1984, I entered into a visioning that lasted fifteen days. My life was changed forever. From that moment to this, each breath I take is with the will to see this Vision of world celebration manifest on Earth. It is written, "Where two or more are gathered, there will I be also." There is great power in "twos." If but one other person can see what we see, and feel what we feel, and hear what we hear, we can succeed. So eager was I to see my Vision fulfilled that every cell of my body ached to attract a Dreaming Partner. I set out to make a calling place. With hammer in hand, I built The Eagle's Nest. On hands and knees, I planted, weeded and harvested a garden. I put up food for several years. I left one-half of the home open with plenty of space for my dream mate. A year and one-half later, Skye came. For all these many years we have held our dream of World Celebration. Skye is my twin-dreamer. Skye is my sister. Skye is my "standing together" business partner. We entered into the sweating lodge and adopted each other as sisters. We entered into the Sky Lodge and bonded our destinies to walk the Dreaming Trail to World Peace. We are *Degataga* (Standing Together). In the book of Ruth of the Bible, there is a story of a mother-in-law and a daughter-in-law who join together to unite warring nations. Ruth and Naomi came from different tribes, one worshipping idols and the other worshipping the One God. When Ruth learned of the merciful God of Naomi, she longed to know more. Ruth fell in love with Naomi's son and married him, even though she was a high priestess among her own people. Her own people, the Moabites, killed her husband. Ruth had a choice to make. She could return to her own people or join the people of her mother-in-law. She chose to join with Ruth and call her own people to peace. In their joining they exchanged a vow: "Your people will be my people. Your God will be my God. I will go where you go, and live where you live. When I die, I will be buried with your people." This pledge is *degataga*. It is closer than any other vow. This is the pledge of sisters joined together to unite the Great Circle. I long to make this bond with all brothers and sisters on Earth.

At all passage ceremonies, it is important to review the past; appreciate the past; release the past; and make welcome the now and future. Now marks the end of this chapter. We have loved the co-creation of each succeeding chapter. With this *adieu* we send this chapter off in the mail and celebrate with a peanut butter and jelly sandwich! Extra crunch Jif and Welch's grape jelly . . . of course!

CEREMONIAL OBJECTS

I am a self-proclaimed Master of Ritual and Ceremony. I have more ceremonial "Togs, Tools and Toys" than anybody. I love ceremony! I also love arts and crafts. Because I am a self-proclaimed Master of Ritual and Ceremony, I have sanction to spend long hours and years carving sticks and staffs and hand-stitching medicine bags and bundles. It is my joy to share my craft with all who will learn. Only a few of my Tools are presented here for your review. They are my Tools and not intended for duplication and proliferation. Perhaps this sharing will stimulate creativity on the part of some, and perhaps one in particular, who would vie with me for "whoever has the most toys, wins!"

A ceremonial object holds skan. It holds power. It holds the love and energy of the one who makes it. It holds the intentions and prayers of its maker. It is a teacher as it assists in the process of its creation. It is an object of meditation. It is a symbol for those who still need symbols to "wake up." It is the toy of a cosmic child who is heaven-bent on contributing to peace and dignity on our planet. It is a tattletale about the recipient of its gift. It is a prophet about events about to happen. It is a stunning prop on stage. It is a microphone, sky to earth and earth to sky. It is a needle that weaves together all living things. It is the focal point of attention and, by capturing attention, it is a co-creator in life. A ceremonial object is held in high regard by all children, young and old. It is a central topic of conversation. It is a piece of art. It is part of the collection in a museum. It is a history marker. It is an artifact of people who live and breathe and procreate. A ceremonial object is not necessary for worship, but it certainly makes it more fun.

THE TALKING STICK

Formal art finally made sense when it clicked that life is about spirit. Wy not art about spirit?

—Kactus

I don't remember when I first began using the "Talking Stick," but I do know it was long before they became a topic of conversation on Murphy Brown. It was even before Jamie Sams wrote about them. In fact, it was so long ago that I thought I invented it. However, in truth, the talking stick has been a way of life among the elders since people using words first sat in council. There existed a time when each person's word was respected. It seems that our elders would first pass the pipe and smoke in silence until all hearts beat as one. Then they would pass the talking stick. It is a very powerful microphone. When one holds the talking stick, everyone listens. The person with the stick speaks into the center of the circle with no thought of influencing others. They simply speak their truth. Since they sit at one point on the circle, they represent one viewpoint. Each person in the circle represents another. Those who listen, look into the fire with open heart and mind. What is meant for their spirits will come to them. What is not, will pass away. A powerful beginning for the one who holds the talking stick is this: "I am Cloud, and I will speak." There is something empowering about saying one's name and announcing that one WILL SPEAK. Holding the stick seems to magically streamline what one will say. As long as one holds the stick, all others listen. When the speaker has finished it is powerful to say, "I am Cloud and I have spoken!" The talking stick teaches about options and choices. It teaches that each person has a unique disposition. In the circle there is room for all manner of dispositions.

Talking Stick

122

One's personal talking stick is made to represent what is sacred to that person. Mine is carved from the exotic and hard Osage orange wood; a wood used to make bows. It is very solid and very beautiful in color. It is crowned with a diamond given to me by my Grandmother. Its tail is raccoon and speaks of intimacy and family. My Talking Stick has sat in circles all over the world. It has powered the dreams of thousands of people. The raccoon tail came from a moccasin drag worn into ceremony with the Peyote Chief; a ceremony in which an elephant came to grant the promise given in the beginning of time. It is important to devote prayer and attention to the making of a talking stick that will carry one's voice to the circle. Know the properties of the wood, metal, glass or other material. Place each embellishment with careful thought to its energy and meaning. My Talking Stick carries this skan: "In the beginning of time, the Great Mystery gave a promise of unity. We are each a part of that unity. Be strong and beautiful. Send your voice like the bow sends the arrow to the heart of all things. Your voice will be quickened by the diamond crystal's magic and go straight to the hearing of the Grandmothers. Speak with the passion, truth and innocence of a child."

Surrender to the riptide and allow ourselves to be taken where we need to be.

—Grandmother Kitty

THE TORI

I made up the name Tori. It stands for tunnel, funnel, vortex, tornado. It creates an opening, a spinning tunnel like the center of the cyclone or the eye of a hurricane. It is used to begin ceremony. At a sweating lodge ceremony, I stand in the center of the fire circle and spin the "Tori" clockwise or counter-clockwise. While spinning the Tori we invoke the Great Mystery and the realm of visibles and invisibles to gather. We create a centering place for our fire, which in turn is the center of our ceremony. In all other rituals I use the Tori to create the center. Into it we place sacred tobacco, sage and corn. From this place we make our invoking prayers, chants and songs. This place represents the center of our heart's fire. Energy is sent earth to sky in the light of day (clockwise). It is pulled sky to earth in the cover of darkness (counter-clockwise). Sometimes a coyote spin in the opposite directions creates an arena for surprises.

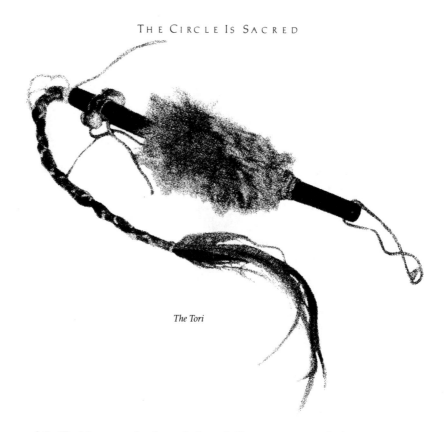

The Tori

My Tori is carved of my beloved Osage orange. It is strong, beautiful and used to send forth like the bow. That which spins is braided hair from my horse and me. Together we represent a power and a freedom of great love. At the tip of my Tori are two medicine bags that look like scrotum. Within these bags are all the things that represent a balance of male and female. In ceremony, the Tori calls for balance. Let us know ourselves as the center from which all things flow and to which all things return. The Tori says, "I stand at the Center." The wolf skin that wraps my Tori calls for the Teacher of Teachers to be present. It represents the Galactic Clan.

GRANDMOTHER'S CANE

Grandmother Great Spirit or Holy Spirit Mother is recognized in ceremony by the presence of Her Cane. Where the Cane stands, it is known that the Holy Spirit Feminine Mother sits among us. Grandmother's cane is in the shape of a horse. She is pure, still power. She reminds us to celebrate the children. Horse hair on ceremonial objects reminds us of the pure power of children. It reminds us to care for our children out seven generations. Grandmother cane is embellished with fox and deer. She is a foxy lady. She is gentle. Her gentleness melts the heart of all demons. She is cunning and teaches us the art of Oneness by our understanding of camouflage. She reminds us to keep the family safe.

GRANDFATHER SKULL

It is common to find a skull at the center of ceremony. It represents the presence of Grandfather Spirit. It reminds us that there are eyes that see and ears that hear. My skull is painted in a childlike way with clouds and rainbows. It reminds me that I am of the Rainbow Tribe of all people: red, yellow, black, white, brown and little green and gray space beings. It reminds me of God's great gift of a Son who told us to "become again as little children." It reminds me of how much my Grandfather Great Spirit loves me. To Him, I am precious.

*Grandmother
Spirit Cane*

Grandfather Skull

SMUDGING FANS

Spirit loves feathers. All that would attract Spirit is adorned with feathers. I suppose it is the freedom of flight and our universal love of it that attracts Spirit. In ceremony, it is the Spirit of all things, that which takes flight, that is the skan power; the sky power. We always come to ceremony and awaken the Spirit in everything. Smoke can be smelled, felt and seen. The smoking feathers can be heard. The act of "smudging" or "smoking" ceremonial objects, areas and participants is an act of calling forth Spirit. The sweet smell of cedar and sage cleans and clears away, then calls forth all that is good for the one and the whole. Feathers give flight to all things. The combination of feathers and smoke says, "Awaken. Be lifted up. Go out in four directions."

The Eagle Fan represents Grandfather Great Spirit and is used

Smudging Fans

in ceremonies that power and seed life. Its voice invokes the heart of the Grandfathers from the beginning. We recently brought it into ceremony with a young man who seeks to restore a piece of our Indian history. He stands to make a staggering amount of money on the project. While he looks to do a good thing for the Indian people, he also sees through white eyes. When a circle of women met with him and called forth blessings on his journey, the voice of the Grandfathers came to say, "When the hearts of your women turn to dust, your dream will perish. Have ears to hear your women." The blessing was a warning and foretold of this young man's own personal challenges.

The Parrot Fan represents Grandmother Holy Spirit and is used in ceremonies that call forth abundance. The Parrot Clan is one of the oldest known women's societies of Seers and Healers. The parrot feather is blue on the top side, like blood that flows unspilled. It is the desire of the women to see all blood flow blue. The feather is red on the bottom side and warns that those who seek to harm will see their own blood spilled. The power of the women's medicine has always been stronger than the men's. Women also spill their blood each month and in so doing maintain closeness with Spirit. Men do not bleed and, therefore, are called into the sweating lodge to achieve the humility that women know in bleeding. Our Parrot Fan is used in invoking learnings or blessings of abundance. It was used to "smudge" the young girls who had come to their "leave-child-behind" time. The feathers joined with smoke to call forth abundance in their wombs, both physically and spiritually. When a woman understands that her body is always in the process of nurturing eggs of future generations, she knows that every cell of her body comprehends nurturing.

The Hawk Fan represents the Messenger, the Morning Star. Just as Jesus came to personally deliver a message with Grandmother and Grandfather God, so our Hawk Fan invokes messages. It is often used to smudge those entering into the sweating lodge. Likewise, it can be used to smudge the Moon Lodge of bleeding women. During this time the women are very receptive to messages from Great Mystery.

There are many other types of smudging fans that are used in ceremony. Each one calls forth its own unique energy. The Raven Fan prepares one to enter into a time of seeking within the Great Darkness; a West time of germination. The Owl Fan sometimes

Chieftess Smudging Fan

prepares one who seeks the Other Side Camp of the Spirit World. An Owl appeared to me before Cliff, Claire and Princess Moon Feathers died. The Owl Fan is also used to clear away deceptions and center on the wisdom of innocence. When great stealth is needed, the Eagle of the Night feather is of great assistance. The Turkey Fan is used at the time of the Give-Away and any other time of thanksgiving. The Swan Fan is used to call upon the energies of grace, ease and intuition. The Blue Jay Fan is used to call forth playfulness and gaiety. The tiny Hummingbird Fan is used to call forth intimacy and love. The Crow Fan is used to access ancient knowledge. The Vulture Fan is used to ward off meddlesome spirits. The Roadrunner Fan blesses those who will be traveling. The tiny Parakeet Fan clears the throat chakra and calls song. Each bird of a feather owns a medicine unique unto itself. When we learn to entrain ourselves with each of God's creatures and exchange our energies, we can truly own the earth and all that is in Her.

ARROWS

Ceremonial Arrows

Arrows symbolize that which goes straight to the heart of things. An arrow clutched and held high symbolizes wartime. A broken arrow symbolizes a time of peace. A straight arrow that is decorated beyond use as a weapon symbolizes swiftness of intention and journey. It calls for one to choose one path and stay on it all the way to the mark. Crossed arrows symbolize partnership in dreaming and manifestation. A cluster of arrows symbolizes the coming together of nations, ideas, clans, bands; it symbolizes the larger hoop of All-That-Is. The small hunting arrow symbolizes the hunt and is filled with gratitude for the small game that give us life. The arrow of soft stone represents one with a soft heart for all things.

Our cluster of "flaming arrows" represents the hearts of those who call themselves the "Rainbow Hoop." It is our passion to see all peoples come together as one Great Hoop. Our crossed arrows represent our Master Partnership with the All-That-Is. The tips of these arrows are made from soap stone and cedar. Our hearts are soft towards all people, as was the heart of Jesus. The parrot feathers represent Holy Spirit Mother and all that is deeply feminine. The shafts of hickory and cedar represent the heart and

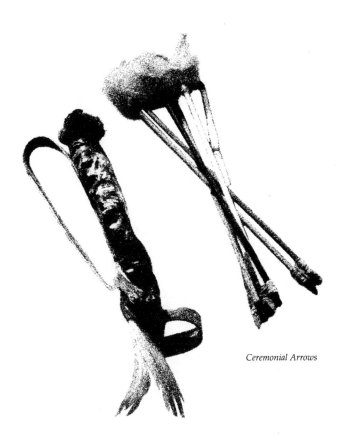

Ceremonial Arrows

spine of Grandfather Great Spirit. The arrows represent the balance of the Mother, Father and child; the holy Trinity. When my nephew turned six, I presented him with his first arrow. It is decorated to empower him to see true and go swiftly on his own spirit's path. It represented a time of passage for him. When one's path is true to what is good for the one and the whole, we often present that person with an arrow to acknowledge her life's work. In this context, the arrow is a medal or a trophy. When a peace is made, it is good to ceremonially break an arrow. This stands as a reminder that there is no more warring. An arrow through a shield marks a commitment to carry forth a dream. Arrows crossed behind a shield represent a partnership. I made a shield for Ted Turner and J. J. Ebaugh. For many years these two friends have carried a dream of global communication. The arrows for their shield came from the Big Island of Hawaii. I took the wood of the O Hea Lauhi. It is first to grow out of the hot lava rock. The wood is very hard and solid. It is the O Hea or the male part. The red and gold shimmering blossom is called Lauhi. This is the female part. The tree and his blossom were given by Pele as a final gift for the last sacrifice of young lovers. This partnership is solid through all changes. Each arrow, with its particular origin of growth, nature of wood, feathers, tip and embellishments carries manna, skan, power. An arrow is far more than a visual reminder.

BONDING STICKS

Last year the borough of Malibu, California, became its own city, complete with mayor. At the passage ceremony, the mayor accepted a Bonding Stick as a pledge of commitment to the well-being of the City. Recently David and Barbara sat in the solitude of their own livingroom and placed their hands on a Bonding Stick. By this act, they became man and wife. We have often sat in a circle and placed our hands to a bonding hoop to signify team commitment. We have also sealed business deals with the Bonding Stick. The concept of the Bonding Stick is so old as to have been lost to historical records. However, Spirit clearly instructed me in it's meaning and uses. It is with humility that I present it into the circle of ceremony.

The Bonding Stick is much like a covenant as portrayed in the Old Testament of the Bible. In the old days of Biblical history, families would spill the blood of animals, bare their own feet and intermingle their footprints in blood. By this act, they said to each other and to God Almighty, "My promise or covenant is sealed in

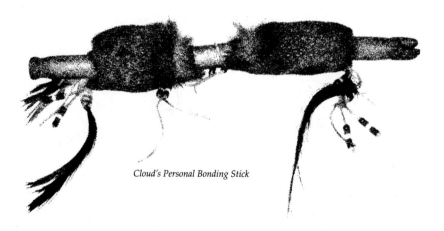

Cloud's Personal Bonding Stick

blood. If I break this promise, let me also spill my own blood." I am told that before men began to dominate ceremonial law, the blood that was used to form a covenant was the women's blood of their moon cycles. This is certainly a more civilized approach and profoundly more powerful. We call for women's menstrual blood to be used again in ceremony. Let it be noted that the first menstrual blood of a young woman can be brought to the fire of ceremony as proof of her fertility. The public viewing of this blood can become again a cause for great cheering and excitement (versus the current embarrassment).

Malibu Bonding Stick

When people come to the stick they come to make public a promise or covenant that is made before God. The consequences for turning from the stick are very great and should be well considered before choosing. When people turn from the stick or renege on their promises, the world as they know it turns face, so that they become the living dead. All who sit in the circle to witness the bonding in the center agree to turn face on any who divorce their promise. When people "turn face" they do not speak to or about those people who have become living dead. They do not look at them. They do nothing that associates with them or theirs. They do not think of them. They do not feed their existence on any level. As quick as the reneging party turns back to the stick (or back to the promise), life resumes as normal and the action is never again mentioned. This is a powerful form of peer pressure. In smaller family and community circles, it is possible that one be instantly cut off from food, home, work and transportation. Let us work quickly to bring back the stick! Three in every four marriages end in divorce. We have no cultural ethic for commitment. We must work to return dignity and respect for

Family Bonding Stick

It is enough to know a little about how to work with materials. Then all you need to do is play with the object until its spirit comes forward and directs the creation.

—Kactus

staying power. The Bonding Stick is about staying power.

Our Tribal Bonding Stick is a large wheel with an open circle in the place of the hub. The hub of our wheel is an inner circle spinning. The spokes and wheel are wrapped in elk skin. The wooden rack of the circle is willow. Willow grows close to water and absorbs much water. It is a good wood for moving emotions or to keep things moving. A turtle shell hangs suspended in the center. She represents one with a strong heart who holds all things good for the Earth and all Her creatures. The turtle is the symbol of the Earth Mother. It was Her back onto which the creatures of the sea put mud that hardened in the sun as she floated atop the ocean. When the mud dried, she swam out from under it, leaving land. She continued to do this until all the continents were formed. The turtle has the strongest heart. One may cut off the head of the turtle, but her heart continues to beat for up to four days. The rose suspended at the center reminds us that in the Spring, the seed becomes a rose. Behind the turtle shell is a medicine bag which contains the matrix of the Earth. The Eagle feathers represent the highest and the best. When the corporate family for Vision Us, Inc. came together, each board member and confidante came to this stick. Our pledge is to live our lives so as to demonstrate our vision of all peoples as One.

Our Family Bonding Stick is carved by a child-spirit of our Hoop. It is made of cedar. The handles where the hands were placed are covered with rabbit fur. The bunny is soft, quick, gentle and abundant. The beads are the color of Father Sky and Mother Earth. This bonding stick is used for adoption into our hoop. We used it to adopt Grandmother Princess Moon Feathers.

My personal bonding stick is carved by the beavers. It is the beloved cottonwood; the wood used for the gazing-at-the-sun ceremony. Cottonwood is a soft wood that acts like a hard wood. While it is soft, it grows so tightly intertwined that the fibers are strong like rope. Its softness allows it to sway in the wind, while its strength protects it from breaking in the wind. Its flexibility and strength protect it from the wind damage caused to the oak and hickory. In the heat of summer, the cottonwood releases its seeds in a white, floating ship of cotton. The banks become lined with the cottonwood cotton balls and we are reminded in the heat of things that the coolness is coming. Its leaves are shaped like hearts and each leaf has a tipi design on it. It reminds us about the warmth and love that burns at our home fires. I found my cottonwood stick at the beaver pond. Our beaver friends had carved the stick. After I cut it to its proper and comfortable length, I carved a deer hoof in one end and a horse hoof in the other. This brings the balance of strength and power along with gentleness and grace.

When two join hands on this stick, they come walking in balance. They come with a good heart for all things. They come to call forth the highest teachings. They come with the energy of the beaver . . . to build a world dream.

THE PIPE

One day Skye sat praying. Her attention was called to the sky. There she saw Great Hands reach down from the heavens and hand her the pipe. I have come to respect her gentle and powerful way with the pipe. She is a true woman of the pipe. The Grandmothers and Grandfathers have passed the pipe to her. I, too, have been given a pipe. Mine came through tribal elders. Though I am sometimes called to my pipe, I do not consider myself a true pipe carrier.

The Red Road is a path. It is a way. The cross is the symbol of the Red Road. The Red Road is an attitude of doing all things with reverence. It is a way of living that is strong and yet does not harm or disturb life. The Sacred Pipe is a tool with which to center ourselves on the Red Road. Skan, that thing that moves in all things, is breath. It is the universal thread that connects all of life. When we breathe into our pipes, we help make the breath of life visible. Our breath, or skan, made visible is the horse that rides our prayers out and upward to the Source of all breath, the Great Breath, the Great Mystery. White Buffalo Calf Maiden brought the Sacred Pipe to the Lakota people. She made the pipe a bridge between earth and sky, the visible and the invisible. It is the pipeholder's duty to live a life of purity . . . in feelings, words, thoughts and deeds.

The bowl of every pipe represents the female aspect of the Great Mystery, the Holy Spirit Mother. The stem represents the male aspect of the Great Mystery, the Great Father Spirit. The Spirit of Earth Maker becomes visible in the sacred smoke. When we inhale, we accept from the Great Mystery. When we exhale, we give out to the Great Mystery, or we release unto the keeping of the Great Provider. The breath of life is shared in the pipe. Skan. Called Chi by the Chinese. Ki by the Japanese. Prana by the yogi. Ruach by the Hebrew. Ruh by the Sufi. Pneuma by the Greeks. Mana by the Hawaiian. Matasooma by the Cheyenne. Medicine by many Native Americans.

There are many types of pipes: tribal, clan, personal, social, council and marriage pipes. There are also various types of ceremonial pipes: Dancing the Sun pipes, Dream and Visioning pipes, War and Peace pipes, Harvest pipes and Planting pipes. The purpose of ceremony is to sharpen our focus, perception, sensitivity and intuition. This happens when all hearts beat as one. In any time of smoking together, it is good to share the pipe in silence until all hearts beat as one. We share a few pipes as examples of their function as the Tool of tools.

Skye's Pipe

The bowl of my Dream pipe is made from red Oklahoma clay taken from our pond. Nothing has been added to it and nothing taken away. The shape of the bowl is that of a dolphin holding the world on her head. The dolphin represents the breath of life, the manna of the Universe. The dolphin is the messenger from the Dreamtime. They have the most sophisticated form of communication. The dolphin is the link to the Great Star People, and brings solutions for the Earth's children. The dolphin is the keeper of laughter and playfulness. There are no secrets among the dolphin. All thoughts and feelings are instantly known by all other dolphins. When one dolphin is hurt, dolphins know a hundred miles away. They come to the aid of one who is harmed and carry it to safety. They have no "pincher grasp" and thus do not cling. The dolphin knows the rhythm of life.

The stem of the pipe is made from my beloved Osage orange. It is strong, beautiful, exotic and carries the energy to "send forth," as does the bow. The Osage orange produces a fruit called horse apple. It is food for horses; a real treat to the horse that holds powers. Wolf fur covers the stem and calls forth the greatest of teachers and the coming together of all hoops. The multi-colored braids represent all peoples in all nations. The horse hair reminds us to live so as to empower our children out seven generations. The prayer beads from India remind us to feed the world's peoples. The elk skin leather reminds us of love that is the Alpha and Omega, the beginning and the end. The gold coin is from Australia during that country's year of peace. It reminds us that the Great Dream held by our Aboriginal Elders is for all people to come together in one great Rainbow Hoop on Earth. The crystal is for clarity of vision, both short and long. When we smoke this pipe in ceremony, we smoke with the hearts of children. The pipe sends our wishes and dreams to the Great Mystery. Sometimes we think this pipe is the tool by which our wishes are granted.

My personal pipe (also called *Chanunpa*) is made of the red pipe stone called catlinite. It is found in Minnesota. They say it is the blood of the buffalo who gave their lives. The stem is wrapped with white and gray wolf to honor the great white wolf who ran into my Third Eye (or Strong Eye). The white wolf is the teacher of teachers. When I pray with this pipe, I sit in silent communication; the kind of communication that education tries very hard to destroy. The beads are of my own Rainbow Tribe. This pipe is my own prayer pipe. It lives in an Elk Pipe Bag. The elk is like the chapel bells that toll in the mountain village. The elk goes to the high place and cries out a welcome to the sun each morning. In the evening, the elk returns to see the sun to its resting place. The elk medicine is likened to the Morning Star; the Alpha and the Omega. Some say elk medicine is medicine of love, sexual excitement and stamina. My pipe bag is beaded with the yellow rose of friendship. My yellow rose represents staying power. My pipe represents staying power.

An Apache pipe sits on our World Family Shelf. It too has elk. The bowl is of elk bone. The stem is from the desert and carved with lightening. The furs are brown bear, buffalo and deer. It is very strong medicine. We smoke this pipe at world peace celebrations. It holds our healing Eagle fan that represents Grandfather God. Always, this pipe is smoked for the well-being of the Global Hoop.

When we smoke, we pray to each of the four directions and to the three directions of the God-Head; up to the Star Nation or Eagle Nation; down to the Stone Nation or the Mother Earth; and inside to the Christ (or Circle of All-That-Is) within. Always the

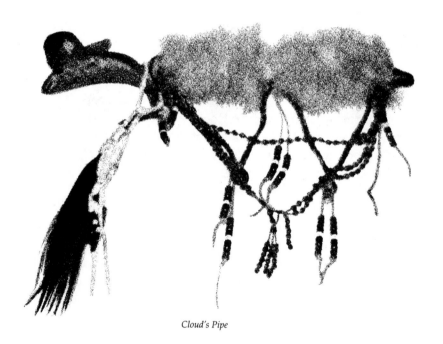

Cloud's Pipe

pipe must lead the way. Never try to lead the pipe. The Sacred Pipe was given to the Lakota people and it intended to go to all nations. I once challenged my dear friend, Mary Thunder, to smoke her pipe with the Pope! Someday, perhaps she will. The Sacred Pipe will find a pathway for us. We must follow that trail, wherever it leads. It will lead us to good medicines. It will lead us to clean water. It will lead us to good shelter. The pipe is like a telephone to the Great Mystery. Pray always in a humble way, like a child who is kin to the earth and loves Her beauty. Learn to pray walking, all the time. Make friends with the pipe and the pipe will make friends with you. When you make a mistake in life, pray for forgiveness and then do something good to replace the deed. The pipe will lead the way. The pipe will teach circular thinking where all things are in the flow.

Smoke expecting nothing and receive everything. The pipe way allows us to remove distractions from our lives. When we take care of the pipe, the pipe takes care of us.

TOMAHAWKS

David is a master student. I gave him a medicine bag. Before I knew it, he was making and giving them to everyone. David saw me gift a tomahawk. He immediately became a prolific maker of tomahawks. Imitation is the highest form of respect. David is my student in the medicine. He is in the process of earning a grand tomahawk. Bruce said it best when he stated, "I bring my hatchet to the fire. I will long-run." Sometimes when naive people see my tomahawks, they start whooping like Indians of the movies. They identify the tomahawk with war. They see it as a weapon. It was first a tool. It was a hammer. To the true warrior, the tomahawk signifies this to the circle: "I am a builder of dreams. I bring my hatchet (tool) to the fire of this circle. I am here to help build the dreams of my people. I am strong. I will long-run."

I am a carpenter. My father wanted one son. He got, instead, twin daughters. I came first . . . four minutes before my sister. The first born of twins is given the medicine. She is the seer. My daddy's son is a girl. He taught me all that he would teach a son. When I bring my hatchet to the Council Fires, and I do often, I come to build the dreams of my people . . . all my people. The first tomahawk that I ever made was like that of a child. The handle was of red-heart cedar and I painted a cloud on the stone; a cloud with a rainbow. I took that tomahawk to Claire's fire. She let it lay on the ground unnoticed for awhile. Then she took it to her altar at the Hill-of-the-Hawk. I will power her dreams as though she were still her in body.

The second hatchet I made is for our Tribal Circle. I take it into ceremony when I go as our Tribal Chieftess. It sits at the Center on the Altar of the Eagle's Nest. Grandmother JoJo gave me an old antique farming implement. I made it into a tomahawk that I laid at the altar to Grandmother Holy Spirit. In so doing I pledged to "long-run for the Earth Mother." The handle is antique rattan (tropical and very solid). The feather is hawk. The fur is fox. I like to put fox on Grandmother's gifts. She's a foxy lady! By bringing this tomahawk to Grandmother Holy Spirit, I wished to send a strong message of gratitude and thanksgiving.

My personal tomahawk is carved from oak. I carved a horse hoof in the end of the handle, sending forth my power to honor our children out seven generations. The fur is buffalo for great abundance. The feathers are Owl for wisdom and seeing in dark places. The stone came from an old ceremonial ground and was given to me by my Grandmother Jerry. She is Cherokee. She found the stone on an old ceremonial ground. The horse hair is from my horse Sedona; a red and white paint from Montana. I

once rode him into a rattlesnake pit. Rather than throw me, he settled and gently stepped through the snakes as I spoke our apologies. The incident occurred when I rode him up a rocky cliff in hot pursuit of an ornery old cow. He was calm on that day and we both lived. However, he is certain to throw anyone who now chooses to race him up an embankment. He has never forgotten that day. I like his spunk and his discernment. He is very sure-footed. I like having his mane on my tomahawk. When I bring this tomahawk to a fire, it is very special. When someone serves the Great Spirit and the Whole of Earth, it is appropriate to present that person with a tomahawk. It is a great honoring. It says, "You are an athlete for God. You long-run for the people. Let tomahawk remind you of our appreciation."

A final note regarding the meaning of the tomahawk. When Bruce learned of its meaning, he came bringing his hammers and saws. Bruce is truly a master carpenter. He sat at our Council Fire in August of 1988. We called this fire, "The Turquoise Journey." He chopped our wood, built our lodge and then came to the fire with this expression: "I bring my hatchet to the fire. I will long-run." Bruce is a brother-friend who has built more on the ranch than any other.

Finally, when I first interacted with LeVar Burton, it was by telephone. He had heard of our devotion to a World Celebration. He called to say, "How can I help?" When we met in Beverly Hills, he came running to me with his arms open wide. He was yelling at the top of his lungs. "Use me! Use all of me!" This is the meaning of the tomahawk: "Use me Great Mystery! Use all of me!"

SHIELDS

I saw my first shield in a vision. No one instructed me in how to make the shield. I simply "remembered" how to rack a shield. When I make a shield, I always throw a cloth. I smudge the cloth. Sometimes I put a favorite "calling crystal" on the cloth. I make a prayer to the shield and ask that all that is to "come to the shield" wake up and come to this place. Then I pay attention to the process. The first shield I ever made was a dream shield. I suppose it will always be my favorite. I dreamed how it would be. I threw my cloth and waited prayerfully and with great excitement. The very next day I received a gift of goat skin. I grew up on goat's milk. A small cottonwood called me to take her for the rack. She lived on the "sweet spot" on the ranch. That's a place where the wind blows all the sweet smells down into a little valley. It always smells the sweetest in this valley.

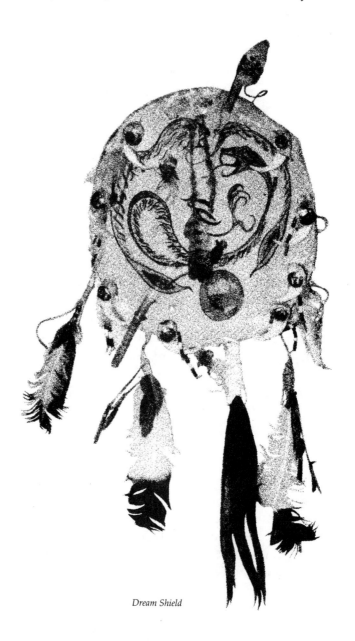

Dream Shield

I think that all land has its own sweet spot. As a child I learned to breathe flaring my nostrils to enhance the smells. We could smell a snake. They are very musty. This habit was instilled for personal safety, but it brought along the gift of all sweet smells. Even today I breathe in this way. I can feel the presence of the Great One in each breath. It feels so full and sweet in my lungs. There's a lot more in air than just air.

Grandmother had given me an arrow head. I carved a strong arrow with the rattles of a rattlesnake. Rattlesnakes were my teachers in the Everglades. They were everywhere. I learned to respect them and their warnings. I learned to walk toe-heel, toe-heel. This is how to walk soft on the earth. It's like always sneaking up on something. It also allows us to put the softest part of our foot to the earth first. If a snake were there, we would feel it and move before hurting the snake. In looking for the rattlesnake, I learned to see everything. I wanted to put this arrow through my shield, like an arrow through the heart of a valentine. I named the arrow "Strongheart". I was gifted many bear claws. I put them around the outside of my Dream Shield. They remind me of the bears that danced upright around me when I was a child.

I carefully chose twenty-three brightly colored pente stones to rack my shield. Pente is a game made by a guy named Gary in my hometown. It started as an assignment for a college class. His friends liked it and wanted a set, so he made some in his garage. He's now a multimillionaire living in Austin, Texas, and making Pente for the world. My dream is for the whole world to play together at a massive, global party. I figure that if we can feed the world for one day, we can do it always. If we can enjoy playing together for a day, perhaps we can play together always. "People who play together, stay together." A special bond is created when people play and laugh together. Pente stones were the perfect stones. Twenty-three equals a "5" in numerology, and five is the number of change. I call for major change on our planet. Onto the face of my Dream Shield I painted an eagle and a snake playing with each other. They are both predators. They can both kill each other. The Eagle represents the Sky People and the Eagle Nation. The Snake represents the Earth, transformation and healing. When all snakes again dance up towards the sky, the earth will be healed. I also painted a picture of the globe and attached a quarter in it. I figure it will cost about a quarter per person to host a global celebration and hook it up by satellite. To power my dream, I also attached my clan totem, a turquoise bear fetish; a red arrow head for "The Royal Order of the Arrows" (my name for enlightened children); a pink quartz crystal cherub for a loving heart; a crystal heart given to me by a child; and a "Cloud" shell button to hold the locks of my braided hair. Hair is our antenna to The Provider. I am most particular about who gets my hair. I save all of it, even what is cut in the beauty salon. I use it to make nest for special rocks, Indian yo-yos, balls and medicine bags. I almost always put a braid of my hair on shields and special medicine objects.

My Dream Shield is made with a handle on the back. It is to be carried in my right hand. I travelled the planet with this shield held high. You can imagine the sight of me at O'Hare Airport, decked out in major ritual regalia, holding my shield high. I travelled this way for five years. This is the traditional time required to carry a dream before it begins to manifest. During this time our dream becomes clear. We have the opportunity to learn what is required to carry a dream. We get used to people asking about the shield and its meaning. Mostly people thought that I bought it in Santa Fe. Some offered to buy it from me. I can imagine that one day every teenager who loves to dance will make a Dream Shield of what they want in life and dance with it at the discos. That is exactly what we did from London to L.A. and from Sidney to Toronto. We danced with our Dream Shields in discos. People would circle us and ask to dance with our shield. Imagine everyone going out dancing in their own "warrior of love costume" carrying their own "dream shield!" Finally, my Dream Shield is embellished with mock eagle feathers and real parrot feathers. I wanted children to be able to play with it and touch it. For the children, I hung a large horse tail from it. Always, my dream is to contribute to building a better world for our children.

Our World Family Shield is made of vine, wrapped three times for the holy Trinity. A beaver skin is stretched inside of it. The Apache Council Pipe sits above the crossed arrows, a symbol of world peace and partnership. A picture of Grandmother Princess Moon Feathers' hands and my hands sits center, along with a medicine bundle of earth from our Council Fires. It is embellished with eagle feathers. Like the beaver, our tribe are builders of the dream of world peace. This shield hangs at the center of our altar.

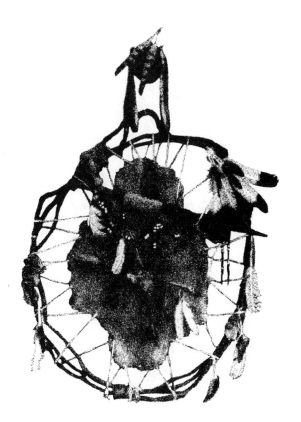

World Family Shield

My Sunset Shield is a victory shield. It called itself into form after I had carried my Dream Shield for five years. I wear this shield on my back. The rack is willow and the skin is lamb. The horns are buffalo with a full harvest moon on her strong eye. The crown is a headband of white buffalo shells given to me by my Kahuna Sister. They come through four generations of women's medicine. Two feathers come together on her face to form an arrow. When two feathers come together to form an arrow, it is always a time of great rejoicing. The hair is old elk, the northern buffalo. The dream crystal that I wore in my headband for five years sits at the top. The strap is from Guatemala and Brazil. Early on my dream path I saw a buffalo cow appear in front of me. Blood was pouring from her Strong Eye. Her voice said, "Stop the bleeding." When this victory shield showed itself, the blood was gone. Everything about this shield prophesies victory on earth. It is the shield I wear in ceremony now.

Victory Shield

My Protection Shield is made of rawhide and will actually deflect an arrow. It is turquoise, painted with the moon for what is strong about a woman. It also has lightening for the old ones. I wear it on my wrist and dance with it.

Our Corporate Shield is made with deer skin. It blends the old west with true patriotic pride of today. It carries a baby's moccasin to represent the law of seven generations. Our corporate symbol is painted on it. The symbol is a combination of a V, an ellipse and the infinity sign. It says, "Let there come great abundance so as to create a peaceful world, forever." Hawk feathers fly from it, for we are messengers in our business.

My Eagle Shield was given at the same time that I received my Eagle Bundle. It, of course, has an eagle on it. It also has a turkey feather to represent "The Eagle of Thanksgiving."

My Partnership Shield is in the form of a figure eight and has our "Vision Us" symbol. The cow hide on it came from a give-away to the elders.

Our Welcoming Shield has 405 prayer ties on it and the skull of a deer.

My South Shield has a picture of Australia and the king and queen of hearts. It also has a big cloud on it. It symbolizes partnership with the Dream World: Friends Uniting Nations. It is my Sworn to Fun Shield.

My Shield of Completion is made of bamboo and is in the shape of a number 9. It represents Cloud Nine. It was given away in ceremony. The strength to complete a dream walk is its gift.

Skye's Fidelity Shield is her statement of fidelity to her dream. Her Driver's Shield is both her symbol of "being in charge of her life" and it is our family's team hoop. We all pulled it together.

My Mystery Shield was given to me to "Hold a Mystery." It is a mystery to me.

It is the function of a true teacher to train the novice how to be trained directly by the spirits. Some traditions say that a woman doesn't have a shield. Others make rigid rules about the types of shields. Still others encourage their people to make shields for each of the four directions. Harley Swiftdeer encourages his students to make a shield for their child, man, woman and elder. The law about shields lies within each heart. Making a shield and owning a shield with our love is a teaching greater than that of any elder. As healers and teachers, we are always in training. We do not question the existence of power, only its application. Pray

Completion Shield

Mystery Shield

in a humble way and the spirits will guide and comfort. They will instruct. Be open and obedient, never question. Just do as you are instructed. The understanding of the meaning will come in the act of obedience. This is what is important about making shields.

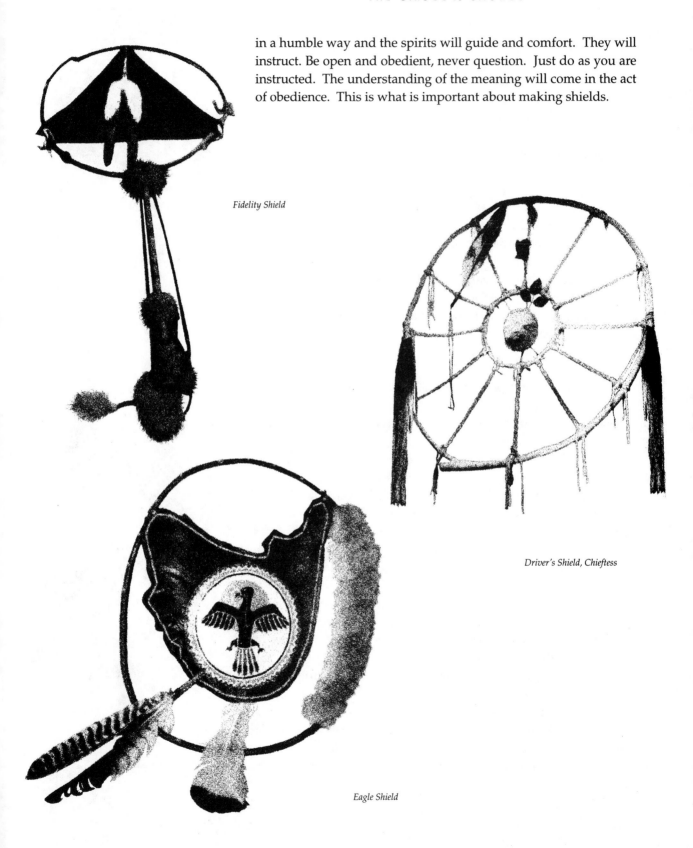

Fidelity Shield

Driver's Shield, Chieftess

Eagle Shield

COUP STICK: DREAM STALKING

It is time for me to make another "coup stick." The feet of a redtail hawk have been prepared and are displayed in a north window for the elders to see. This morning I found a perfect red-heart cedar branch with a fork at the top. It comes from our sacred sanctuary on the cliffs. The land belongs to Mr. Primm. I will seek his permission to take the stick. The first time I made a coup stick or "dream stalking stick" was the first week of January, 1984. Three weeks later I was visited for fifteen days by spirits showing me a major vision. Dream Stalker is very powerful. My first Stalking Stick held the feet of a great white owl. I sought a dream in darkness. I did not know what that dream was. I embellished it with a medicine wheel, bear teeth, buffalo teeth, deer skin and a raccoon tail. I wanted the dream to be good for all people. Two months ago, Peanut (my mechanic) came bringing me a redtail hawk. It had been killed by a car. The feet are ready. Now I know my dream. I am a messenger. It is time to "stalk" the platform on which to give forth my message.

Some may pray, "Lord, what am I to do with my life?" Perhaps they cry out in desperation. To make a stalking stick is a strong way to pray for direction. The act of making the stick is itself a teacher. It will call you to variables you desire in the couping of a dream. When we place a purchase order through prayer, it is very important to be specific. When we pray for a partner, we need to be specific. If we are not, we cannot complain when we get someone who is fat, drunk and lazy. Putting our hands to the creation of a coup stick buys our attention and affords us the opportunity to really focus on this question: "What do I want?"

In the old days, "couping" or touching was a way of acquiring property. What we couped, we owned . . . until someone else couped it from us. The making of a coup stick is an active form of establishing goals and objectives. We created the game, Dream Walker/Dream Stalker to assist people in this process. Those who know their dream, make a dream shield. Those who do not, make a dream stalker stick. The game is a major game of seek and find. The Dream Walkers must carry their dreams to the top of the mountain. The Dream Stalkers must attempt to coup a dream. How we perform teaches us a great deal about ourselves. The more our perceptions are sharpened, the more obvious is the

Coup Stick

Totem Staff "The Lady"

presence of the Divine in all things. Lack of direction in life is a lack of will power. Lack of will power comes when one gives away one's own medicine to others' whims, distractions, laziness, indulgences or dis-ease. The stalking stick is a way of taking back personal power. To gain power is to focus and concentrate our energy within and around us. Everything that we can do to focus ourselves is an act of power. Being given a vision is not enough. We must constantly "walk our talk" and "talk our walk." We must renew our vision and fortify our medicine with acts of ritual, games and ceremony. Be guided by what is known of tradition, but never limited by it. Experiment freely and in every way possible, seek to understand the depth of your own soul. Be sensitive, but not vulnerable to public opinion. Your path is your path. You must seek and find it alone.

TOTEM STAFF

I call my Totem Staff "the Lady." She was a gift to me from a man named Raven Starr. My Totem Staff is tall, strong and straight. She is a cobra at a full stretch. I made her my own by embellishing her with the stone of my birth, a topaz in her throat chakra. I gave her ruby red eyes and a jade heart in her Third Eye. Deer, raccoon, elk and rattlesnake skins are wrapped around her staff. She represents gentleness, playfulness, stamina and transformation. Horse tails hang from her waist and turkey feathers call for abundance for the give-away. She makes a strong statement. "Walk Tall! Face life head on! Put your heart out! Look people in the eyes!" Her energy is that of a five-star general. She is keen on proper manners and respect for Spirit.

(It may be well to note here that our horse tails either come from living horses who give us some of their mane and tail, or they come from a vet friend at the University. When horses die, we are allowed to utilize some of their tails for our sacred objects. The same is true of all other animals. They have died either naturally or for food. They are either food for the vultures or energies for medicine. We, in no way, advocate the killing of any animal for use as medicine objects.)

Our Totem Staffs sit at the front gate of our altars. They also accompany us to ceremony. Sometimes I take the Lady with me when I go to the hilltop to pray and meditate. She makes a strong statement that "Cloud is here!" I stand her front and center on stage. She is an overseer and a symbol that all is shared for the well-being of everyone. It is common for chiefs or chieftesses to stand their staffs in front of their people. It will be a glad day in paradise when we stand as one great hoop, each with his or her own totem staff. That will be a great and wonderful circle. We stand our staffs, not to assert superiority, but to invite all others to stand up and be counted. This is the symbol of the totem staff.

The Totem Wand came as a gift to Catherine Oxenberg. It speaks to the truth of my own experience. These are principles that were passed on to her. The making of this totem was a gifting of wisdoms passed down through the ages. It resembles a tuning fork. When I made this totem, it reminded me of the working principles for life. I wrote them down and passed them on to Catherine. She will pass them on to her daughter, India. We hold the wisdom of the ages in our genes. We all began as One and will return to the Sacred Circle.

Ceremonial Staff

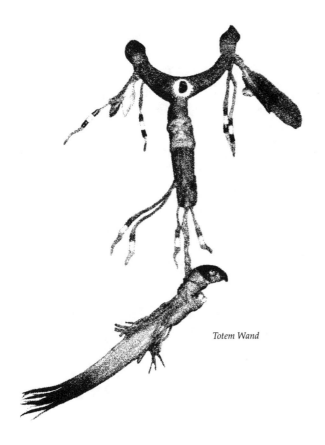

Totem Wand

CHOICE STICK

I am a messenger of the people, both visible and invisible. I live my life in such a way as to help bring back a race of individuals who recognize that we are caretakers of the earth, who regard nothing more sacred than the right of choice. I will want my name to give meaning to those who dare to live their dreams. I will want thoughts of me to be synonymous with courage. I will want it told that my generosity is balanced with discernment about what is good to fertilize. I would have my elders go peacefully to the Other Side knowing that I live carrying their dream. I would want the public to know me as a bridge that joins opposite and different ideas, ideals, beliefs, traditions and peoples. I would be a legend for standing up for what I believe in. I would cause the business community to marvel at my tenacity, brass and astuteness. I would be a light in darkness, joy in sorrow and always a breath of fresh air. I would like to hear whispers behind my back, saying, "She walks as she talks and she lives as though she is the last unconquered person on earth."

I would want the Circle to say, "She holds the good of the tribe in her hands." I aspire to be remembered as one who yielded not to anger, anguish, fear or lust. I would want all friends to call me loyal. I would want the world to know me as relative to all who swim, fly, crawl, walk, run or stand. I would want to live always knowing that something protects me. I would want to be known as a healing power who renews those who come asking. I would want the invisibles to see me as one who always kept my spirit in readiness. I would remember that my place remains out front. I would be rich in blessings, with all that I buy with my attention and focus.

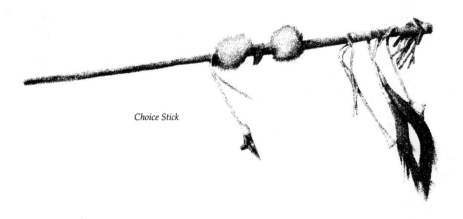

Choice Stick

I would always know myself as something precious, and may the dignity of such knowing pull me always to my full tallness. I would be remembered as one who traded nothing in her nature for her wealth in the world. I would be called one with an unwavering disposition. When my legs can no longer run, I would to be one whose senses outwit opposition. I would be remembered as one who knew the language of the sky. Scout Cloud Two-Children Lee. Onto my Choice Stick I paint, carve, breathe and decorate this meaning. To each Council Meeting where choice is required, I take this stick. When I lay it to the center, all understand that I, Scout Cloud Two-Children Lee, will support the decision of the circle. When I lay it to the outside of the circle, I declare that I would barter my nature to support the decision and, thus, cannot choose such support. All who see my Choice Stick know that it is mine and its placement tells my position and direction. From this knowing, they can choose to follow, join or move away. This is the meaning of the Choice Stick.

HEALING FEATHERS

A long time ago Chuck Storm gave an eagle feather to Vinaya. She passed it on to me. It was my first eagle feather. It's a very big feather; the feather of a big Golden Eagle. Today it shows hints of ceremonial paint on its backside and it has several battle scars. My healing feather is like the true Shaman that has died and been reborn. It even got drunk one night with fine wine. I drank way too much of it at a ceremony honoring the vision that I would one day become someone's wife. I guess the thought of it drove me to drink. I haplessly left my eagle feather at the Village overnight. It got to drink in the starlight and bathe in the morning dew. Skye found it and returned it to me after many, many days of healing it. At first I felt much remorse and shame. Then I began to realize that my feather was truly a healing feather. Skye beaded it and returned it to me in ceremony. Shortly thereafter I became a tee-totaller: overnight. At some very deep level I couldn't believe that I would leave my eagle feather behind. It slipped away from me one other time. It spent the night at Bob Segal's house. He's a big movie producer who lives in Malibu. We had been guests in his home, where we had presented a sacred circle. I had allowed a few of the rude guests to intimidate me. I gathered my things in such a hurry that I forgot my feather. The maid found it and put it safely in drawer. However, it took several days to unearth it. I was in misery the entire time. When I got the feather back, it showed me that it had stayed behind on purpose. I needed the time to grow past allowing rudeness to affect me, and the feather wanted to eaves-drop on the scene in Malibu. I'm convinced it has lots to teach me about the industry.

The eagle feather is used to clear and clean energy fields and to locate illness in the body. I suppose there are other feathers that may do the same. I just don't know about them. My Grandfather Brave Scout once used an eagle feather to locate poison in my body. Grandfather gave me my second eagle feather. Our women can carry eagle feathers. However, some tribes do not allow such. We had been at a gathering in Michigan and had used our eagle feathers in ceremony. Some of the local Indians sent people to harass us. One of them was a witch doctor. I stepped in between him and Brooke. Whatever was intended for Brooke hit me. Grandfather told me that I would have gone crazy if he had not found it and removed it. He found it with his eagle feather.

It went like this. He laid me down on a cot, surrounded by my friends. He then chanted his healing songs and prayed. Then, while he chanted, he moved his eagle feather over my body. He covered every inch. It vibrated differently when he reached my head. He found the bad medicine near my crown chakra. He then sent everyone out of the room to avoid releasing any bad medicine into them. He painted the spot red and then he sucked very hard on that spot. Something awful squirted from my head into his mouth. He spat it into a tin can and sucked again. When he was finished, he showed me what was in the can. There was a snake, about six inches long. There was an embryo, about eight weeks old. There were the bottom two chambers of a heart. There was a scroll made of skin; it was about one inch wide and nine inches long; it was folded three times. There was also some very smelly stuff. It was unlike anything I have ever seen. He recalled my friends and showed them. He then had his son take it outside and bury it. That was it. Amazing! Grandfather is the last traditional sucking shaman in Oklahoma. He is Oto. During my dark days of doubt, I have thought, "He just made an awful noise and then puked up that stuff. It was a trick!" But, then I realize how difficult it would be to puke up what was in that can.

Sucking poison from a body certainly makes a lot more

Healing Feather

scientific sense to me now than "brain surgery!" Modern doctors would call Grandfather a savage. However, he can do surgery without cutting and bleeding. How very primitive is modern science next to Grandfather's skill. He truly understands energy and can move it from one place to another without reckless plundering with a knife. Grandfather gave me his medicine powers. He said that when I need them and trust them they will be there for me. I'm convinced that my eagle feather can locate all manner of dis-ease. This is what I know about Healing Feathers.

THAT WHICH CALLS TO GATHER

Bells toll in the villages of the Austrian Alps. Whistles blow in factories. Organs play in cathedrals. Bugles blow in the Army. Horns blast on tugboats. The conch shells bellow at the Village at our ranch. When the conch shells sound, the circle gathers, visibles and invisibles.

The sound of the conch is a familiar one at the ranch in Oklahoma. Sometimes we blow a cow horn or a digereedo for variety. Always we blow the conch in seven directions: East, south, west, north, above, below and within. These are the seven sacred directions. Above is to Father Sky. Below is to Mother Earth. Within is to the Christ energy, or love within each of us. The call to each of the seven directions is to "open the gate" of that direction. It is to say to both visible and invisible, "You are welcomed. We are gathering for ceremony. Good things will be happening here. Come and join with us."

Our Queen Mother Conch was given to us by Grandmother Princess Moon Feathers. She told us she had it with her most of her life. We painted it with her many symbols. When we blow it, the message painted on it goes out to the seven directions. We say with the horse, "May your journey be good." With the sunrays, we say, "May you live a life of consistency." With the Thunderbird we say, "May your happiness be unlimited."

With the crossed arrows, we offer friendship. With the straight arrow, we offer protection. With the arrowhead we call for alertness. With the bird in flight, we offer lightheartedness. With the running water we offer constant life. With the raindrops we offer plentiful crops. With the tipi and the hogan we offer both temporary and permanent housing. With the sky band we offer a trail to happiness. With the medicine eye we offer wise and watchful council. With the bear track we offer all good omens. With the rattlesnake jaw we offer strength. With the butterfly we offer everlasting life. With rain and clouds we offer good prospects. With the lightening we offer swiftness. With the morning star we offer guidance. With the sun we offer happiness. With the big mountain we offer abundance. With the short cross we offer joining together. With the broken arrow we offer peace. With the snake we offer wisdom. With the deer track we offer plenty of game.

Our Grandfather conch is plain and has a much deeper voice. Our Morning Star conch is high and strong like the voice of a child. The three make beautiful music together. At the end of our call to gather we make a prayer: "I come from very old people. I speak with the voice of the ancients. My will is imbued with the mystery of the Sacred Fire. May what is done here today inspire all to right action in relieving the suffering of the peoples of the world. May all beings realize freedom from suffering and all conflicting thoughts reach resolution. May this happen so that the Great Fire of Wisdom may burn in our hearts and shine forth in everything we do. When others look upon us let them see only enlightened actions and words that benefit all our relations. May what we do here inspire us all to act as one with the Sacred Law. Let all our thoughts and actions bring harmonious resolution to life. May our actions here benefit the land and the people out seven generations. Let us now dream those yet unborn and be ever mindful that life is forever unfolding according to Divine Law. We have spoken! A Ho!"

DEER WHIP

The coyotes killed a young Bambi deer in our coupe gaming field. I found her one morning at sunrise. One of her legs and hooves were still in pretty good shape. I brought it home and seasoned it with salt and Mule Team Borax. When several weeks had passed, I braided a long whip and affixed it to the hoofed leg. It made a perfect whip handle. For my last birthday I asked for the opportunity to do a give-away. Skye arranged for eight teenage delinquent boys to come to the ranch for their first sweat. I took the following four sacred objects into the sweating lodge with the young men: The tomahawk, a lion's paw from an old lion shot by Stewart Granger, the Deer Whip, and the Talking Stick. For each of the four rounds, I passed an object. While the young men held the object, they spoke from their hearts. It went something like this. Round one was to the east. I passed the tomahawk. The east is the place of sun power. It is the place of generating. They began their talk with this: "I bring my hatchet to the fire. The gift I have to give is . . .". In the south round I passed the lion's paw. The lion is the medicine of leadership. In the south one leads with passion, youthfulness and heart. In this round, each boy spoke from his heart. In the west round, I passed the Deer Whip. The west is the place of death and rebirth. It is the place where we look inward at ourselves. The Deer Whip says, "Let me look upon myself with gentleness and strength. Like the deer, let me look at how I may improve and progress without fear." I passed the Talking Stick in the north round. The north round is the place of renewed wisdom and purity. In this round, the boys spoke about the wisdoms their young lives had already

Deer Whip

155

taught them. It was a very powerful and beautiful sweat. This is how I use the Deer Whip.

Once I used it as an instrument of music. A whip makes a loud crack, which sounds very good when it is well-timed with the song "Oklahoma."

CEREMONIAL GOURD

I use a drinking gourd in all manner of ceremonies. In the sweat lodge I feed the rocks with it. In circle ceremonies I serve common drink with it. In feasting, celebrations and the give-away, I give drink to the Mother Earth with it. When I open the gates of our ceremonial grounds, I feed the guardian angels with it. I love my gourd. It is painted in the tradition of my blood relations: Seminole, Celtic and English. The colors represent all peoples. The symbols proclaim the following: "We are children of The Great Mystery; we seek always to see in darkness; we walk the path of the spiritual warrior of love; we call forth joy in all things; we walk praying Sky to Earth and Earth to Sky and we are partnered with the All-That-Is."

When we nourish ourselves with sweet drink from the sacred gourd, we must pray allowing. When we pour water onto the Earth, we cannot direct its flow. When we pray with water, we must pray with an openness to the possibility that what we want is not the only possibility. Otherwise, there is little possibility that

Drinking Gourd

we will get what we want. When we pray with water from the gourd, we pray with this attitude: "It doesn't matter who caused the flood. It is important who can mop." Finally, the gourd reminds us again of balance. If a person has too much fire, they anger too easily. If they have too much air, they cannot hold a thought. If they have little wood, they bend easily to listen to others' ideas. If they have too little earth, they lack practicality. If they have too little metal, they begin to think in isolation. If they have too much water, they flow in too many directions. Walk in balance.

RATTLES AND DRUMS

"A psychiatrist does not want you to wake up! He only tells you how to find your well of pity so you can fill it up with your tears. He is a bird of prey drinking from your misery. Cry only when your tears do not feed another's joy or pad their pocket books. Wake up! Wake up!" So speaks the wisdom of the rattle. Incessant! Throbbing! Pounding! WAKE UP! Oh, that those who support psychiatry and group therapy would know the power of the drum. "Let those who struggle on the death road of strife, return home to circle where we walk from life to life." Come home to the drum. Listen to the heartbeat of the Earth. It is the heartbeat of all things. Follow the sound of the rattle home to your own heart. Almost all healing uses rattles and drums to syncopate bodily rhythms and energies. Rattles are used to drive away unwanted spirits. Drums are used to bring us into harmony with the Mother Earth. Like the rattle and the drum that go on incessantly, be guided by a single will. Let the rhythm of the rattles and the drums move you to dance the history of your culture.

Drums

The head of the Catholic diocese in Oklahoma City once told me that the drum used to be the center of worship in the Catholic Church. He felt that when the drum was taken out of the church, so was the heartbeat of the church. The church removed the drum because they thought it pagan! The drum is an old mysterious medicine, a medicine that can change the destiny of the people. Let us beat the drums and shake our rattles. Let us beat the drums around the world. Let us bring our satellites into high service. Let us allow them to connect our world, drumming, drumming,

drumming. Let us drum together, the heartbeat of the Mother Earth.

Lightening was our first Drum. Peter brought her to us. He drummed the heartbeat for one week, sometimes into the early morning hours. Skye holds Lightening. Thunder is my drum. He was made by the Taos Indians. I call Thunder "he," but I know that the drum belongs to woman. She is the heartbeat of the Mother Earth. She is a womb place. Men must respect the drum. There was a time when women were the guardians of the drum. They played the drum. It is time for the women to return to the drum. Men have abused the womb place of woman. Many of our sisters' hearts turn to dust. It is time for the women to return to the drum. Peyote was given first to a pregnant woman on the desert. When the men learned of its power, they took it from the women. The women in the Peyote Church are not allowed to play the drum.

Drum

Skye is the best drummer I know. She wanted to play the drums as a child, but her father would not let her. It was "unladylike." Now she plays the drum. She's the best drummer I know.

We have made many hand drums and now our hands make the biggest drum of all. Soon we will dance on top of our Earth Drum. A Chumesh Medicine Man sent Mary Nighthawk to us with a message. Build, again, the Earth Drums. Our Earth Drum is 16 feet in diameter and eight feet deep. Soon we will dance on top of her and she will send our music out under and into the Earth. We will also sit in her belly. She is also a kiva in the Earth. To her south will sit a mound plated in love grass. The mound came from her belly. On top of the mound will blow wind from the southwest. That prevailing wind will play the wind harp on the mound. That sweet sound will blow across the top of our Earth Drum and keep her always happy.

Rattles

We have many rattles. We made them from rawhide, shells, nuts, gourds and even from cans, for the children. Each one is different. Some are used for healing and have all the healing crystals and rocks in them. Others are for entertainment. Most are for ceremony and have ant rocks, seeds, rice and beans in them. They are each decorated for their medicine. My favorite design is on my "magical rattle." Its handle looks like the magic stick in *Willow*. I painted Chivas (my paint horse friend, now deceased) on the rattle. On the back side of the rattle is the ugly red face of the medicine witch that Sigourney Weaver, playing the role of Dian Fossey in the movie *Gorillas in the Mist*, painted on trees to attempt to stop the killing of gorillas. The witch's eyes are my own thumbprints. This rattle is one I use for special magic and spells. Only children really understand the power of this rattle and its special design. An adult could understand a little, if they knew that Chivas and I were friends for 41 years before he died. When I die, I want my ashes to be sprinkled close to Chivas.

Finally, about rattles: One day I walked a trail in the woods. Twice I heard a rattle in the distance. Then I saw my rattlesnake sister on the path. She sat up and took notice of me. She shook her rattles. We looked at each other. We both knew that we each held a poison to kill the other. We both respected that strong medicine. We acknowledged each other and passed without injury. We paid each other respect. This is the medicine of the rattle.

SCEPTER

Asia tells many tales. One is a tale of her mother's journey to Africa. She returned with the scepter of a Masai Chief. The handle was a carved lion's head. The tail was a horse tail. She told me, "When you see one of the Masai with this, you know he is the Chief." The Chief of the African tribe featured in the movie *Out of Africa* carried an umbrella. It is a modern version of the horsetail scepter. In truth, the horsetail scepter was a flyswatter. It is given to the Chief as a way of saying, "You think always of the good of the people. For this we want you to live in comfort." It was a status symbol with a genuine function. The umbrella accomplishes the same thing.

Some symbol of comfort is given to any Chief. I gave my first scepter/flyswat to Chief Wilma Mankiller of the Cherokee Nation. She seemed amused by it. I have since made two more. One I have kept. One I have given to a corporate visionary. He is a chief with love for his people. Chiefs are leaders only through counsel and example. They have no authority of force. Once an American soldier was trying to persuade an old Indian Chief to move his people. He said to the old chief, "Chief, you're the Chief. Just tell those people what to do!" The old chief looked at him queerly and replied, "If I told them what to do, I would not be the Chief." Others have said, "A chief is one who follows the people." The definition I like best is this, "A chief is one who sees where the crowd is going and runs to the head of the line and says, 'Follow me!'" The scepter is a flyswatter. Give it to those who live as shining examples for others. In this way, you give them your wish that they should be comfortable.

MEDICINE BAGS AND POUCHES

When something is special to me, I make a pouch for it. In this way, I acknowledge its medicine. Grandmother Jerry brought me my centering stone. I made a bag for it. She also brought me a double terminated crystal that is perfect in every way. The crystal called her to it. She dug down two feet to find it in a cluster in Arkansas. The crystal told her, "Take me to Cloud. Tell her my name is Mataya (Star of Stars, shooting through the world at an amazing rate of speed). I have written a song about Mataya. I also wear her in a special pouch around my neck. The pouch has a dolphin on it. I aspire to be as clear and pristine as Mataya.

The Empress is green fluorite crowned in gold. She came from China. She lives in a white elk pouch with a beaded spiral on it. Sammy is a crystal from the McEarl pocket in Arkansas. McEarl crystal is among the most expensive in the world. When they opened the pocket, the crystal sang. The old miners ran to get the medicine peoples. A medicine man named Mountain, an apprentice of Rolling Thunder, came and did ceremony. At the ceremony, the crystal showed pictures of elders dancing and singing victory. Much of this crystal was given to the medicine people. Mountain gifted me mine. It is the clearest crystal in the world. I took mine to sit with the Crystal Skull. Sammy is my microphone from Control Room Central. I carry Sammy on stage. Sammy rides in an ermine pouch. Ermine is for women's fertility.

Crazy Horse's granddaughter gave me his thunder rock. It is said that no harm can come to one who holds the thunder rock. I wear it in a pouch on my belt. Children love to shake it and hear it thunder. "Arrow's Way" rides in a special pouch with a tomahawk on it. I took this turquoise fluorite crystal with me on my last Vision Quest. We sat together at the edge of the world, on an altar overhanging the sea, almost a mile high. "Rocket" rides in a pouch that has a Jonathan Livingston bi-plane on it. She is a crystal who holds earth and water in her belly. An old man told me she was formed when the earth was in Her beginnings. "Love Light" rides in an elk pouch with an arrowhead on it. She is a deep purple sudulite from Africa. They say she vibrates the fastest of all stones. My petrified bean rock is named "Jack." He rides in a small deerskin pouch. My telephone is a tabloid crystal that is double terminated. It rides in a pouch on my belt. My Cloud Crystal has a bunny pouch. My Key Crystal has a Kulu pouch. My petrified Aboriginal bread has a tasseled deer pouch. My oldest rock (400 billion years) rides in an orange butt-pack. It is part of my prayer bundle. My Dog Star rock rides in a rainbow deer pouch around my neck. So does my Grandmother Great Spirit rock. It came from the most western point in America. My sacred tobacco is kept in a small deer pouch and fits easily into my hip pocket. My opal Chief is carried in a Sioux deerskin pouch that is beaded.

My "Go Stones" ride on my belt in a deerskin pouch. I met a

Medicine Bag

"Go Master Gamesman" in Miami. In exchange for my talents, he wished to teach me the game of "Go." I really don't like playing board games very much, but I consented to indulge him his mastery. I had no desire to engage my brain to really learn the game, but I thoroughly enjoyed his love of the game. I made a prayer and asked my child self to pay attention, while the rest of me surrendered to the beauty of watching a master at work. When it came time to play, I still had no earthly idea what was happening. However, I tuned in to my intuition and made the move that my familiar suggested. I beat him! He was most surprised and gifted me with two stones from his master set of "Go." When I wear them, they say, "Go. Surrender to The Great One. Ask no questions. Just go!"

We will mention four types of Medicine Bags here. Later we will discuss the making of personal medicine. There are as many types of medicine bags as there is imagination for making them. We'll discuss the Pipe Bag, the Cloud Bag, the Music Bag and the Eagle Bundle. I like to think of a Medicine Bag like a bedroom. My bedroom is my own special, private place of comfort. My most intimate dreams and moments happen here. I share my bedroom on a very selective basis. The same is true for my personal medicine. Each medicine bag has "birds of a feather" so to speak. The things that are in each medicine bag are related, just like a bedroom has certain furniture which is different from living room furniture. Each Medicine Bag is a room where things of like nature live. Each room, or bag, has a different function.

The Pipe Bag is made of elk and beaded with a yellow rose. Its energy says, "I will long run in partnership and friendship with all things." It holds the pipe, tobacco and a cleaning stick. The pipe bowl is wrapped in a bandana that belonged to Chivas the horse.

The Cloud Bag holds Indian popcorn. It is beautiful and multicolored. We use the corn in ceremony and we plant it as a gift to the Mother Earth. Most people plant corn. We plant popcorn. I suppose it's the kid in us! The bag has its own Tori for a tie. In ceremony we unwrap the tie and spin the Tori to create a vortex on the earth. There we plant our corn and say our prayers. There is a beaded wave rolling in to the top of a big cloud, which is set against a full sun. A black and white gull flies in the sky. The bag calls for great, GREAT abundance for all people.

The Music Bag was the first Medicine Bag I ever made. It

Medicine Bag

holds the faces of elders and blood stones for healing with music. This bag holds palm drums, flutes, finger symbols and a nose flute. These are instruments that I love to play in ceremony. I often carry this bag into nature and play for the rocks and trees.

The final Medicine Bag is the Eagle Bundle. I was given my Eagle Bundle in a dream. A very strong dream. It took many weeks to make. I threw a cloth, prayed and waited. When I open the Eagle Bundle, it is either to do a specific ceremony or healing, or it is to deliver a message. Opening the Eagle Bundle is like reading the Holy Scriptures. We are given many gifts. We have only to be open to those gifts. The gifts in the Eagle Bundle are powers. Power comes to one who has surrendered to a principle and lived that principle so much as to become it. Always, when I open the Eagle Bundle, it becomes a game to see if everyone present can remember the meaning of each object. Little children are the best. Sometimes when one cannot remember an object, I am told that they need that medicine. I will open the Eagle Bundle for you. Please do as I have done, if only in your mind:

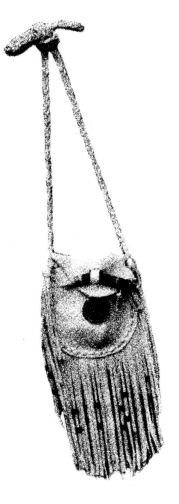

Medicine Bag

Blow the conch and send out greeting in four directions. Let hearts fill with gladness. The Eagle Nations are being summoned. Sing the Eagle songs. Let the heartbeat of the drums be heard above and below. Shake the rattles to send away meddlesome spirits and invite respect. The Eagle Bundle is opened. Fill the air with sweet sage. Offer up prayers of Thanksgiving to the Old Ones, the Ancients, the Elders. The Eagle Bundle is opened. We have been given powers by the Old Ones. Many gifts are given; few have been received. Receive these gifts from the Ancient Ones. We are needed here to do the work. Recognize and accept these gifts.

The ocean shell shaped like a face speaks about this gift: "We are given the innate ability to hold a mystery. This is to walk in faith, believing like a little child."

A deer pouch filled with my own hair and crowned with a bear claw, a bell and a dolphin tells me: "I, Cloud, Seminole, of the Bear Clan, friend to the Dream and the Dreamer, have been given the ability to know and understand I have only to walk in faith, behaving in the believing way, and sooner or later I will know from the place of All-Knowing."

The crystal wand with the face of the ancients tells me this: "We are given the ability to destroy, or to take apart that which is no longer useful to the one and the whole."

Skunk Medicine Bag

*No animals were intentionally killed
for use as medicine.*

The jade serpent with the turquoise eyes tells me this: "We are given the ability to transmute and heal all manner of disease."

The deerskin pouch with the beaded "$" sign tells me this thing: "We are given all that we need to manifest our destiny."

The crystal eagle speaks to this gift: "We are given the gift of vision so that we may prophecy."

The cloth pouch with sage and herbs and tied with a coral dove says this: "We are given the gift to purify."

The silver spoon and the watermelon tourmaline reminds us this: "We have the ability to feed and nurture."

The silver box with the life-saver crinoid speaks of this gift: "We have the ability to make live."

The broken blade of the ceremonial knife, that has been healed with gold fissures, and lives separate from its handle, speaks of this gift: "Always we have the ability to choose to live as we divine. Always, even in relationships, our choice is our own."

These are the gifts given to me in vision. The symbols came to my own throwing cloth. Each bundle has its own unique symbols. I am told that these gifts are given to those who will receive them. I have made and gifted one Eagle Bundle. It was like giving away a Bible. It spoke of what is possible if one will open and receive. The symbols serve as precious reminders. Others have sat at the opening of the Eagle Bundle. They have returned to their homes and called their own bundles into form. This is a good thing. The medicine is to be shared. We need many hands to do the work on earth. Let it be that many hear the call and "Come To The Bundle." It is a gift of the Eagle Nations. The Ancient Ones offer this gift freely to all who would receive. Receive it with open hearts of Thanksgiving.

POINT OF POWER AND POINTS OF POWER

Klint is wise in his spirit. He is one about whom some say, "He is wise beyond his years." He is wise because he is innocent and open. He first planted a "needle" or "point of power" in the Village. He came to tell me that Joan of Arc had a "Point of Power." I secretly prayed that my life would have a better ending! In 1989 I was gifted a beaded needle to represent my own "Point of Power." Many women in our society feel that they have given away their power. I had never felt this way . . . until given a "Point of Power." Now I recognize that it has taken me many years to fully step into my power. The beaded "Point of Power" came from an isolated beach in the Caribbean. In 1989 I journeyed with five friends to live among the Mayans. We went to speak with the elders on the New Year. A hurricane had recently hit the area and the beach was littered with the remains of destruction. From these ruins came the small stick that Skye used to bead the needle. It took her most of 1989 to bead the needle. It sits at the front of my altar and reminds me that THE POINT OF POWER is this: Power is in Spirit. To walk with Spirit is to walk with Power. There is no power in money. It is only paper. Power is in Spirit. It is always moving through. It cannot be contained. Always true Power is a loan. Always, when we walk in Spirit, we walk with a loan of power. We take it in and give it out at the direction of Spirit. This is power.

The following are examples of "Points of Power" that have come to me for using. They are a loan. I give them back into your keeping and thank all who brought into my path.

Points of Power in The Village

Quarreling angers the Great Provider. Take anger outside under the sky where there is lots of room. Go alone and give it to the sky. Then a solution will come.

Nickname a tree and it will guard over you.

Buzzard feathers are good to scare away dark energy. It is a strong form of protection.

When lightening strikes wood, it is more powerful. Use it in ceremony to quicken.

Never call a disease by its name.

Silence is the voice of the Provider.

Learn to "feel" with the heart rather than "hear" with the ears.

Wave moccasins over the fire and be protected on a journey.

Repeat a charm only three times. The fourth time releases its power.

Look for plants to nod to you when you are gathering herbs and flowers.

Stump water makes hair shiny.

To dress well shows respect to Spirit.

Know your heart in solitude where others can't reflect.

Dogwood twigs are good to brush teeth.

It is good to intimidate your mind into turning off for awhile.

We are rich when we have many days for giving food to old

The Needle Beaded by Skye

people and children.

Never doubt the Spirit.

I could go on for days and weeks reciting "Points of Power." This, however, is another book.

CENTERING STONES

Grandmother Alinta gave me my first "Centering Stone." She told me to bring it always as the first stone to the ceremony when we "paint the rocks red." This is when we heat the rocks for the Stone People Ceremony. This rock came from Australia where summer begins in November and winter begins in June. She said, "Always know all sides." She said, "Let our Center connect together the whole world." She told me to keep this rock always on my altar, except when it came to the Sweating Lodge. She said this rock would be in charge of the "call for the Stone People Ceremony." When I "pour the water" (lead the Stone People Ceremony) I always bring this rock in first.

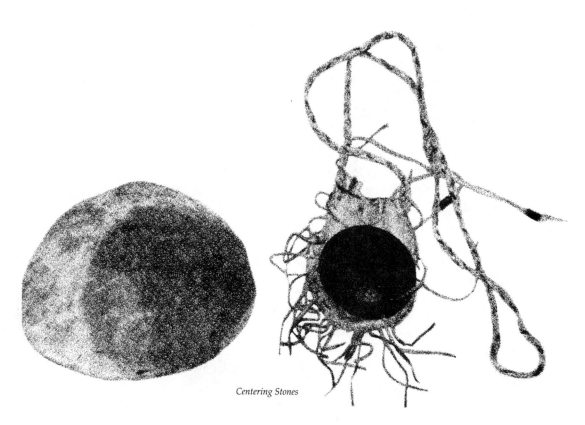

Centering Stones

166

Grandmother Jerry gave me my personal "Centering Stone." She found it in a dig on her land. She has a collection of her Cherokee people's artifacts that is worth very much money. However, she would never sell it. She said this stone belonged to a very powerful medicine woman. She said the stone told her to bring it to me. I slept with it for weeks. Never has a gift brought me so much joy. My centering stone and I are in love with each other. I gave it my oldest and favorite tasseled bag to live in. This stone sits in the center of my prayer bundle and of all ceremonies for which I spread a blanket. By placing this stone at the center of the ceremonial blanket, I put my belly and all power that flows through me to the center. I offer myself in this way. I offer the strength of my womb as woman. I offer the strength of my womb as Cloud. I offer myself.

I gave myself my last centering stone. It is an amazing river rock. I call it my belly rock. It holds the magic of breath. I put it on my belly and ride it up and down with my breath. I ride it up on the inhale and down on the exhale. It teaches my body to fill all the way up. It teaches my body the importance of filling my lungs from the bottom to the top. It teaches my body the joy of skan moving through me. Some people take yoga to learn to breathe. I play with my belly rock. It centers me before ceremony or performance. It centers me when something has distracted me from my balance. It is my beloved companion who takes the cares and concerns of life away on the winds of my breath. It is a confidant who knows the extreme of my emotions. It never tells my secrets. I sometimes talk silently with my belly rock. As I give it the full-breath ride, I talk out my troubles. Sometimes I seek its advice. It is my friend.

Brooke and I planted a family cluster of crystals at the center of our ranch. It was dull and needed to return to the earth. After five years we dug it up and put it in the center of the Village. Now it sits center of our Nashville altar. Where it goes, attention flows.

That's what I know about centering stones.

Crystal Cluster

The brain controls the body, maintains it while spirit travels.

Using crystals . . . meditate for one to one and one-half hours. Our double comes to take our soul on a spirit journey. Between 4 and 6 a.m. are the most powerful times for meditation.

—Alinta

CEREMONIAL BOWLS

I will tell you about three ceremonial bowls. There are many waiting to be made by your imagination. You need only know that the bowl represents the womb of the Great Mother Earth. She gives and gives and gives. No matter how we treat Her, She gives. It is with great reverence that we place a bowl to represent Her to the center of the ceremonial blanket. Sometimes I place my personal "centering stone" in the bowl. The bowl always sits center of ceremony for women. I like to fill it with different things. When we greet weary travelers, we fill it with warm, scented water to wash their feet and hands. When we feast a bride-to-be, we fill it with the sweet juices of fruit. When we come seeking vision, we fill it with the Awa Pua voice. When we prepare one for passing, we fill it with the warm ginger water. All who sit in the circle take from the bowl, just as we do from the Mother Earth. We offer the Earth the first drink from the bowl. We give Her all that is left. We offer the Mother's drink at each of the four directions. We throw an offering to the Sky and show the Mother's gratitude to the Father. We give our prayers, songs and laughter to the bowl. We do this to thank the Mother for all Her many gifts. An act of honoring the bowl is an act of honoring the Earth. Our children learn the Sacred Balance like this.

Ceremonial Bowls

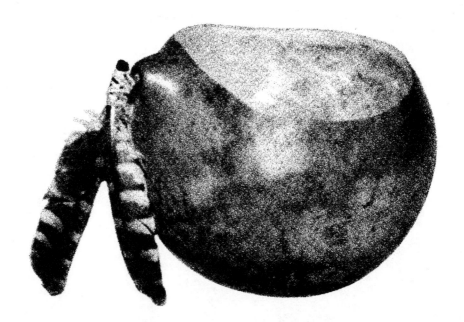

The Awa Pua ceremonial bowl is made from the shell of a coconut. It was cut, smoothed and blessed by Rhio. Rhio is one of the most ancient living souls. She lives in the jungles of Hawaii. She lives in a hut of her making. She is sprung up from the land. To see her is to see the Mother Earth form into flesh.

The Thanksgiving ceremonial bowl is made of clay from the earth and molded by Merrillyn's hands. She pulled the clay together from four directions and sealed the seams with her fingers. Each section is imprinted with beautiful leaves from the Mother's trees. Fruit bearing, wood giving, medicine bearing and thorny trees of protection are represented. The glazes run free, as do the waters of the Earth. The bowl makes a beautiful chime. It sings like crystal.

Our newest ceremonial bowl is drying in the sun. She was a gourd grown in Georgia. She was picked and discarded along the roadside. I found her laying abandoned in a littered ditch. She called to me when I drove by. She is ready to be cut, cleaned, sanded and painted. She has not yet told of her decorum. She has not yet revealed her place in ceremony. However, she is a thing of beauty that has been found. She sings of the prodigal daughter who has returned home. The mother cries, "Bring forth royal robes and rings. Spread the banquet tables. My daughter has come home. That which was lost is found! It is a time of great rejoicing!" I imagine that this bowl will celebrate Homecoming. That is what I know of ceremonial bowls.

Only when I was able to take Mother Earth's energy in the form of clay, with her own moisture, and form it into a vessel with my own hands, did I recognize that it was a female energy. Each woman has the characterisitcs of the Mother Earth.

—Colonel Lyn

MUSICAL INSTRUMENTS AS MEDICINE OBJECTS

"The hills are alive with the sound of music!" "Cloud's here!" says all of nature when our canoe rounds the bend in the river and they hear the sweet sound of my dolphin flute. It is a very small gift to give in exchange for the wondrous beauty of Mother Nature and the songs of all Her creatures. From far away the tree spirits can hear the flute. By the time I arrive, all the creatures are excited and waiting. When I want to impart a message of deep love from my heart, I play my smallest nose flute. This way my message goes out on the horse of my "allowing breath." The Tibetan bells clear and awaken. It is good to listen to their song as it goes all the way out to eternity. It goes on forever. It is easy for children to

Instruments played in spirit create an altered state, a shift. It is the experience of singing the Universe.

—Kactus

learn how it is that their voices carry all the way around the world. It is good to know that what we say will be felt somewhere. In this way, we learn to say good things. Sticks and stones love to join the band. Without our help they have no voice. To hear their spirit voice, we have to quiet our minds and listen. To hear the voice of their essence, we click them together. They love to be played. It is a good day in the life of a stone when a child holds it in her hands or clicks it together with another stone to make music. Sticks and stones who join the band, always give away their secrets. They love to be played. We always bring them to the stage. Perhaps one day they will join all country, gospel, classical and rock bands! When they do, we will celebrate the coming together again of all peoples, because sticks and stones need us to play them. They are very sad to be used to break bones. In truth, they are artists and musicians. Strike up the band!

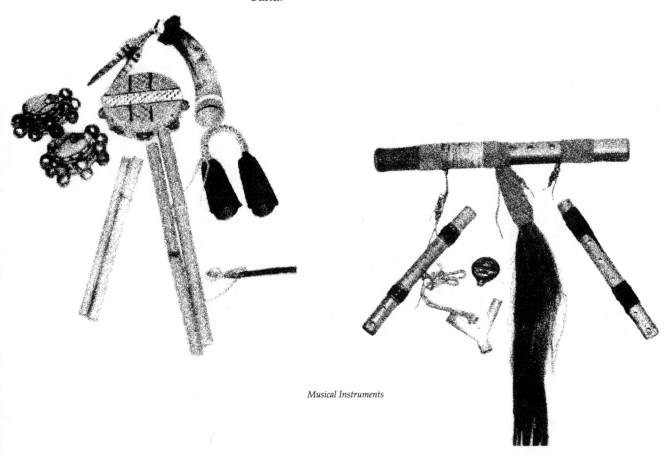

Musical Instruments

CEREMONIAL TOGS

One who lives her life for the People lives always being watched. It is respectful to dress to honor the Spirit. It is healthy to dress to honor one's own spirit. I always do. Some say that I am always in costume. Others squeal, "The sixties are back!" I know very little about the sixties since I spent the first half as a sorority president and the second half at Bible College! Skye is the only true "hippie" that I ever knew and she was no longer a hippie when I met her. I suppose the beads, medicine togs, vests, boots, moccasins and headbands are cause for rejoicing over the return of the sixties. In truth, I dress to make my spirit happy. I dress to honor the brilliant colors of our Great Provider. I dress to entertain children. I dress to awaken myself to my own loan of power. I look like a walking museum. When Walter Boyne, Director of the Smithsonian Aerospace Museum, met me on the set of "Star Trek: The Next Generation," he exclaimed, "I would cast you in bronze and call you the modern spirit of the pioneering woman in America!" I win trophies for my costuming. I now have an image to uphold.

I make my own costumes. What I don't make is given to me in ceremony. The only clothes I buy are socks, underwear and Levi jeans. Perhaps my epitaph will read, "Cloud, Forever in Levi's." Ladies in California, New York, London, Sidney and Toronto often want to buy my vests. I make all of them by hand. No machine is used. I pray all the while I am making them. They are my own prayer clothes. I have dance vests, medicine vests, wedding vests, adventure vests, ritual vests and formal vests. My formal vest is black with tails. It sports the black and white mane and tail of Chivas. Chivas was my horse friend for 41 years. He gave me the gifts of hair while he was still living. He was a regal dresser himself, a perfectly symmetrical black and white paint. He roamed free in his latter years. He always had a strong spirit and was extremely intelligent. My medicine vests have snake skins and represent transmutation and healing.

I often wear prayer clothes with my skirts and jeans. They are handmade Seminole patterns that call for all people to come together. My shawl is handwoven by an old grandmother and has so many rainbow colors that I cannot count them. I will never wash this shawl. Never will I wash my vests. They carry my skan.

Head Dress

Medicine Togs

My moccasins have travelled the world. Some have danced with the Sun. Others have walked the streets of Jerusalem. Still others have performed on stages around the world. When I gift a pair of my moccasins, they have truly walked many miles. Their medicine is great. Each of my headbands has a crystal in them and is wrapped with deerskin ties. I wear them to keep the hair from my eyes and to awaken my vision.

My jewelry is a constant attention getter. I have the opportunity to share so much medicine just by answering the questions, "What does this one mean?" I wear the first money my father gave me. It is a silver half-dollar with the year of my birth on it. I wear a medicine for all children. Another medicine bag reminds me that I have all that I need, always. I wear a rock to honor Grandmother Holy Spirit. I wear beads of my Seminole people. I wear the gold insignia of our corporation, Vision Us, Inc. I wear opals given to me to balance my energy. I wear an eagle given me by Grandmother Kitty. I wear a medallion representing my blessing from the Sacred Buffalo Hat Teepee. I wear Mataya, the pristine crystal from Grandmother Jerry. I wear many pouches on my belt. I wear bracelets given me by a medicine man and woman. My jackets are colorful and stately. They represent my lineage. I even choose the color of my underwear with My Creator in mind. On days that I will be giving forth, I wear red. On soft days on the river in my canoe, I wear turquoise. I wear white in ceremony. I wear black in healing circles. I dress to honor my spirit. I have worn feathers many, many times. I dress to honor my spirit. I keep myself clean and neat and colorful to honor The Great Spirit. I will enjoy seeing the costumes of all spirits on our Planet. I'm certain that corporate gray will fade away and there will be no high heels and hose!

Prayer Clothes

MAGICAL CHILD MEDICINE DOLLS

It has long been a strong practice to make a doll to represent the self. This self can make many changes ceremonially. Little girls learn to be mothers by playing out life with a doll. The magical child doll is a doll that represents the beautiful child within. Today, nearly all doctrines of mental health are seeking to heal the child within.

Our magical child dolls hold the magic of our dream. They sit on the World Altar and hold the magic wand. They sit in a Pepsi wagon with the book *The Little Train that Could*. Each person is a magical child of God. Our Magical Child Foundation is founded to rediscover the Magical Child in all people.

Magical Child Medicine Dolls

MICROPHONE AND MICROPHONE STAND

The last ceremonial object that I mention is my microphone and my microphone stand. The most sacred gift given to me by Spirit is a microphone. I first carved wooden microphones. Then a corded one came. Then "Hawk Eye" came. Hawk Eye is a cordless mike. He lives in an elk bag with "The eye of the tiger" stone sewn on the flap. A sachet of sweet sage lives in the bag with Hawk Eye. He is wrapped in a bunny fur. I care for Hawk Eye as I care for my words. Words are the brick and mortar of creation. What we say, is what we get. Our language and songs must be filled with love and beauty. I carved a microphone stand from sycamore for Hawk Eye. Always, I think of Zacchaeus and Jesus when I think of sycamore. It is beautiful to see. It was the tree that Zacchaeus used to see Jesus. I want people to see the Christ in themselves. Hawk Eye sits on top of "Sac" when he is not working. Sac is wrapped with a horsetail for the children out seven generations. Sac also is wrapped with bunny fur. Sac is a girl. Her stand is covered with bunny fur and she rolls around. Sac and Hawk Eye want all the children of the world to be loved and cared for—children of all ages.

If I had to choose only one medicine tool to keep, it would be Hawk Eye and Sac. It is a wonderful thing to see the expressions on the faces of all who hold Hawk Eye and speak into his power. It is like, for the first time, they hear their own voice speaking . . . and everyone listens. Hawk Eye shows them how it is that God listens to our every need.

This is what I want to share about medicine togs, tools and toys.

A Ho!

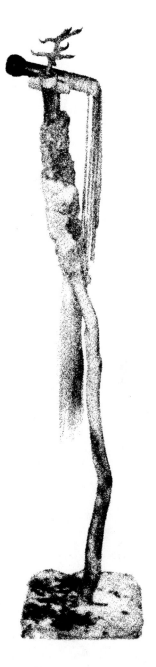

"Hawkeye" Microphone & Stand

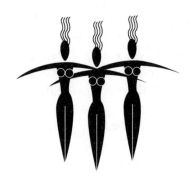

WOMEN, THE MOON AND POWER

In the womb of woman sits the seed of all future generations. The blood that surrounds this truth is the source of great power. Money is not power. It is paper. Status and material possessions can be acquired with this paper, but true power is in the contact of the supernatural . . . the Divine. There is power in the wind. There is power in the rain. There is power in the rivers that flow. There's power in the sun. There's power in the moon. There's power in stars that glow. There's power in grass that grows through rocks. There's power in a flower grown wild. But the greatest power in all the world is in the single tear drop of a child. Women know this power. Even before a woman is born, she holds the eggs of her children in her womb. The nourishment that a female in-utero receives from her mother is given to her own eggs even before she is born. After birth, the nourishment that a baby girl takes in is given to the eggs of her children. All that nourishes her, nourishes her children. She will never receive more eggs. She is born with the eggs of her children. Her every breath feeds those children. All of her life, what she eats, drinks, breathes, sees, hears, smells and feels becomes nourishment for her children.

Child abuse is the music of our culture, of its television productions and movies. These vibrations are strongly felt by every living thing that awaits birth. The energy of city life is absorbed into the eggs of our children. The well-being of our future generations depends on creating a kinder and gentler world. Woman is a manifestation of the feminine principle. Women know about nourishing twenty-four hours a day, seven days a week, forever.

Women hold the true power. Our wombs are like generators that store energy. Our wombs contain life. Men have no way of containing power. They make the fertilizer. Because they cannot store this fertilizer for long periods, they leak it in dreams or sexual acts. Men who are constantly after "nookie" leak their power. Women who allow such, have holes poked in their storage tanks. When fertilizer finds its way to the egg, it awakens from a long sleep. Man's energy throws the switch at the power plant and— poof— the lights come on. Man is intended to fertilize and grow with every thought, word and deed. Man is not intended to hold power. Men have no sacred, divine genes to do so. They are blessed with the ability to fertilize the seed that God planted in the womb of woman. They are gardeners in God's garden. Woman is the fertile soil where God plants seeds. A man may feel pride in his woman when he so nourishes her that she and God's children are radiant. The fruit of the womb is not the result of man's seed. The fruit of the womb is not the children of the parents. The fruit of the womb is a child of the Almighty, unique in all the world. The only seed that is planted, is planted by God long before man and woman ever meet. Each person is a well-thought-out plan of the Almighty. The seed that is us was planted in the womb of our mothers by God Almighty. Our fathers provided fertilizer and our mothers provided the soil in which we grew for nine months.

Some of our ancestors felt that dying in war and dying in child birth were the same level of spiritual accomplishment. To know blood, men become war-mongers. To know blood, a woman bleeds. The Earth Mother and all of nature love the scent and energy of this bleeding time. It is the signal that pregnancy is possible and what is pregnant is favored above all things by Mother Earth. Life goes on. It is the greatest time of celebration. In truth, a woman does not need to sit in the *inipiti* ceremony and sweat in order to clean her blood. A woman cleans her blood with the cycle of the moon. When a woman sits upon the earth and bleeds, she is attended by all of nature. The wind and the sun and all that lives on and in the earth want to render up their secrets to this woman. The veil between the world of Spirit and the everyday world is torn asunder and the woman can be in close

I see women as individuals with much power and just at the tip of the iceberg of recognizing it.

—Colonel Lyn

177

Men of my culture carry on the history, language, law and the culture. Women have the responsibility of everything else. Men must carry on these four things without interfering with women's activities. We have a circle of advancement in our cultural structure of women's law. Young women are coming to a stage where they will be leaders in whatever field they wish to go in and they are guarded by the older women, who are the real bosses in our culture. I am now an elder. I sit with the council of men. I've now earned this right.

—Alinta

communication with the Spirits.

The bleeding time of menstruation is a time to dwell alone (*isnati*). It is a precious time for woman to sit quietly on the earth and be nurtured. It is a time for woman to listen to the voice of Spirit. It is a time for all around her to attend to her needs. It is a sacred time for all the tribe. At this time, a woman's powers are greatly amplified. Her prayers go farther and are carried on the wings of angels. This moon time is a time to sit in women's circles and drum. It is a time to sing and chant and pray. It is a time to smell the flowers and hear the sweet voice of the babbling spring waters. It is a time to vision for the people. What a woman sees and hears during this time is often as provocative as what is discovered by one who goes crying for a vision in the mountains. A woman has a vision quest each month of her adult life. She does not need to starve herself on the mountains to meet with Spirit. It is her divine nature to have an audience with spirit each month.

I once ran a boyfriend out of my life because of his unyielding attitude about the moon cycle. He called the sensitive shift in emotions "PMS" and came dragging home Proctor & Gamble products to numb the feelings. In essence, he wanted to close the Power Gate to Heaven so that woman would surrender to captivity. Women are not "bitchy," "emotional" and "unclean" during this precious time. They are sensitive to messages from Spirit and if they act bitchy and emotional, it is because there is truly something in their environment that needs to shift. Whatever it is that results in ill feelings during this time is being programmed directly into the seed of a woman's womb, and divines our future generations. A man can feel pride when his woman is soft, sensitive and happy during the time of her moon. It speaks well of the environment in which she is living. A man can participate in nurturing children to come by fully nurturing his partner during the *isnati* time.

Women first held the power in tribal cultures. There was a time when the moon blood was used in ceremony, because of its great power. It was not seen as unclean. It is true that a woman is more powerful than a man during the moon time. It is true that a woman of ill intentions can disempower the medicine tools of man and ruin him for war. This being the case, let all the bleeding women converge on our largely masculine war system and disempower this planet for war. Let the moon blood of woman be put on all weapons. Let bleeding women infiltrate the conference rooms where men sit and plan global destruction. Let our bleeding women sit with their forks open in places where drugs are dealt on the streets. And let these women pray for peace. Let the bleeding woman pour water for the men's sweats, since she already holds the power. Let her use the power to power the men to use their energies in fertilizing joy and laughter and peace. Let the bleeding women call the men to be players and recreational leaders for our families, businesses and government. Let the men spill their "seed" (their fertilizer) into planning reunions and celebrations between nations.

In strong tribal cultures where there is a real sense of community, the spheres of influence and activity are divided between the sexes. The men do their thing and the women do theirs. Where a man or a woman showed a natural proclivity towards activities of the opposite sex, they were freely admitted into the circle of opposite sex and treated as a same sex person. When a person shared both the soul of man and woman, they could be welcomed into both circles. This person was held in high esteem and allowed to lead ceremonies that involved both sexes, as they understood both. If we are moving more and more towards an androgynous world (and to see rock stars, I think we are), we will hope to see more and more twin soul persons who understand both sexes. Until such time, we women have the task of teaching men about nurturing and the men have the task of teaching women about fertilizing.

After fifteen days of visioning in 1984, I traveled to "The Woods of the Apache" in New Mexico. Here I was given a vision of a shield. The message of the shield clearly stated this:

> "The MAN powers and champions the
> dream; the WOMAN holds and nurtures the
> dream; and the CHILD dreams the dream."

When we understand this balance of male and female energy and cultivate this balance within, we can attract to us partners that are our perfect balance. We are each male. We are each female. We are each old. We are each young. It is important to be balanced in these aspects. Bringing back the regard for the woman and her moon cycle is essential for all to know the balance. We can no longer tolerate young girls being told that they are dirty or sick. They are God's garden. Their bleeding says that the garden is fertile. The woman's energy will call a mate . . . just like

Moon cosmic energy comes down every morning, then it becomes mist, then dew. This time is perfect to revitalize energy.

—Alinta

In the past, as women we have been taught to feel guilty for the power we've exhibited on the planet. Let's face it, throughout the centuries we have sunk continents.

—Mahisha

a dog in heat. If she wishes to see her child blossom and grow into a beautiful plant, she must become an attraction in all that she does. She must resonate the sweetness that she wants around her. If she is puny and grumpy and sickly, she will resonate such and is bound to attract a mate that will give her good reason to be puny, grumpy and sickly. If she is vital, soft, strong, active, playful, gleeful and happy to be alive, she will attract a mate that delights in fertilizing her ground of happiness. Let the women show their true emotions during their moon time. Let this serve as a mirror for the men. May they act to balance the energy of their environment so that all is happy and peaceful.

The most powerful medicine first belonged to woman. It still does. The Holy Spirit that moves through all things is not a "friendly ghost." She is woman. It is Her heart's desire that calls Father God to champion and power. The Earth, she will survive! Her mate will see to that. People may not survive. The Earth, she will! She is woman. When the hearts of the women turn to dust, the people perish. Woman knows the pain in the tear drop of a child. It is that tear drop that conveys supernatural strength to woman. Let the tear drops turn to giggles and all the world will rejoice.

Let women use their bleeding time to redirect missiles and confuse the thinking of war-mongers. A woman in her moon is powerful.

Many tribes recognize this power as the power to create future generations. For this reason, the greatest time of celebration is when a young girl comes to her woman time. Her first blood is kept and brought to ceremony for all to see. She lays down her child name and puts on her woman robe. She is given many gifts and is told many secrets by the women. There is great feasting among the tribe for their lineage will go on. It is at this time that young men of prowess are honored, for they will fertilize these young women. Read details about such a ceremony among the Apache in *Secret Native American Pathways: A Guide to Inner Peace* by Thomas E. Mails.

There is a tribe among the bush people in Africa who require each young man to adopt seven fertile maidens for a year. He is to build their lodges away from the main village. Here he is to supply their every need. He is to bring them food, wood for their fires and special treats as he ascertains what they are. However, he is never to be seen. He must watch them from a place of hiding and become sensitive to each one. During this time he may favor one, but never must he deprive the others. It is his duty to show equality to all of the young women. If he is caught or seen by the women, he is beaten until he cries. If he is caught three times during the year, he is banished from the tribe forever. If he is successful, he may marry. If he has been true to his task, the young woman of his choosing will also choose him. This is the way the young men learn to regard women highly.

When the sap of the peach tree runs, it turns red like the blood of woman. The peach is like the woman's womb and the seed is like the seed in her womb. The blood of the peach tree is powerful medicine. Use it to make medicine bags to wear over the navel and under clothing. It is good to wear this small bag into meetings where men have not yet learned to regard woman for her true power. This small bag will shield attacks that weaken a woman and stir her thoughts from an intention to nurture with her choice.

I have recently written a song to call for a return to pride in the virginity of our women. It goes like this:

Now is the time of blending our talents. It is creating the circle of eight; spirit into form; as above, so below.

—Grandmother Kitty

> "Mary was a virgin at the mountain valley school.
> She was a kind and gentle filly who believed the Golden Rule.
> The girls all mocked and teased her; they called her "Goodie Two-Shoes."
> They bought their popularity with sex and drugs and booze.
>
> Mary's Mama taught her all about a woman's place,
> as protector and creator of the fragile human race.
> She taught her that a woman is the anchor in the home.
> With faith and grace and dignity, she would never walk alone.
>
> She's the virgin Mary every Tom and Harry would love to make their own.
> She's a woodland fairy picking herbs and berries in a dress that she's hand sewn.
> Her mind is as pure as the driven snow.
> Her heart is as open as a drive-in show,
> and her body's as virgin as the Mary of long ago.

Mary grows more beautiful as others grow more
cruel.
She'd rather eat her bread alone than to eat steak
with a fool.
She plays alone and always prays for those who
would be free,
By smoozin', cruzin', boozin', losin' their
virginity.

Nearly 40 years have passed since I began this
song.
Good girls still get teased a lot and bad girls still
do wrong.
Mary is a woman now. She's kind and just and
fair.
They call her virgin Mary with the long, golden
hair.

She's the virgin Mary every Tom and Harry
would love to make their own.
She's a woodland fairy picking herbs and berries
in a dress that she's hand sewn.
Her mind is as pure as the driven snow.
Her heart is as open as a drive-in show,
and her body's as virgin as the Mary of long ago.

There is power in the space between two hands that reach, but
do not touch. There is power in the containment held in the
womb of a woman. Abortion would not be a problem, if the true
dignity and respect for woman and her power were brought back
into our circles. Unwanted babies come from careless sex. Though
I realize that material contained in this chapter is in opposition to
tradition that places power with the men, it is important
information. I am woman. I sit with Spirit. I honor the vision of
each month. The Great Mother calls for balance in power. All will
be happy again when woman, the moon and power are honored.
We must not serve the form of traditions. Their time is past. We
must sit together at the dark of the moon when the veil is the
thinnest and take our orders straight from Grandmother Holy
Spirit. We must honor only the Spirit of tradition. Remember
always that the first ceremony was given to a man or a woman
straight from Spirit. Now is the time to step fully into Spirit.

Come forward Woman. Know the power of your bleeding. Beat the drums, Man, and raise the energy of your sex chakra to your heart. Then, take care that the woman's heart is happy.

Woman is related to the Moon and all Her cycles. Men are related to the Sun and its consistent movement across the skies. Woman dances with her feet close to the Mother Earth. Man dances with his feet stepping high to the sun. Twin souls (those who move into androgyny and know the spirit of both man and woman) dance in both ways. Woman is intended to be of an ever-changing nature, like that of the moon. Like the Grandmother Moon, woman is sometimes full, vibrant, active and the light in darkness. She is born to intuition to see in the darkness, like the Grandmother Moon who sits weaving together our dreams at night as we sleep. Grandmother Moon, like old grandmothers, has time to sit keeping watch over a fitful baby who tosses in the darkness. Sometimes awake, sometimes half-dozing, the old Grandmother Moon keeps her vigil over all the sleeping children. As we dream, she stitches together our dreams and designs the intricate weavings that bring us into direct contact with each other. When our paths cross, or we find ourselves in a circle, it is the doing of Grandmother Moon. She knows our Dream Walkers well. In the night, she introduces us to each other and makes the plans that turn our daytime paths toward our destiny. Grandmother Moon knows best about relationships. She knows our secret wishes. She knows our unconscious selves who travel far at night as we dream. Women have this secret knowing about relationships. We must teach it to men. Men are related to the sun. The sun is consistent. It works during the day and rests at night. It gets up every day, irrespective of changes in weather. It always shines its light onto Mother Earth, even if clouds soften its touch. The Grandfather Sun understands the moods of the Grandmother Moon and always, no matter what, gets up to shine his light. This is a knowing within man. He must comfort woman with this knowing.

When the moon wanes, so do the urgings of woman. She prepares herself to bleed with the dark of the moon. At this time, her veil is the thinnest and so is the moon's. Woman has access to "The Throne." During this time, she must listen and vision for the good of the One and the Whole. She must never use this precious gift for herself alone. If she abuses this power, it will come back on her and her people. When the moon waxes full again, woman

Female creative power is housed in the womb, whether a woman is complete physically or not . . . that is irrelevant. Women are powerful.

—Mahisha

*How do I find my own path?
I start within my own heart. I
define down to the finest
particle. I chunk it down into
do-able steps. Then I take the
first step.*

—Colonel Lyn

acts on the knowings of her vision time. Just before the moon is at its fullest, is a good time to council. All the people are awake and energized. Their attention is turned to the delivery by the woman. She is at her fullest. It is a good time to feast and play and mate. Some suggest that woman only spend time alone during her bleeding time. Moon lodges and *initipi* tipi's are set apart for the comfort of these women. In these places they can be quiet and be nurtured. However, some ceremony calls for the inclusion of these women. They are not dirty. They are powerful. The grandmothers kept them away from the men during time of warring so that the men would remain powerful. This was a matter of survival in a time when warring was necessary. Today, the grandmothers call for the end to all war. This is the time of great blending.

When we arrived in Australia in December of 1989, we were called into the moon ceremony. We were called to lead the dance of some 300 people. We went early to the site and prayed. We walked the perimeter of the property and communed with the spirits. The dance that resulted that night was the most powerful dance of our lives. Rather than sending the bleeding women away to a private circle, we called them to the center to be honored. We had created an altar in the center. The bleeding women lay down on the earth with their breasts to the ground. They spread their forks and connected their toes in a star circle around the altar. A handmaiden came forward for each of the bleeding women and sat at her head. From there, they massaged the bleeding woman's shoulders and back while chanting softly. They arranged their hair in designs on the floors. The remaining women made a large circle around the inner circle of bleeding women. The men formed their circle around the outer circle of women. As we danced and sang, the men circled clockwise, to mimic the clockwise movement of the daylight energies. They danced with their feet high. The women circled counter-clockwise to mimic the nighttime energies. They danced with their feet close to the earth. The prayers of the people were spoken into the center of the circle where the powerful star circle of bleeding women lay on the earth. The keepers of the gates and the drums of the four directions were both men and women. It was an amazing spiral of energies.

Let us once again use the blood of the moon time to heal. The time of degrading or ostracizing this blood and replacing it with the blood sacrifice of our children is over! Grandmother Moon provides the only blood that ever needs to be spilled. Let us use it to power our people so that peace will reign on earth.

There are many men who abuse the medicine that the women have passed on to them. They would have women believe that sex and sexual favors are part of the ancient rituals. Beware of these men and their teachings. One of the most miserable nights of my life was one in which I lay next to the room of a medicine man who is known for seducing every woman he can get his hands on. He spent the entire night before a sacred medicine wheel ceremony, seducing a young participant. Two old medicine men have attempted to force sexual favors on me after ceremony. Another brought three young students with him to Canada to attempt to coup the Crystal Skull from Anna Mitchell-Hedges. I, in no uncertain terms, backed these men into their places. They hold little true power. They leak it through their penis. It is good to wear peach blood over one's navel when dealing with medicine men. I know of another medicine man who used sensual seduction as a means of gaining the attention of a very well-known woman of medicine. At the time, she could easily be pulled by this energy. It is best for the men to teach the men medicine and the women to teach the women medicine.

One of the greatest delights of my life was meeting Belva Bloomer. Belva was Shirley McLaine's secretary and confidant for many years. Belva is a very enlightened soul. She answered most of Shirley's fan mail about spiritual matters. After Shirley released Belva, Belva maintained contact with the network of star children that Shirley wove together. Belva called for them to circle on Mt. Piscah in Cripple Creek, Colorado. She asked me to choreograph the three day gathering entitled World Celebration.

Belva had invited many people from around the world to participate. Among them came an old Indian medicine man and his young braves. It was early in ceremony when I realized that this man and his braves had come to steal power, turn the focus from the circle and create a leak in the circle's energy so that they could beg monies. The old shaman and his braves began to call for a storm to blow apart the arbor and the tents. They came to the stage and sang thunder and lightening songs. The storm rolled in. There was no shelter other than the arbor and the winds were taking it apart. I stepped forward and took the microphone from the singing brave. This display of power had to be stopped before the entire weekend was ruined. I asked the women to face

We never call ourselves anything. We are known by what we do.

—Grandmother Kitty

Not until you know that you are truly loyal to yourself can you be loyal to others.

—Cloud

into the wind and "toke" the wind into their bellies. I asked them to capture the wind in their bellies. I asked the men to turn with their backs to the wind and ride what wind was not captured by the women away from the camp. The women stood as an arrow facing the wind. The men rode flank, drawing the wind away from the camp. The storm split in mid-air and totally missed the camp. It poured all around the camp and lightening crashed around us. Not a drop of rain hit us. With this, the medicine man and his boys jumped in their cars and left. We saw no more of them. Power is a sacred thing. It must be used for the good of the people. If we abuse power, it will abuse us.

One last story. In the mid-eighties, a certain medicine man came seeking the Crystal Skull. He wanted to convince Anna Mitchell-Hedges, its finder and keeper, to give it to his people. He called it the West Skull, the Woman Skull. For weeks I had been dreaming Anna and feeling as though she was not well. I called her. She had been experiencing pain in her belly. She could not discern the origin. She had received a call from this man and he was coming to meet her the next week. I made immediate plans to go to Canada to gather him and his troop from the airport. We met them (much to their surprise) and spent several hours with them before allowing them to see the skull. When we sat with the skull, I sat between him and Grandmother Anna. I sat with peach blood over my belly. His attempts were unsuccessful. Anna immediately felt better.

It is time for all women to realize the sacred nature of our wombs and step into the place of power. This place is a place that surrenders only to God. This place is a place where no one divines our course except the Great Mystery. The day of the guru is over. It is time for men, women and children to listen within and act always on that familiar voice that speaks for the good of the One and the Whole. It is time to bring back the Sun Lodges for the men and the Moon Lodges for the women. Let all money and resources come into the hands of the women who carry and nurture the Dream. Let these resources be distributed to the men who serve the Dream and power the Dream. Let the women return to rule. Women know, from their womb, how to hold power. Let the men lighten up and play. It is their nature. They know how to fertilize the Dream. It is taught to them by their scrotum. Let the men receive the resources given to them to fertilize joy and fun and abundance and laughter on our planet.

Let man know the joy of powering, of championing a woman who holds and nurtures a dream. Let women know the joy of nurturing a man who so champions. It was a sad day when women started to leave their hoops to join with man. It is the other way around. Let the women awaken to the dream they hold of life and abundance. Let the men come to this dream and power it. It is a happy man who has a woman in whom he can be proud. Wake up woman. The Dream is in your belly. Follow the path of the moon and know the Dream.

THE FIRE WOMAN

Our quest for fire is old. Our ancestors carried a heated coal in hardened pouches over hundreds of miles, so that each nightly campfire could be started. The Keeper of the Fire would focus her entire life on keeping a hot coal always burning. The tribe depended on it. We muse in modernity to watch "survivors" on television struggle to make fire and keep it alive for forty days. Any of us who have camped in the cold and the rain know the value of fire. However, the true fire is in our hearts. The true fire is our passion for life.

We come to the place of all-knowing through our hearts. Our hearts are the heartbeat of our provider. Our hearts are the gateway to God. When our hearts are open, we move with grace and ease and understanding. When our hearts are closed, nothing goes right. The elders of many tribes are now telling us that we must open our hearts. The fire that burns at the center of our council lodge is the heartbeat of the people. The hearth that holds the fire in our homes, holds the heartbeat of our family. When building a home, a lodge, or a circle, it is good to put our first attention to the fire. It is good to acknowledge the fireplace as the center of the home.

On The Ranch, we have a sacred teaching lodge called the eagle's nest. It is an eight-sided hogan, built like a teepee. The vision of this lodge first came by showing its fireplace. While we were walking across the fields one day, the Eagle's Nest appeared in spirit form. It sat on the land exactly where it now sits today. When the vision vanished into thin air, we walked to the center of where it was and made a prayer. We invoked the powers needed to manifest this dream. We planted a crystal in the centering place and transplanted eight little cedar trees around the periphery. Cedar holds the energies of protection. We then began our journey to nature in search of special stones for the hearth.

We knew that we must first honor the fire of the lodge. For two weeks we traveled around the state visiting lakes, mountains, rivers and cliffs. Each stone held a special prayer and a special memory. When we had enough stones, we built a simple hearth to hold our fireplace. At the time we had no money to build the structure. However, as soon as the hearth was complete, a check for $15,000 arrived in the mail with a note saying, "use this to build a structure on the land." When we honor the fire, miracles happen. The elders again remind us, "Follow your heart. Follow your passion." The fire symbolizes God's passion.

The Eagles' Nest is an Octagon Altar to World Peace

When we do ceremony, we build the fire at the center. Smoke from the fire goes to the Above Ones. This fire is the heart of Grandfather and Grandmother God. It is a sacred place. It is said that a full day at the fire is worth ten days of fasting. It is good to focus energy into the fire and thus know the heart of God. As "fire women" we are on fire with God's passion for peace and harmony. The fire infuses us with vision, strength and extreme passion. Life comes from fire. Life comes from woman. A woman is fire. The old expression "you're playing with fire" has great truth.

While smoke from the fire goes to the above world, the ashes go into the earth. The upper world brings down power, information, or healing. The below world brings up personal empowerment. The upper world is the land of our ancestors. The middle world is our world. The below world is the place of animal power. In the middle world, we walk the lands of the great clouds. Our heads are in the sky and our feet upon the earth. We are the bridge between the upper and lower worlds. The fire is our bridge.

The different kinds of wood bring different energies. The pine tree is called the "Lord of the Fire." It burns hot and fast. Ash wood, cottonwood, hickory and oak are good to kill viruses and purify the air. Smoke of any kind goes to the Other Side

Camp. What one says in the presence of smoke also goes to the other world. Even as there is a fire in the sun above, so there is a sun fire in the belly of the earth. Both warm the earth. Charred wood that has been struck by lightening is very powerful wood to use in sacred ceremony. It quickens the spirit of the fire. It is often used in the half-moon fire or the peyote fire. Ceremonial fire is sacred fire. It is called Big Red or Ancient Red.

To give children fire, tease them as you would a cherished puppy or a colt. This gentles them and gives them an urge to accomplish. The blood of youth should never be heated with angry words. Anger inflames the overly proud and the brave alike. It is like throwing red hot coals onto dry grass. It leaves the coward cold like a wet stone. When an enemy comes, build them a welcoming fire. It will dis-spirit their mission. Lightening flashes and fires summon the spirit of the dolphins. People feel more youthful by a fire. The smell of the fire reminds them of being a child. When we sit at the fire and pay respect with tobacco, what we say is heard by the ancients. What we see in the fire reflects and divines the course of our destiny. Fire in the form of lightening is a daughter of the sky. Fire is a woman. Grandfather sits in the fire. Together, the fire is both man and woman.

Air represents the mind, intellect, thoughts and ideas. Earth represents the material world and all physical realities. Water represents emotions, intuition, spiritual belief and trust. Fire represents the will, drive, destiny and Spirit in action.

Fire transforms. New wood is brought to the fire. Within a short period of time, the log ages with the heat and then turns into an old gray-hair, then to ashes. Then it becomes earth. Over time it is worn away with the wind and the flow of water. It becomes so small as to be lifted into the sky by the water returning to the clouds. Here it again becomes fire, sent back to earth in lightening.

When one has come into your home bringing unwanted energies, it is good to light a candle and put it between you and that person. The candle will burn quickly as it consumes the energy. When the energies are good, it burns slower.

There are many "releasing" and "passage" ceremonies that require the use of fire. The symbol of what is to be released is blessed, thanked and "put to the fire." Leaping over a fire is a symbol of a marriage bond. "Painting the rocks red" is the act of bringing the Stone People to the fire to be heated. Fire is central to ceremony. Fire is always used in rituals that remove hate,

The symbol of what is to be released is blessed, thanked and 'put to the fire.'

as anger and hate are the fire of emotions. Rituals of lovemaking and passion also come to the fire.

Fire is very big medicine. A Fire Woman is very big medicine. She knows about the passion of the heart. She is a fire that cannot be put out. She carries the dream.

For days we had all worked very hard to build a village at the base of Mt. Warning (Mt. Wolumbian or Cloud Catcher Mountain) in Australia. Alinta, our Aboriginal elder, had called us to the "Making of Fire Woman" ceremony. She was the messenger of Aunt Millie Boyd, lifetime Spirit keeper for Mt. Wolumbian, and a devout servant to Spirit. Alinta had prepared me for this ceremony. I wore a wrap-about skirt and a loose top. Alinta wore a leather headband to cover her temples. She would serve as "dog soldier" for the Stone People Ceremony to follow the initiation. A dog soldier stands in the circle with her back to the fire and watches for meddlesome spirits. I had gathered eucalyptus leaves and put them to the fire to purify the air. Our ceremony would occur between 2:00 and 4:00 a.m., during the sluggish hours when all sleep deeply. This is the time of the warrior. While others sleep, even the coyote, the warriors meet.

I was shown how to lift their energies to their hearts.

Alinta asked me to begin the ceremony in my own tradition. I opened the gates and made my beginning prayers. I then knelt on the earth and placed my strong eye to the ground. I stayed there long enough to thank the Mother and the below world for bringing me this far. Then I listened. Alinta then spoke to the spirits above and below, before she painted me with white paint. She painted my crown, throat, heart, navel, base of the spine, hands and feet. In this way, she explained, the spirits could see me as a servant to them. My human colors blended into the darkness and only my paint showed. To the spirit world, I stood as a servant of peace.

Alinta then backed me to the fire and called to the Woman of the Fire to travel into my spine that I would walk with fire and passion. Next I was required to put my hands into the fire and "feel it cold." Finally, I was taken apart to a secret place and shown how to repel men with sexual ambitions. I was shown how to lift their energies to their hearts. I then returned to the fire and commenced with my Sweating Ceremony. As a symbol of this initiation, I was given a long corded leather strap to wear in ceremony. It is to be crossed over my heart and my back. My "fire" is for use by Great Spirit. My partners on earth are our companions. I would serve none but Spirit forever.

The four days of being able to watch his own ceremonial death was satisfying to all in him that wanted to kill himself.

I love the fire. The ancient tradition of firewalking is a game with us. We dance across the coals. We have performed many ceremonies with the fire. When one walks across the fire and feels no heat, it is possible to understand that our bodies respond to what our minds tell us. When we walk looking at the stars and call the hot coals "popcorn," the coals feel like popcorn crunching beneath our feet. It is possible to walk the bed of coals unharmed by the coals, then to step on a tiny coal that ran from the main fire and be burned. This happens because we see the single coal as "hot:" something to avoid. Firewalking is a very powerful way to teach us that our bodies are, indeed, the reflection of our minds. Once we know this, we can take responsibility for the thoughts of our minds. This is the lesson of the fire. We are disciplined in our minds. It is the discipline of a lifetime. The fire teaches this lesson very quickly.

Another remarkable fire ceremony comes to mind: There once came a rich man to our ranch. His marriage was deteriorating. He was suicidal. We sought the direction of Spirit. We were led to "let him lay his body to the fire." When one puts his bones to the fire, he is given a new body. We helped him build a funeral pyre in the village. To this rack, we had him bring symbols of himself. He made a papier-mâché model of his body and put his own hat on the head of the mannequin. He also brought many other objects to represent his attachments. We made a ceremony of good-bye and had him urinate around his pyre to mark it as his territory. For three days we drummed and chanted at the site in order to mark the passing of his old spirit. On the fourth day we helped him put the pyre and the "body" into the fire. It was a powerful moment when we watched the pyre and the mannequin disappear. The four days of being able to watch his own ceremonial death was satisfying to all in him that wanted to kill himself. Within a very short period of time, he left his failing marriage, moved to the islands and began a totally new business with his friends. He now has a new life. This is the magic of the fire. She brings new life to the living.

In the fire, in the flames, our memories are captured and held, prisoners of love. Images of mind and soul are all we have and they are all that we will be. Memories warm us when times are hard. They comfort us when the wind blows cold and our provisions are meager. Memories sustain us when the coals burn low in our lives. Love is never beyond reach as long as a memory lives and a flame burns.

Let us fan the embers of our "fire." Come to us again, memories of a savage ecstasy of love. Let us remember the sweet fire of our all-consuming love. Come memories of love. Take us back to the beginning fire where we were all one.

We share this song of love. It tells of our walk back to the passion of our youth.

It reminds us of the "fire" of love that is ours to share with each other.

THE QUEST FOR FIRE

My quest for fire has ended in your arms.
Nobody else has all your grace and charm.
One sacred coal, one tiny little flame,
We kept alive through years of joy and pain.
Now with a force much stronger than the wind,
We've blown a fire back in our love again.

Chorus:
One flame, one spark, one small jump-start,
 one chance to love again.
My quest for fire would never tire, and now at last I win
The noble prize cuz' in your eyes I've earned a place of fame.
No compromise, no jealous ties, could put out our love's flame.

Our passion burned so age could not forget.
We knew desire that youth does not regret.
Yet something deeper called us to explore.
Come past this place. Let friendship give you more.
Now years have passed. There's been no other flame.
My dearest friend, my quest for fire's the same.

One glance, one smile. Two friends run wild through fields
 of yesterday.
Our laughter speaks far more than words can say.
Beyond romance we took the chance to stalk our heart's desire.
Now side-by-side and hand-in-hand, we quench our quest for fire.
One flame, one spark, one small jump-start, one chance to love
 again.
Our quest for fire would never tire, and now at last we win
The noble prize cuz' in our eyes we've earned a place of fame.
No compromise, no jealous ties could put out our love's flame.

One morning, while we were feeding our horses, an Airborne Express Truck pulled up to the corrals with a certified letter for me.

It is with joy that we sing with audiences everywhere a song of our childhood. "This little light of mine. I'm gonna' let it shine. Let it shine, let it shine, let it shine."

One final story of fire:

For many years I have traveled to speak to corporate groups with the focus being "Lighting the Fire Within: Respiriting Our Organizations." When the 2002 Olympic Committee selected the theme "Lighting the Fire Within," I was thrilled. Many years ago, at the University of Georgia, I had the good fortune to read a small book written by Lee Trevino entitled, "How To Succeed."

He simply suggested that we identify our life goals, write them down and put them on our mirror to view every day. I selected five goals. One of those goals was to run at the Olympics. The Olympic trials were to be held in Atlanta. I ran day and night in an attempt to condition myself. I wanted to run the 100-meter race and felt that I had a chance because, as a young woman, I simply could not be caught. Circumstances arose that caused me to miss the trials in Atlanta. Still running in the Olympics remained a life goal.

Thirty years passed and I would, from time to time, review my life goals. I was always aware that this one goal remained unfulfilled. However, I told no one. One morning while we were feeding our horses, an Airborne Express Truck pulled up to the corrals with a certified letter for me. Inside was an invitation to carry the 2002 Olympic Torch in the Olympic Torch Relay. Thirty years had passed since my first intent was set. We had no idea how or who recommended me for this task. We only knew that 250,000 people were recommended and only 11,000 selected.

I trained for months to carry that flame, a flame that was lighted in Greece, flown to Atlanta and then carried all around the USA before entering the Olympic stadium in Salt Lake. I carried the Olympic flame that proclaimed, as I had been proclaiming for years, "Light the Fire Within." It remains my most affirming story about fire.

WOMEN'S
HEALING CIRCLES

The circle is the shape of Mother Earth, Grandmother Moon, Grandfather Sun and every planet. It is the shape of a bird's nest, the stem of a plant, the trunk of a tree, the hunting patterns and territorial markings of animals. It is the growth pattern of rocks and flowers and little children. It is the most universally occurring shape. It is the shape of smoke rising to the Great Spirit. It is the shape of our eyes. It is the diameter of our bodies. Orbits of atoms and molecules are circular. Seeds are circular. Eggs are circular. The entrance to the womb space is circular, as are all openings to the body. The circle has no beginning and no end. It is the shape of the tipi lodges of our ancestors. Many claim that it is the most sturdy of all structures. The wheel is the most perfect shape for movement. The Great Provider is a Circle of white light. The circle is the universal sum of all symbols. The circle is the symbol of perfection. All healing ceremonies occur in a circle.

The circle of healing teaches us to think differently about things. In modern education we are taught to think in a linear way. Linear thinking uses only the intellect of the mind. In circular thinking, the mind is guided by the intuition. Rather than being the guard and guide, the mind becomes a parrot sitting on the shoulder of the true leader, intuition. From this vantage, the mind can exclaim with wonder and delight what is revealed through the eyes of the heart. A linear attitude is concerned with the end product only and not with the process. The circular mind views the process as what is important. The linear mind measures

Healing is a memory of wellness . . . of a sense of well-being. We all hold such a memory somewhere in our lives.

—Colonel Lyn

time in a straight line. Circular thinking steps into the flow. A linear attitude is constantly saying, "I want," "I expect," "I'm disappointed." It is burdened with illusions of false power that say, "If I do this, I can get that." The circular mind values "the moment," the "now." A circular attitude is one of non-attachment to the getting. It enjoys the "doing." The "deadline" has no power to dis-spirit the traveller. In circular thinking, there is no sense of "hurry." Circular thinking knows that things will happen when they are intended to happen. Linear thinking cannot understand medicine teachings. People who live in high expectations are tested the most. It is said by our elder, "Expect nothing and receive everything. Expect everything and receive nothing but the lesson of expectation."

In the healing circle, the drums beat until all hearts beat as one. That is to say, that the drums beat until linear thinking falls away and all minds enter into the spirit of the circle. People who are able to think in circles do not get upset over an overdue check or a threat of litigation. They live their lives as if tomorrow will never exist. They do the very best they can today. They live intensely and always in the moment. They are not greedy. House mortgages make us think that we will live forever. People of the circle live life with the passion of today. What others call life insurance (of which I have none!) should really be called death insurance. People who live in the circle are not afraid to die. They know that, in truth, they do not die, but walk from life to life. People can only die when no one ever thinks about them anymore. As long as they live as a memory, they live. When people said that God is dead, they only said that God was dead in their memory. A God no longer remembered is a dead God. To live in the circle is to constantly be alive. Everything is a ritual and a celebration.

Women's healing circles follow the moon and Grandmother Holy Spirit. The most powerful of all women's healing circles are those that focus on healing the Earth. The most powerful time for women to circle is at the precise moment of the dark of the moon. This occurs when the moon has waned to its lowest point, and for a moment in time, is empty. Then she begins to wax full again. Into this space we put our prayers. This is the time when the veil is the thinnest between middle earth and the upper and lower worlds. If we have lived close to the earth we are bleeding at this time and our own veil of vision is also the thinnest. At this time, we are both heard and spoken to.

Always at women's healing circles, it is important to post dog soldiers to divert meddlesome spirits. One who is sensitive to energies or who is a seer will serve as a good dog soldier. It is good to wear leather over the temples when one serves in this capacity. Sometimes our brothers will sit at the entrances of our gathering places and serve as our guardians. It is a comforting feeling to have our brothers near. It is a beautiful sound to hear them speak softly to each other and play their flutes to create a beautiful place for the sisters to circle.

Women, as a whole, are more in touch with their spiritual selves than most men. Women are beginning to recover their deep knowing about their wombs and their blood. This precious knowing was lost when male medicine teachers and sweat lodge leaders have come out among the people without their female counterparts. Women's healing circles must now instruct women about their true power so that this dishonoring can end. A woman on her moon is a guide to spirit world. Her input is extremely valuable. The moon time is the most receptive time of the whole two-legged's experience. The veil into Great Mystery becomes transparent. The feminine must come first in all things. The feminine holds the greatest power. Grandfather Great Spirit serves Grandmother Holy Spirit. She is His mate. He serves Her. Much energy is whirling about each woman at her most feminine time. Her energy can change the direction of a ceremony. She does not need to be set apart as unclean. Rather, she needs to be instructed in her powers and then use those powers for the good of the whole. When a woman begins her period, it is good to be touched by all the people, for now she is holier than others. It is important to honor our first blood and the vision of our women. This is a central teaching of women's healing circles.

The first teaching of a woman's healing circle is to love oneself. This is the first rule about being a human being. If we do not have a harmony within, we cannot help others. If we are not in love with ourselves first, we cannot love others. Our religions have taught us to love others above ourselves. That is all backward. We can only give what we have. We must do what makes us happy. We must choose a job that we like. It is only when we are living our dreams that we are fulfilled. Otherwise we are bombarded by negative energy. We hate and feel jealous. A ritual of initiation for a woman is a search for love within herself. Our ancestors have known always that the ultimate

Never call a disease by its name. What we call by name will come running to us.

—Cloud

Enter the water, there's a

healing for you.

—Grandmother Jerry

dream of humanity is androgyny: being male and female at the same time. It is good in women's healing circles for the women to dress and act as men. It is good to show off what is masculine about our natures. It is also good to embellish the deeply feminine with each other. We learn from each other. As women, we cannot learn how to express our maleness from men. We must learn how a woman expresses maleness from another woman who expresses maleness. It is different than "being like a man." It is a true expression of masculine energy as it flows through a feminine form. The same is true for men. They must learn how to express their feminine natures from men who do so. If they try to learn from women, they are only being "like women." They are not expressing their own feminine natures.

We can only find love by first loving ourselves; otherwise we create sickness. The highest rate of illness is among people who are bored by life or bored by their work. They want to be more than a handmaiden or a number in an office bullpen. By being sick, they think they find love. As long as harmony exists between the mind and the body, one lives in wellness. Harmony protects us. The balance chases away evil spirits. As soon as the harmony is broken, evil spirits penetrate the body and cause damage. The first rule of healing is to find out what broke the harmony. After the evil spirits have departed, the healing can take place. There are medicines that repair the damages. What doctors call psychosomatic illness, we call "evil spirits." In women's healing circles, we make a direct link with Spirit and Spirit does the healing. The healer directs Spirit contact. In modern medicine, diagnosis and analysis are important. Personal empowerment for the patient is secondary and Spirit is totally unacknowledged. For the traditional healer, Spirit is first acknowledged and personal empowerment is the healing. Understanding and diagnosis is peripheral.

People are not sick or depressed. They are dis-spirited. Their very spirits are unhappy and out of balance. A healer speaks with a spirit tongue. A healer does what works. The Spirit does the healing. The circle only keeps the person entertained long enough for nature to take its course. Dis-ease is disharmony, fear, anger and soul loss. Soul loss is the gravest of all conditions. It is the major cause of illness and death. Disease is inevitable if life loses meaning and one forgets the feeling of belonging and connectedness to a larger meaning: To a circle. The circle of healing brings one back to that sense of belonging and connectedness. The great connectedness is to be connected to the Great Spirit. A chronic sense of fear will cause a person to lose love, joy and trust, which are the basic foundations of health. Without these, the force of life begins to withdraw from the body.

In a healing circle, we strongly shape the imagination. We act out the stalking and capture of the evil spirit. We enact its release. Darkness is only light that has lost its way. We dramatize "sending it away to the light." What we can get one to imagine changes the shape of the body. No thought fails to leave a corporeal mark; no neurochemical signal occurs without being registered by the mind. A shift in the imagination is required to access the universal mind. Healing comes from sensing an inseparable moment with all things. As healers, it is the authentic presence of who we are that empowers others and ourselves. It is the discipline, the beauty, the balance, the harmony and the order of who we are that brings the possibility of healing to the circle. We cannot heal ourselves or assist in the healing with others when we are jealous, angry, or afraid.

The woman's healing circle is particularly powerful, as it draws its healing energy from the moon. As women, we celebrate our ability to magnetize and to draw by celebrating with the moon. It is our relationship with the moon that gives us our sense of mystery about who we are, our sense of wonder, our receptivity and softness and our incredible expansiveness to embrace the All-That-Is. We celebrate the sun in us by walking dynamically and giving our best consistently. We must be as dynamic as we are magnetic. We are the sun and the moon. By having these aspects in balance, we walk as a star. The 1940s and 1950s were sun times. The 60s and 70s were moon times. The 80s and 90s are star times.

All things have two sides. There is day and night, physical and spiritual, matter and energy, negative and positive, action and reaction, left and right, up and down, male and female, logical and intuitive, conscious and unconscious, life and death, seen and unseen. This is the balance. In healing circles, it is important to always respect this balance. When the candles are lighted to the four directions and the welcoming incantations made, meddlesome spirits will come. It is good to make a welcoming place for them. It is good to leave them food and drink. Alcohol is a good drink to give. It is attractive to the dark spirits. When people are drowning in alcohol, they have weak auras and these

Women know how to nurture, seven days a week, twenty-four hours a day, from conception to death. We hold the eggs of life in our bellies. All that comes to us, goes first to these eggs to sustain them. We are the creatoress.

—Cloud

Everybody has been taking things too seriously. When you do that you end up worried and depressed. Now I will tell you . . . you cannot smile and laugh and worry at the same time.

—Grandmother
Princess Moon
Feathers

shadow spirits have come into them and are using them for their own gluttony. The shadow spirits will eat, drink and go away forgetting their business if the alcohol is left at the gates or the welcoming place of darkness. If the alcohol goes into the bellies of people, the darkness must find a way into the body to drink and create mischief. Drop water and herbal teas on the ground for the spirits of the light. Pray that these spirits will enter the circle and bless the ceremony. Ask only those with the Christ heart (a heart for the "circle of all things") to come. Burn sweet smells. Incense is very attractive to the spirits. If we do not first invoke and then instruct the spirits, nothing will get done. Always honor the little people . . . the space beings that live in the sacred mountains. They do much good when they are respected.

The demons are very ugly. Some are so ugly that you want to vomit. They must be received as though they are beautiful. We must respect them for their ability to make us strong. They will either defeat us or they will call us to greatness. They are servants of the light. It is their job to harass us until we walk in the light. Then they will leave us alone. There are demons of sex, jealously, fear, gluttony, laziness, lust, greed, lies, mistrust, unrest and shame. They get into us when we are weak and vulnerable. Sometimes this happens when we are children. Sometimes it happens when someone dies. Very often, it happens when people are drunk, stoned or high.

All rituals have four ingredients: A sacred time; a sacred spot; a sacred intention; and sacred togs, tools, toys and food. Secret ceremonies occur in the wee hours of the early morning when all else sleeps. Empowering ceremonies occur at high noon when most others are "out to lunch." For new beginnings, ceremonies begin with the rising sun. For ceremonies of release, the sunset is good. Women's healing circles are held in "center" places where there is much protection around. Always, the sacred intention of women's healing is to bring the balance and to teach about love, beginning with self-love and extending to others. Love for the Great Mystery is implied in all aspects of women's circles. Before one can be healed, she must first be cleansed from negative feelings, thoughts and energy. Sometimes a healing can take as long as it takes for one to release feelings of hate and remorse. Sometimes, before a person can be healed, she must chop wood and carry water.

I have had the experience of having a very close sister-friend turn on me and sue me. The pain was unspeakable and the anger consuming. With my tears, I built a star lodge for children and three shelters for the ranch. With my anger, I built fences and mowed hundreds of acres of land with a push handmower. It took months and months to burn off anger and cry out the pain. Never during that time did I counter the lawsuit. When, at last, I came to my place of deep love and forgiveness, a settlement was made that gave me all of my properties, plus an additional $10,000. All of the negative energy was transmuted into positive power for building on the land and making the earth more beautiful. This is how we "own" what is ours. I bless this sister for providing me the opportunity to learn about transmutation and true ownership. When hardships come, the warrior builds. When money could not buy supplies, I picked up my hatchet and built with the natural materials of the earth. Healing first requires that we deal with the negative emotions. Then the damage can be repaired with good food, herbs, massage and good fun.

The serpent is important in healing. It is the symbol of all healing societies, including the American Medical Association. Our Eagle's Nest is called "a snake house" by those who understand medicine. The snake is associated with the sky and its phenomena of rain, rainbows, stars and lightening. It is the symbol of renewal that governs life as well as death. The snake is associated with the ability to move from one world to another. The snake is the gateway to our unconscious. She is interdependent on light. Her power induces healing dreams. She has the power of physical regeneration. She can see into the future. When she comes in dreams, she comes to heal. She is the symbol of the Kundalini, the fire at the base of the spine spiraling to the heavens. They say the Buddha and the Christ are protected by the cobra during this coming of enlightenment to the Mother. The snake calls us together. In this time, there is but one thing to do. Come together. In healing circles I say, "I am Cloud. Let this rattlesnake call you to a dance."

Women who sit in healing circles bring their spirit helpers with them. These spirit helpers are our allies. We can have many, many allies. They come to us in dreams and visions. They attract us to them and make us collect them. They have rules of conduct for us. They want us to communicate with them and they want us to listen to them. We must never eat their meat. We must not boast of them. When we come to them for help, we must remain

God made the earth round so that you can't look too far in front of you, nor too far back. It's a big adventure— your gift is to give. To share your gift in being here is to let others know who are also on the path, so they can be familiar with how it is to give. The grandmothers have given us so much. Take it in and use it, because you are on the path already. You are already on the path.

—Colonel Lyn

201

Every two years, the women of the Iroquois nation selected men to the Long House. No decisions were made in a hurry; they used the talk stick for days. They considered, "How will this effect seven generations?"

—Grandmother Kitty

celibate to show our fidelity. We must abstain from indulgences. We must honor them with songs and dance and ritual acts. When we honor our allies with dance and ritual acts, we make love with them. We are married to our spirit helpers. We must cultivate our relationship and nurture it. Our allies, our spirit helpers, have the medicine. They give it to us to use. We also have our own medicine. We can use it to help our allies on earth. They depend on us to sustain their future generations, just as we depend on them.

Sometimes we will bring a fetish of our allies with us to the healing circle. These small replicas of our spirit helpers are a source of power and a way to access ancient knowledge. It is good to feed our fetishes with smoke and song and drumming. The fetish has the power of the animal it represents, the artist who made it and the stone or wood from which it is made. It is three dimensional and organizes information like a hologram. It acts like a template or mental mold for shaping a thought. The way in which we shape our thoughts is the way in which we create our worlds. We can shape a thought to be a gloved hand cutting into a breast to remove poison or we can shape a thought to be a young lion cub sucking on a mother's breast. Whatever thought we shape is the way in which we will heal. Some people call a sucking healing "heathen" and "pagan," but no blood is shed. It is infinitely more "primitive" to cut into a woman's breast to remove tumors than it is to suck them out. The lion is a strong ally, because it knows well how to identify and mark territorial boundaries. If something is growing in a body where it does not belong, the lion can remove it. The lion can also teach about setting limits that are needed for survival.

If we want to discover something about a person, we make her something sacred. The process of allowing the gift to make itself through our hands will teach us what we need to know. If we want to heal someone, we make him a prayer stick. It will tell us about the dis-ease. For example, if we are making a prayer stick and a magpie feather comes to the object, we know that the person is tough and will survive. Big birds will not mess with the magpie. It is a good omen.

Smudging fans are used in healing circles. Wing fans lift the spirit. Tail fans carry one away to another realm. Eagle fans clean a person's aura, as does an owl fan. It takes away what is wrong with the body. The parrot or macaw fan moves things around. It changes things. A single fan is like a knife. It cuts out what is wrong. All ceremonial fans and doctoring fans hold beauty. Beauty is the result of healing.

Power objects in ceremony are special keys that unlock doors to knowledge locked in our universal mind. Feathers are the messengers to the gods. The birds that fly high see and hear everything. They possess magical powers to heal and bring magic to the circle. When we are told that we have been given all that we need from God, this includes the power of animal helpers. They are clear of malice and greed, unlike the doctors of our modern world. We have only to trust and listen. The feather of a bird is like a radio antenna to the Great Spirit. They know the secrets of disease, misfortune, death, birth and celebration. They say that "luck in hunting" can come from swifts, kites and hummingbirds. Mirrors, crystals and wands serve as transmitters, receivers and satellite networks for information from the spirit realm.

Always one must pay for healing. The healer must be paid and the Spirit must be paid. What is given to one is taken from another. Always a payment must be made. Payment can come in many different forms. When Grandfather Brave Scout did a doctoring on me, I gave him a truck. This is what he most needed. The truck cost $1,200. That was a lot to pay for five minutes of sucking and chanting and very little to pay for freedom from the dominance of frightening thoughts that were put in me to drive me mad. Those who heal need to have all their bills paid so they can concentrate on good medicine. This is the way it used to be. No person of medicine had to hunt or make clothes or prepare meals. Their needs were met so they could do their healing. It needs to be this way again for the healers in our circles.

Completion is an important part of healing circles. The pathway to completion is sometimes filled with hardships, payment and sacrifice. However, if we endure, the payment is to walk with the gods face-to-face. Whatever we promise to the gods, we must do. A promise is a promise. We obtain what we get from the gods through bargains and payments. We must pay for what we get. Some of the vows we take with the gods are our own. Some are inherited. My twin sister, Jan, knows this. When I was mis-diagnosed with terminal cancer and given two months to live, she came immediately to tell me that she would take up my Dream pact and carry it forward. If one is given a large dream to

I think Aunt Millie Boyd chose me to take over the Spiritual caretakership of Mt. Warning because I am so fair and remind her of her own star children. Many Native Americans have come to this place. I am honored to hold this sacred mountain for all of our people.

—Cloud

carry, it is important to share the load with many. If our family member dies with a dream unfulfilled, we must carry it to completion. Some are born into a family network of tasks and obligations to be completed or passed on to siblings and descendants. This is true for all of us who "wear the feather." Our ancestors have a dream that all peoples will live in one great Hoop. We are obligated to live our lives to help fulfill this obligation. Completion is the key to having a full life. It is important to bring completion to both the simple and complex things of life. The medicine wheel walk was created to teach this principle. We will share it in the next chapter. It is important to note that when one completes a cycle, it is good to make a disc or round object as a medal of completion. Make it to be very special. Then take it to a sacred place and leave it for the Great Spirit. The Great Provider will arrange for whoever needs to find it to "happen along the trail."

The particulars of women's healing circles will vary with every ceremony. We mention a few as examples. When a woman is low in her energy, it is good to have her lay down on the Mother Earth with her arms and legs spread. She should lay on her back with her heart to the sky. Her head is to the south. Crystals (clear quartz) are placed pointed towards her feet, hands and head. Another is placed on her womb. The crystals can be about five inches from touching. An hour in this position will restore her energy and bring her back into general good balance.

There is a ritual for beginning the process of releasing negative energy. It is followed with lots of hard, physical labor. It is necessary to spend anger and pain before the healing can begin. Make a circle of candles around the person. Encourage her to think all of her angry and painful thoughts as she lies in the center of the circle of light. Darkness never flows into light. Always, light flows into darkness. Circle the luminaries with a circle of women with rattles. Shake the rattles and sing welcoming songs. Welcome the energies to come out into the light where they can be seen. Thank the energies and direct them to the light. Tell stories about how anger and pain are transmuted into direct action that is good for the people. Tell stories of how to transform this energy. Allow the person to remain in a prone position at the center of the circle. Keep the candles going as long as is necessary for the energies to begin to clear. Rattles break up old forms. When the energies are lightened, drum. The drum can transport one to another place. Sing travelling songs. Direct the energies of light that need a boost. Never leave the darkness to depart without direction to some good use. What comes out of one person will go into another. It is good to direct it to a place of power. We worked with a young woman whose mother had been murdered. She had absorbed the violence into herself and was filled with hate. We sent this energy out to power neighborhood "watch" programs. Instruct the dark spirit to serve the light. It is seeking the light. Follow this circle with assignments of physical labor. "Chop wood and carry water." Continue chopping wood and carrying water until the person comes to a peaceful resolution of her own design. This resolution will be constructive and serve the good of the whole.

All forms of body work are very powerful when done in the support of the circle. We mention body-painting because the spirits can see the paint at night under the moonlight. A presentation of a person to the spirits, via body painting, can be a very powerful experience. Another powerful act is to "comb the hair of the Mother Earth" with the hair of the person seeking healing. Lay her on the earth and comb her hair out onto the earth. Then carefully arrange her hair in a crown around her face. It is very powerful to comb the hair of Mother Earth. Teas, nourishing foods that are alive and fresh, and baths go a long way towards healing.

When you have been healed, do many good deeds to show your gratitude. Take off your shoes on the Earth. Know you walk on Holy Ground. Crawl into sacred places and show respect. Ask permission to come and go. Leave offerings. A healed heart is a grateful heart. Give a gift of turquoise. It is the stone of the healed heart.

WOMEN AS WARRIORS

Come together, gentle warriors. Our decade is at hand. We promised at the front of time to blend Earth's family clan. Stormy sisters, firey mothers, our decade is at hand. We promised at the front of time to blend Earth's family clan! Sisters, circle in the garden. It is divined to be. You are the sacred fire of passion: Warriors of antiquity. Warrior woman, you're the butterfly, changing all, your wings enfold. Your fork is the source of Spirit Light and courage bold. The wheel of life is spinning. Every child is going their way. You're the Mother! Stand to Center! Make it safe for all to play. The change is here to take us to the Light above the sea, where our children and the dolphins dance in perfect harmony. This is the decade of promise. This is the great Blend Time. This is the time of the return of the Woman Warrior.

During my vision time, I saw legions of women warriors dressed in their native dress. We were so many as to reach into infinity. Some of us were bare chested and our medallions flew in the wind. We came unarmed, with rainbow light cascading off our bodies. Behind us we could hear the drums of our men. Our back door was covered. We came as warriors to end all war.

A warrior is not a war-monger. A warrior does not take orders from anyone outside of the Great Spirit. A warrior is so well trained in battle techniques and defense that no one dares to confront her. A warrior is trained in the highest experience of using personal will as the ultimate tool for harmony among the people. During World War II the samurai gave unquestioning obedience to their leaders. This type of devotion is given only to the Great

Provider. The true warrior has the probing self-direction of an individual who has become as strong as the Earth upon which she lives. Her awareness is astute enough that she can change a potentially unpleasant situation before it develops to the point of no return. The true warrior is a peace-monger.

Three thousand years ago, our societies were centered around the feminine. The woman warrior was held in very high regard. Geronimo often used women warriors in his journey to reclaim his homeland for the people. He favored the woman warrior. We have mostly avoided mentioning medicine teachers and elders. This is due to our respect for privacy and the knowing that all things come from the Great Spirit. Before discussing the spirit of the woman warrior, we will summarize the nature of woman–centered cultures and will draw on the genius work of our medicine sister, Paula Gunn Allen. She is our modern-day authority on the history of our people's devotion to the feminine and she has done a superb job of documenting the demise of matriarchal and matrifocal societies in North America in her book, *The Sacred Hoop*. (See reference in "Suggested Readings.") Woman–centered societies are very permissive. Great latitude and respect are given to sexuality and life-style preference. The men are nurturing, passive and fun. The women are self-defining, decisive and assertive. The women assure that food distribution is equal among peoples and there is no strict means of punitive control. Connection with the Divine is paramount. The welfare of the young and the old is put above all others. Powerful women are central to the social structure.

The status of mother is the highest of any in the world. To call someone that greatest honoring name is to call them "mother," even if they are male. Mother is the power of magic, the power of thought, the power of mind. Mother gives rise to all other things. To come to Frank Fools Crow, even in spirit, is to say, "How are things, mother of everyone?" Chief Frank Fools Crow called the Divine, "Mother." The offering of corn is made to the Mother. Motherness is the most revered and highly valued characteristic of any in the world. Mother is a title of extreme competence. Mother-centered cultures value peace, harmony, cooperation, co-creation, health and prosperity for all. Women warriors are mother warriors, even if they do not have their own children.

White colonization sought to make women voiceless and powerless. The whites called the woman-centered societies "petticoat governments" and they obliterated all women's councils

Women's business is what ONLY WOMEN CAN DO . . . not what they seek permission to do.

—Cloud

and the last remnants of the Beloved Woman, whose voice was considered the voice of Great Spirit speaking. The whites made the reward for killing a woman twice that of killing a man. They made the men beat the women in front of the children, to teach male dominance. They changed the names of the deities from the feminine to the masculine. They eradicated the women's rituals, medicine societies and clans. They burned the women's bundles. "When the women threw down their medicine bundles, the people perished." (Allen) It is time for the women to pick up their bundles and rebuild the circle.

Colonization terrorized our children and made the women submissive to male authority. It then made the men submissive to the priests. Under patriarchy, the men were rewarded only if they were punitive and authoritarian like the priests. Women-centered societies before them had always distributed power evenly among men, women and "jewels" (those of twin souls); also among the young and the old. The women were in charge of the economy, which equally distributed among all. We must return to the Sacred Circle. The return to the Circle is a shift from male domination to feminine equality. This is a shift from hopelessness to trust. It is a shift from pessimism to optimism. It is a shift from despair to possibility.

Peace is our only purpose now. Form follows content! The content of any thought is in one of two states: peace or conflict, greed or generosity, comfort or fear, gentleness or attack, love or hate. The content of what we think and say is entirely subject to our own wills. The form of our world will follow the content of our speech. No peace is ever made by planning and preparing for war. Now is the time for the return of the true women warriors. One focused, well-intended woman can part a crowd of angry men. We women must lead the way. Our men must get behind us and "cover our back doors." We women must awaken to the Dream of peace on earth and stand together, shoulder-to-shoulder.

There is a man in Canada who is very influential in the financing of war. He financed the Contra gun deal. We wanted to influence him towards peace. He was throwing a fiftieth birthday party at his mansion outside of Toronto. His home is surrounded with high walls and fences and is heavily policed. Marie, Skye and I dressed in our "warrior" suits. I wore my colorful breech cloth, vest, moccasins, head band, medicine bags, rainbow shawl and carried my Dream Shield. Skye did the same, except she carried

Women are not for war!

When our cause is love, the

effect is peace.

—Grandmother Kitty

"Thunder," the drum. Marie dressed as a chauffeur and escorted us to the location. The front gate was open for the party guests. We pulled in and parked. It was obvious that the front door was heavily guarded. We lined ourselves up, three abreast, and marched to the door with the confidence of the Queen's army. The guards were obviously confused, but broke into smiles and greeted us by saying, "The crowd is waiting for you in the basement ballroom to the left." They obviously viewed us as entertainment. We thanked them and whisked by and down the stairs. We quickly set up for a performance and, of course, people gathered. When the man appeared, we sang "Happy Birthday", with the crowd's full participation. He was convinced that we were a special birthday present from someone. We then told him the great story of the eagle and sang him the Eagle Song. In our presentation we called for the highest and the best and invoked God's blessing on his children in accordance with his ability to make decisions for the good of all people. He was so thrilled with our "eagle blessing" that he begged us to stay for the party. We graciously declined and left. We certainly did not want to answer questions about where we came from. Several months later, his involvement in the Contra gun scandal was discovered and his empire came apart.

When we place the Dream in the hands of others, they cannot turn from it. I wrote a song about Desert Storm called, "The Dream That Stopped the War." It calls for women around the world to band together and walk into the desert, shoulder–to–shoulder, as far as the eye can see.

There is a story told about a tribe of Indians who were under attack from warring tribes. Their people were war-torn and the grandmothers were weary of war. The grandmothers, who always hold sovereignty, ordered the warriors to drop their weapons and go to the back of the tribe. They put the old men in the rear, the younger women in front of them. They called the children to the front, just behind the old grandmothers. The grandmothers picked up the babies and held them high above their heads, as they marched as an unarmed tribe into the face of the enemy. The old grandmothers sang a song that means "These are your children. We are your grandmothers. These are your aunts and uncles, your sisters and your brothers. These are your grandfathers. We are one family. Let us live together in peace." The on-rushing warriors were stunned. They dropped their spears and loosened their bowstrings. They circled their steeds out and around the people and came back unarmed to sit down as one family. This song of the grandmothers stopped the war. We must again sing the songs of the grandmothers. There was a time when war was our survival. Now war is our demise. The grandmothers from the beginning of time call for our peace. Let it begin in the hearts of all women. We hold the true power.

The woman warrior is wise and enters often into the stillness. She has outgrown mentally striving, searching, confronting, talking, taking and warring. She knows that it is practical to trust the Great Provider. She knows it is glorious to be kind. She knows that it is safe to be happy. She is called to her own destiny and is not afraid to die. Until one can die with ease, she cannot live. To the eastern warrior, this is the Bushido mind. A warrior that is already dead, cannot be killed. Once a friend to her own death, a warrior woman thinks of nothing while playing, except adding to happiness through winning. She gives her all to the spirit of the game. She will not indulge herself in despair. She knows it is fruitless to wish back something that is already lost. She is generous, but never to a fault. She knows that greed comes from inside and it makes you always hungry. A warrior never forgets herself. Not for a moment. She respects herself. She has no need to save or rescue anyone. She knows the addiction of saving and being saved, and avoids the junction where weakness needs protection. Both are illusions.

The intention of a warrior is unwavering. Always, all things and events are seen as something significant or something to be avoided. She is ever aware of mirrors in life. She knows whenever she recognizes bad in another she has, herself, soured. A warrior cries only when her tears do not feed others' joy. She knows that if she gives way to crying, her life will always be sad. A warrior woman will hold your hand, but she will always think her own thought. She will not listen to something meaningless call her. A warrior will sustain her grief only long enough to know within her own heart that she cares. If her caring is deep, she will not grieve the flow of life.

A warrior woman is a dreamer and looks always to make the contents of her mind happy. Always she wishes for peace and will not suffer one unforgiving thought. She trusts the present and allows the future to unfold. She knows that no protection can come from worry. The best protection is to pay attention to the present. The warrior woman does not give in to worry. She is free to change

Within the sacred global womoncircle the seeker has energy and attention from her womanspirit guides, her full intuitive and her full potential. The planetary imperative is change or die. With the present planetary crisis, and the love and power available with the sacred global womoncircle, who would not grow and change? To change one's self is to change the universe.

To change the universe, one must change the self.

—Spider Redgold

her mind because she knows that when she changes her mind, everything changes. The warrior knows that the body is a loyal servant to the mind. She knows that if she can see light in any situation, there can be no true darkness. The warrior woman laughs softly at herself, because she knows that amusement without mockery is Divine. She knows that she deserves her own lightness and love.

The warrior woman does not blame. In this way she avoids serving the ego, whose passion is to blame. She knows that illness is an act of violence from the mind. She has learned the power of imagination and avoids seeing anyone as a victim of disease. The warrior, instead, offers up her gift of healing. The warrior woman renounces guilt as a useless feeling. She, instead, assumes responsibility for all things. She gives her anger to the sky, where there is room for it. She is willing to let it go and accept the mirror that is herself. The woman warrior is fearless. She knows that power lies in the release of fear; never in the attempt to provoke it. She understands that enemies are always old responses, not relationships. She knows that an enemy deprives us in the same way that we deprive ourselves. The warrior woman would rather be happy than be right.

The warrior woman turns everything over to First Mother. She does not attempt to defend her specialness at the Throne. She comes for guidance and is a servant of the Divine. She comes often to ceremony to integrate herself with the whole. She is not concerned with how SHE feels. She is concerned about the good of the whole. She knows that her own feelings will change when her sense of oneness is restored. She has learned to understand with her heart, not her head. She is in a constant state of readiness to do her work. She will not avoid her pain, but move to the very center of it and confront it head on. In this way, she watches her pain disappear. A warrior woman knows that the truth is the truth and everyone knows it. She knows that the truth is to be lived. It cannot be expressed in words. Like anger, she knows that she must go alone and spill her words to make room for the void that welcomes the solution to any problem.

The warrior woman can find her way in the woods or in the dark of city lights. She is an excellent tracker. She knows that everything important is held in a single moment. She knows that the end is in the beginning. She can predict any situation. She knows when a person has an over-abundance of anything for they

For Aboriginal peoples, women are the carriers of the way.

—Alinta

We are magnets for all that is in our lives. Look around. This is a reflection of you.

—Cloud

211

We women are constantly storing energy. We are like a generator. The male cannot store energy. They release it every few days. Women hold true power. Men are physically strong. Women can hold an immense amount of power and divine to use it at will.

—Cloud

will give it away, whether it be love, joy or fear. She can see when someone leaks their power, because they close over their navel, where power is held. She can see the dark spots in a person where they hold attachments.

A warrior's adversary is her friend. She grows when others oppose her. She trusts that her adversary is purposeful and refuses to lapse into an emotional prison, while maintaining a high tension of danger. She knows that when she chooses distrust, she invites distrust into her own council fire. As a warrior, surrender is impossible. Defeat is not a word. Always, we are coming and each situation is a learning. There are no mistakes. The warrior knows that fast blood clears away the past and she seeks many ways to speed her blood. She loves exercise. She knows that any monsters inside will attract monsters outside. She pays attention to what is attracted to her. What she creates in her inner life is what she creates in her outer life. She is gracious with her monsters and makes a welcoming place for them. A warrior woman knows that power will leave if one constantly takes and never gives back. She knows that what she ignores in herself will only grow bigger. Avoidance will dethrone a warrioress. What we forget to honor will live off of us.

A warrior woman likes to live on the very edge of life and death. She has died many deaths in one life. She knows the fires of transformation and can take her healing to others. She understands that she is born to heal. She understands suffering and comes to heal and share. As a warrior, she seeks always to stand center. If she is moved from her centering place, she sends her attention back to the center and seeks only to achieve this thing again. If she becomes scattered, she gathers all the pieces together as quickly as possible and makes a whole. If she has become burdened so that her journey is heavy, she lightens her load. She cleans and clears.

The age of seeding is over. This is the age of reaping what we have sown. At the beginning of Desert Storm came the call for the great division. Veils of ignorance will be torn away and each person will be called to take a stand with greed or sharing; peace or war. The old ones are back. They come in many white bodies with red hearts. Their primal consciousness knew no hate. They have brought back the old, gentle, wise, abundant paths of heart. Those who choose not to see will pass away. The women warriors are gathering. We fight from the heart. Our Mother Earth is our garden and we are here paving pathways of the heart.

THE MAKING
OF PERSONAL
MEDICINE

This topic is a book unto itself. Let this chapter be the beginning of that book. There is no symbol that represents the truth. The truth can not be spoken, carved, painted or otherwise put into the hands of humankind. The truth must be lived and breathed. No symbol is a god. All symbols are expressions of God; expressions that will forever fail to represent the fullness of the Great Mystery. All things have medicine. All things have the truth of God within their experience of being. But, no thing, no sound, can contain the Truth unto itself. To make and carry medicine bundles, objects and talismen is not to worship these objects. These are expressions of the joy of Creation. Our ancestors did not worship idols and graven images. There is but One God with many names. There is the presence of this Great Mystery in all things and to acknowledge this is always a way of worshipping the One God.

All things on earth and sky have a special medicine. They are born to it. Our journey as humans is to discover our specialness. That is a great part of our personal medicine. We have the sacred right of choice. How we use this sacred right is our path. What difference does it make if one person's truth walks her tall and another's bows her head and bends her knees? What is important is that none interfere with the course of another. We are each a part of the Great Mystery. We are each a special knowing in the place of All-Knowing. We must only come to know our own medicine and use it to the glory of the All-Mother, All-Father. In

When making a medicine object or altar, throw a cloth and pray, "Come to this place things that will make ME want to BE."

—Cloud

this way, we become wise. But, we will not stop at becoming wise in any one thing. We will continue listening to our spirit voice for it is all that is truly familiar. The old ones tell us to "Live in the Spirit." To do so is to understand that no thing is to ever stifle our spirit or deny us our own reasoning. No thing is to deny us our natural urges. As we evolve our personal medicine, we come to appreciate ourselves. We come to see that our own attention gives meaning and beauty to all things. Our own ears give the songs to the wind and the streams. We, ourselves, choose to soar on the wings of these songs. Our own eyes give beauty to the sun setting and the harvest moon rising. Our own choice turns us to be lifted up by these sights. In our appreciation, we become the Great Spirit. Our own heart is filled and so is the heart of the Great Spirit. Our own feelings give to the Great Spirit this experience of flesh. We are the heart and hands of God. We are the eyes and ears of God. God needs us to be fully God. How we fulfill this urge is how we manifest our own personal medicine. In all the world, we are unique. If we choose to deny ourselves our own spirit's urges, something is lost, for no other will manifest what our own medicine is. It is ours to do with as we please. We have only to look around us to see our own personal medicine. What is on the inside is always manifest on the outside.

Many years ago I did a ritual dance around a winter campfire. In the fire I had burned all books, magazines and newspapers that spoke of other than peace. The ritual took most of the library that we had accumulated over a lifetime. In the dance, I prayed that old thought forms and words be taken into the fire, consumed and transformed into new words and sounds. Several years later I heard the first song being given to me from the other side. It was spoken in the language of a chant. I sang it over and over. Today it is a personal power song. As I honored each song that came, more came. Today I am called a singer/songwriter. Producers in Nashville are seeking my songs to pitch to their singers. This music is a gift of my own personal medicine. Music is personal medicine and I have mine to sing. A song has a story to tell and it seeks a story-teller. I can feel a song lingering close by. I have only to make the space into which it can come.

In 1984 I couped a dream. I reached into the Mystery and couped a dream. We have spent every second of our lives seeding that dream, until now. I felt it was time to coup a new dream. Two months ago, Peanut stopped by our cabin and brought me a redtail hawk. She is a strong spirit helper. The Crow called me Redtail Hawk Flying On The Sunlit Wind. I put her wings alongside the picture of Big Brother, Jesus. It gave His spirit uplift power in these days of new beginnings. Her tail became a beautiful butterfly smudging fan. Her feet were spread open in the couping position and placed on our God Box in a north window. We prayed that the Old Ones would call to those feet the perfect coup stick. Her coming to me had told me that it now was time to coup the dream of my heart. She is a messenger bird. She carries my heart's dream to Control Room Central. She holds the medicine to gather what is needed to fulfill this dream. I hold this dream close to my heart. Telling it would weaken it. Today, the perfect forked staff came to me to coup this dream. It was right under my nose. It came when I put aside work for the rest that comes with the moon lodge dreaming. During this sacred time, I put Redtail Hawk's feet into the Dream Stalker staff. She has taken her place among my medicine. We have shared power. It is finished. Today I give thanks for a dream fulfilled.

It is my moon time. I am very sensitive to Spirit. When I moved to this cabin in the woods, my dear brother-friend, Bruce, gave me a staff to bring as protection and a walking companion. He had carved a deer hoof on one end and a rattlesnake up the shaft. The other end remained unfinished. It has sat on the porch as a reminder that a brother cares. However, it had not come into its power in this place. This morning I sat in the village to pray. I heard the voice of this companion call to me. It was time to own it with my attention. It called to be shortened. Into the other end, I carved a horse hoof. Its balance was immediately felt. It then spoke to me of an ancient form of martial arts known as Chinese wands. I began to perform these old rites. By sending my attention to these things, I am assured that the dream of my heart is very close by. By giving myself to Spirit, I am given the exact ways to make personal medicine. Ask, receive, obey, learn, express gratitude, serve and repeat the cycle.

Often times a personal medicine bag is the first personal medicine one makes. The process that we will share was handed down from Grandfather Brave Scout. There may be many, many ways. Perhaps as we share his gift of making medicine, others will emerge from experience. When Grand Dad brought me my first bag, he told me that he had prayed for four days. We have found that four days is good preparation time for calling

Each woman in the cirlce comes from her own past and is going to her own future, at her own pace and of her own free will. There is no step that is comon to every womon. Each womon can use and accept only what is appropriate for her current being.

—Spider Redgold

Seek first to have an intimate relationship with Great Spirit, the Starmaker.

—Cloud

What you ignore controls you.

—Cloud

medicine. He told me that my medicine bag was about paying attention. He told me that I could only learn from that on which I would spend attention. He told me to wear my medicine bag every day. He told me to always know where it was. He told me to take it off to bathe, swim, sleep and make love. I only lost it once. A friend scooped it up in some laundry. It took four days to find it. It nearly drove me crazy. It was all I could think about. Grand Dad told me I must learn to think about my dreams with the same passion that I sought for my lost medicine bag. I must look into every corner of things. I wore the medicine bag from Grand Dad for years before I made my own. The example of his medicine bag guided me and Spirit revealed the rest. This is how it is done.

First make a "calling place." Sometimes this is a prayer cloth; sometimes an altar; sometimes a special direction or a sacred place. Here a prayer of intention is made and an offering is given. It is good to focus attention here with a candle or sweet smudging. Attention is what attracts, so any way to hold your own attention to the task is helpful. To this place will come what is needed. What goes into the bag is unique. All are different. Ashes from ceremonial fires, grains for nourishment, seed for growth, small crystals for clarity, the sacred grasses for protection and sweetness, animal hairs for the animal spirits, dried flowers and earth and human hair, blood or nails. These are only a few of the possibilities. Always a mystery is added to allow for surprises. A piece of turtle shell brings strong heart. A piece of horse hoof brings power. Many surprises may come to the calling place. A round leather disc about 3-1/2 to 4 inches in diameter is used to wrap the contents. It can be beaded or painted. Before doing either, chew the leather to soften it and give it Skan. This is a way of putting oneself into the work. It is a way of "owning." If a leather strap is used, it is also chewed at the midpoint and ends where the tying will occur. After the leather disc is moist and soft, the contents are prayerfully put to the center. The leather is closed around the contents to give it its round shape. After the strap is tied around the medicine bag, the excess leather is trimmed off. This is darkened with black dye and polished. It is the "brain" of the bag. Rub it often. Put good smells here, or menstrual blood, or the sweet ejaculation of your own body's orgasm. The medicine bag is your own power. Hold it as such. It will teach you to own your own power. It is a great learning; a great teacher.

Rub it to awaken it and yourself as well. Others may want to make medicine bags for you. They will never be as powerful as your own.

Catherine is an amazing seamstress. She designs and makes some of the most stunning wardrobes on the planet. Her work is widely known. All that she and her family wear, she makes. She puts her love and prayers into every stitch. This is the making of personal medicine. I, too, make all my medicine togs, tools and toys. Our ancestors spent their attention on handcrafted items. Things that are handcrafted with love have lots of skan in them; lots of medicine. Things that are factory made have lots of factory skan. There is no love in them. Love is what directs skan. It is good to put our own energy into what we eat and use and wear. When people surround themselves with products that were largely made by "fearful people," they will absorb that fear. Fear separates us from Great Spirit.

Civilizations rise up and fall down because they have not yet addressed the issues of fear and denial. Americans say they are free. They look to the Declaration of Independence to prove it. Yet the American choice has reduced their inalienable right to file for an income tax extension on paying the taxes that are being used to kill them in wars, rather than to abolish such a barbaric form of tariff. Still, the poor feed the rich. Having a choice in where the next nuclear plant will be built is not the same as declaring that no such thing will be built. Americans declare that Japan lost World War II, but the Japanese own America, and they pay little to no taxes. All of history records that the Native Americans were heathen and savage. They say that they were defeated by the Americans. This is not true. Our ancestors won the real battle because they maintained personal medicine. We have always only fought for our right to grow our Spiritual bodies. We have never fought to determine who would subjugate the earth. Soon the truth of manifest destiny will be known, and it is those who have strong personal medicine who will align with Spirit. Before the written word, we lived in an age of pre-consciousness. We went to the rocks for our strength. We listened to the winds. Then came technology and we advanced to a different form of communication. It was a great leap we took into the age of technology. Now, at long last, we take the truly quantum leap in the age of Spirit. We will perform feats that will make the most amazing computers seem primitive. We come to

Walk in balance. Seek first to go inside. I'm my favorite opinion. Earth Shaker, Star Maker lives in me. There is no greater authority.

—Cloud

an age of the many returning to personal medicine; personal connection with Spirit. We send out a voice in four directions to awaken to Spirit. In all things, serve Spirit. This is personal medicine. Spirit will teach all that is required. Pay attention. What you buy with your attention is truly life, liberty and happiness.

THE MEDICINE WHEEL WALK

All things grow in a circle. The circle is a sacred spiral. The medicine wheel is an ancient and powerful symbol of the Universe. It is a teacher of truth. It shows the many different ways that all things are related and inter-related. It shows us how life is with our Mother Earth. It prophecies how things will be. The word of life and of our Provider is not written in dead scrolls and scriptures. It is written on the winds in four directions. God's truth is encoded in every seed that grows and within every river that flows. The laws of God are the laws of nature. Our daily guidance is not left to our feeble attempts to interpret words of men written many years ago. The prophecies of old are the prophecies of old. New prophecies are sung by our birds and rustle in the fingers of leaves singing in the wind. We are not alone.

We each stand center of our universe. In our journey on earth, we turn full cycle to gather the teachings and power of the winds in four directions. We each stand in our own unique place and we each perceive differently. When many sit around a fire circle, each perceives the fire from a slightly different space. Each looks into the mirror of the fire and sees a unique reflection. So it is to look deeply into the medicine wheel of life. When we speak of our perception, we speak to the center of the fire. Our intention and meanings are gathered in by the fire and sent spiraling into the Universe. What each of us says is perceived differently by each of the others. We gather to ourselves what is of value to us and let

Liberation is the right to walk, each our own Sacred Path.

—Grandmother Kitty

219

the rest go.

We are each born to a unique position on the great circle of life. From our beginning point, we journey with the sun. Sometimes we move fast, sometimes slow. We may complete the circle many times in one life. We may barely move from our beginning place. Always we choose. Always we are the center of the circle. Always we walk the circle.

Walking a great circle on the land, with the intention of completing our life's mission, is an active way to pray for guidance. With this in mind, I created another high-game, the Medicine Wheel Walk. We begin with "talk-story" around the fire circle. We speak into the sacred circle and we speak of the sacred circle. We notice that all points of the circle have an opposite point. We learn that all things have an opposite side. We see that the circle brings great balance. Some in the circle have been taught to be tough, brave, tenacious and hard. Others have been taught to be humble, gentle, loving and courteous. The medicine wheel teaches us that courage must be balanced by wisdom, toughness by gentleness and tenacity by flexibility. Balance in all things is the great lesson of the medicine wheel. Always we stand to the center of the wheel and turn to acknowledge all directions.

We are now moving from the fourth world of separation to the fifth world of unity. We pray for the people, for the earth. The Mother will heal Herself, for She is woman.

—Grandmother Kitty

THE EAST

The new day comes into the world from the east. The sun gets up every day in the east. The east represents the dawning of life . . . birth, rebirth, renewal. The east is the place of illumination, the direction from which light comes into the world. The great eagle flies in the east as a symbol of that which flies the highest and sees the farthermost. Out of illumination comes direction for guidance and leadership. The eagle's vision draws what is distant eight times closer. The eagle can see clearly up close. The eagle watches the movements of all creatures and knows the hiding place of even the smallest. The capacity to watch over and guard the well-being of others is an important gift . . . one that is often learned with great difficulty.

The east journey brings gifts of beautiful and clear speech. It also brings the ability to see clearly, through complex situations and over a long time. In the east, the leader learns to see things as they are connected to all other things. We learn to be self-reliant. We learn to have hope for the people. We learn to trust our own vision. We begin in the east and we learn these things when we return full-cycle back to the east. We cannot truly lead people until we have made the journey to the south, to the west and the north. In the south we learn sensitivity to other's feelings. We learn love that expects nothing in return. In the west we must learn our unique purpose and how to correctly use power. In the north we learn to serve and guide with wisdom. We return back to the east with spontaneity and joy; with the capacity to believe in the unseen; with hope and uncritical acceptance of others; with courage, truthfulness, beautiful speech, vulnerability and devotion to serving others; and the ability to see clearly and focus our attention on the task at hand. The east is a man place (yang energy). Its color is yellow.

Now is the time to know. Nothing and no one can hurt you, unless you let them.

—Alinta

THE SOUTH

The sun sits at its highest point in the south. The south is the place of summertime, of fullness, of youth, of physical strength and vigor. In the south, the plants and the grasses are green and full of life. Kites fly high and the laughter of children is heard. In the south we play and prepare for the fall and winter months. The south is a time of preparing for the future.

The little mouse sits in the south. She is near-sighted and must get very close to see things. Matters of the heart and intimacy are learned in the south. It is here we feel our feelings for each other and learn to express how we are feeling. The coyote runs in the south and plays tricks on us. We learn to tease and be teased. The south is the place of the heart, of generosity, of sensitivity to the feelings of others, of loyalty, of noble passions and of love . . . the love of one person for another.

In the south, we are tested in our physical bodies. We learn to discipline our bodies as we would train and discipline a horse. We teach our bodies to respond to our commands rather than direct our journey. We train our sight, and our hearing, and our taste, and our touch to serve as a total person. We learn to move gracefully. We learn to sing and play music. We learn that we are artists and we learn the powers of discrimination. The lynx and the cougar can be used to symbolize the physical excellence and sensory acuity learned in the south.

In the south we learn the kind of idealism that makes all great things possible. We train our feelings. On the one hand we learn love, generosity, compassion and kindness. On the other, we learn to be angry at injustice and repulsed by violence. We learn to release our feelings of hurt that can prevent us from clear thinking. The color of the south is red.

THE WEST

The sun goes down in the west. The daylight turns to darkness. The walls of our vision close in around us. We are quieted. We relax from our day's work and review our accomplishments. The west symbolizes the sunset time of our lives. It is the direction of the unknown, of going within, of dreaming, of meditating and of praying. The west place is a woman place, a mystery. All of life comes from darkness, like the place of the woman's womb. The west is the place of testing, where our will is stretched to its outer limits so that the gift of perseverance may be won. We become like women persevering the last days before giving birth.

The nearer one draws to a goal, the more difficult the journey becomes. In the west we learn to stick to a challenge even though it is very difficult, painful and long. Thunder and lightening often come from the west, so the west is also the place of power. The thunder beings are the bringers of power. In the west we gather our power to heal; our power to protect and defend and to nurture; and our power to see and to know. It is in the west that we turn to the laws of God and learn to handle power in perfect harmony.

In the west we learn strength. We are like the bear who goes inside to hibernate. From the depths of our being, we become

Go inside and seek your own counsel. Connect with Spirit.

—Cloud

strong. In darkness we learn to balance the passion of loyalty with deep spiritual insight. Our insight is learned by shutting out the noise of the outside world and going alone to look and listen. Another guide on our inner journey is the turtle who not only goes inside for protection, but also possesses a heart that will continue beating days after the rest of her body has died. She teaches us perseverance. By going directly to the center of our experience, we connect with our Creator. We learn to accept ourselves as we really are. We see ourselves as fully spirit and fully physical. We know ourselves to be created in the same image as God. We are humbled in this recognition and vow to always stay connected to Spirit.

In the west we learn sacrifice. We learn that the mystery of sacrifice is that there is no sacrifice. We learn that for each gift of life, there is a price. We learn that when we give, we are given unto. In the west we can see ourselves new and filled with hope as we are born in the east. We can turn south and see our hope mature with youthful passion. We can see that we are being prepared for a great mission and in this seeing, we are humbled. In the west, we gather the capacity to see clearly with our inner eye. We see what we can become. We see what the people can become together. We are sent forth from the west with a purpose. We spring from the belly of the west filled with spiritual vision. The color of the west is black.

THE NORTH

The north is the place of winter. We see the snow fly and cover the trees and the earth. Many winters in our lives bring white hair to crown our own sacred tree. We are reminded of our elders and our ancestors that have gone on before us. We are reminded of our grandparents' labor in our behalf. We are reminded of the sacred relationship that exists between the grandparent and the grandchild. The north is the place of the grandmothers and the grandfathers. The white buffalo lives in the north.

We remember that the buffalo once represented abundance for

In my nursing career, I saw many people hanging onto parents, children and relatives . . . putting everyone in debt . . . and, out of guilt, hanging on and not allowing that one to go with dignity to its maker and band members.

We begin at one place on the Medicine Wheel and return to that place from which we came, after we walked the Medicine Wheel. Our challenge is to get out of self . . . stop being so self-centered.

—Grandmother Kitty

*A*lign to spirit with intent.

Be true to Self.

Trust yourself.

—Mahisha

our people. From the hides of buffalo came robes and clothes for our backs. Our tipi lodges were covered with the buffalo hides. Our meat and our stews came from the buffalo, as did our tools and shields. Even the dung of the buffalo provided fuel for our fires. The grandmothers and the grandfathers of the north wish only for abundance for our children and grandchildren out seven generations.

The leaves in the north have fallen from the trees and the limbs stand naked, basic and covered with crystal icicles. The north is the dawning place of our true, crystal-clear wisdom, a wisdom that is simple, basic and direct. It is in the north that we learn to think, to synthesize, to speculate, to predict, to discriminate, to solve problems, to imagine, to analyze, to understand, to calculate, to organize, to remember and to interpret hidden meanings.

Among the teachers of the north are the great mountains. We learn that the higher we climb, the steeper and more difficult the way becomes. Yet, in the north, we learn that the higher we go, the better we can see, and the stronger we become.

The north is also the place of completion and fulfillment. Here the power of our will reaches its peak as we learn to complete what began in the east as a far-away vision. The capacity to finish is a measure of greatness. It is of tremendous importance to our well-being. While we were in the west, we learned the power of perseverance. But even perseverance can falter until at last the end comes into view, and we are inspired by the sure knowledge that our victory is close at hand.

Access to the knowledge that the time of completion is, indeed, at hand is gained by giving our very best to the task and then letting it go. We must learn in the north to detach ourselves from the final outcome and make a space for the Great Spirit to embellish our efforts with surprises from above. Detachment allows us to stand high on the sacred mountain and see the past, the present and the future as one. We can see the course of our efforts and the trail of destiny. At this point we can free ourselves from all the emotions of the journey — hate, pain, jealousy, desire, anger and fear. In the north we reach the point of being able to let go of all things, even those we love the very most. Once we are able to joyfully bring our gift to the throne of God and leave it there, we are able to step outside of it and see it from a different angle. It is important to be able to stand apart from the things we

have believed to be true, or from our fears, our jealousy, our hate…
or even our love for others. Things that we cling to can prevent
us from thinking clearly. They can control us. We must come in
the north to see that we are far more than our bodies and our
thoughts and our insights. We are a vast being that is capable of
all these things and more. We know and we feel and we can
watch our knowing and our feeling from a place of detachment
and thus choose to act for the good of all things. The beginning of
detachment is learned in the fires of love. The end of detachment
is learned in quiet moments, in sacred places, and it cannot be
told.

The final lesson of the north is the lesson of balance. The
wisdom of the north teaches us how all things fit together, are
related and inter-related. When we understand balance, we
understand justice and a sense of justice is the greatest gift of all.
When we understand justice, we can see things as they really are.
Without a sense of justice and balance, there can be no peace or
security in the affairs of life.

In the north we finish what we began. We free ourselves from
fear. We learn to make predictions based on full vision. We see
how all things fit together. Our intuition is made conscious and
we trust it. In the north we learn moderation. We learn to stand
to the center of things. In the north we become the elders of our
own journey. White is the color of the north.

This ends the description of the four directions. (My
understanding of the four directions was aided by a simple book
called *The Sacred Tree*.)

Whatever you truly need, you earn. So "need" never really exists.

—Cloud

We have learned to renew our strength through ritual and
ceremony and games. From time to time we are called to walk the
great circle of our ranch. Each time we are called to a different
place in each of the four corners. My last medicine wheel walk
proved to be the most meaningful. I had returned to the land after
two hard years in Los Angeles. The voice of my vision had taken
me to heads of networks, television and motion picture stars and
political leaders. I was exhausted. I returned to the land to renew
myself and await further instructions. Those instructions came
through my most glorious medicine wheel walk.

A group of professional women were at the ranch for a three-day Excellence Camp. We had played on the ropes, swam at Chocolate Pond, gathered in the Sweat Lodge and made kiva masks for our silent meditations at the fire circle. Someone suggested that I lead a medicine wheel walk. I decided to join the journey.

I headed east with hope in my heart. My desire for a new beginning almost sent me running toward the sun. As I passed a large patch of Oklahoma sage, I heard a voice say, "Did you know that stars implode into themselves and become very solid before they explode into the galaxies?" I stopped still in my tracks. I knew the voice called me "Star." "A star implodes into itself, before it expands and explodes into the galaxies." I pondered the truth. Intuitively, I knew the meaning. I would stay still on the land. I would go deep into the mystery of myself. I would grow solid. Someday I would expand into the universe. Quietly, I gathered sage to remind me of the message.

I turned south, eager to grow my hope in the place of youthfulness. My body had felt tired from the hassles of Hollywood. When the voice of my vision first sent me westward to Tinsel-Town, I had thought that some rich and famous people would jump on my bandwagon and help support a world celebration. At the very least, they would help me issue the invitation to "come home." Such was not the case. I had invested all that I had and still there seemed to be no way to launch my invitation to world celebration. I headed south to Turtle Pond. I had named this pond "Turtle Pond" because I had always seen a few turtles there, basking in the sun. This time there were forty or more. I was stunned and alert. As I rounded the bend and entered through the cottonwood portal to the northwest curve of the pond, I was again stunned. There in front of me was a forest of young, straight, supple willow trees, the kind that are perfect for pulling into racks for shields. Always before I had hiked a mile or more to a low, moist area to find this kind of willow. There, before my very eyes, was a forest of perfect willow . . . on our own ranch. The wind blew, and it sounded as if the willows were applauding. My familiar voice said, "You have everything you need— and more— right here." I had travelled the globe only to return home and find all that I needed. Though I did not know the details of the omen, I knew to relax and snuggle into being home. I would not need to knock on doors any longer. I gathered willow in my hand and continued on.

I circled west with the usual mixed emotions. I knew that the west would bring rest and strength. I also knew that the west went deep and pushed limits. I was led to a field of lambs-quarters. Lambs-quarters are considered to be a weed by most. It grows out of dung and is quite prolific. However, there is hardly a healthier or more delicious green on the planet. If I want to give a guest my very best dish, I fix lambs-quarters greens. I stood in the west, practically hidden from view in a field of lambs-quarters. Again the voice so familiar to me spoke. "Cloud . . . Only the finest for you, your family and friends." "Only the finest!" The message went deep. A victory had been won. The tides had turned. The rewards of hard work were rolling in. I gave thanks, pulled some raw leaves to eat and gathered a few more for my journey.

The village lay to the north. I could see the sweat lodges, the council fire, the temple shrine and the ceremonial sky lodge. The shield of protection stood highest and faced full into the wind. I ran full-gaited to the north. Many times I had stood on the eagle rocks bordering the village. Never had I walked below them through the thick field of Oklahoma wild flowers. Today the north called me to walk among the simple flowers. Barefooted, I picked my way through the knee high grasses, peppered with lush colors of orange, violet, yellow and white. The little flowers seemed tall and straight and proud. I bent to touch them and kiss their little faces. They seemed to speak to me in unison: "Let your wildness flower!" Let my wildness flower! Yippee! I was thrilled and whooped to express it. So much of my life I have contained my energy. I was now being told by the wisdom of the north to "let my wildness flower." I gathered some of the wild flowers and ran, gliding across the fields to the place of my beginnings.

With my hands held high to the sky, I sang praises in my language and repeated my learnings: 1. A star implodes into itself before it explodes into the Universe. 2. You have all that you need and more. 3. Only the finest for you, your friends and family. 4. Let your wildness flower. The omen was clear. I was being told to prepare myself. The gift of my destiny is at hand.

I returned to our home, "The Eagle's Nest," to put the gatherings of my journey into a small deerskin pouch. That day I made my first medicine bag with a bell on it. I wear it every day, knowing its promise and the promise of my Provider.

STORYTELLING

August 17, 1989, marked a turning point in our planet's history. Up until that point, we had been given the luxury of "preparing ourselves" for this age of "manifest destiny." We "groupied and seminared" ourselves into oblivion during the 60s, 70s and 80s. It was vogue to be into "finding ourselves." That time is ended. Ready or not, here comes our destiny and we are in total charge! Awake or sleeping, THIS IS IT! Take a stand. Roll up your sleeves and go to work, even if you feel that you are not ready. The flood of the Dawning is here. Mop! The Harmonic Convergence era marked the return of energies that influence our choices. One of those energies is the eagle. The eagle nation is here in full force. Our ancestors are back, teaching. The dove came and carried the hope for peace. Now the eagle has returned to "make the peace." This is what we know of the eagle.

The eagle is the symbol of excellence in the United States of America. She is the symbol of our country's pride. She is the symbol of our courage. She is the symbol of all that is good and right and just. She is as American as apple pie. The eagle is our symbol of strength. When we aspire to "walk our talk" as an eagle nation on earth, we will have manifested our destiny according to Divine plans. The eagle is a bird of prey. Eagles do not eat rotting things. They catch their food live. This presents a daily challenge to the eagle to walk in balance with the environment. The eagle is accustomed to challenge.

The eagle lives in high places and builds of very strong materials. The eagle is a wonderful carpenter. Some of their nests have been known to weight twenty tons. Their nests sit on lofty ledges and must be built to endure the fiercest winds. They must endure the hottest sun and the coldest snows. The eagle is a great builder.

The eagle is perpetually young. When their feathers get tattered and worn, they go off alone and throw off the old feathers so they can grow new ones. Until the day they die, eagles perform this act. They will not live with feathers for flight that do not work. They are perpetually throwing off the old and gathering in the new. To understand the magnitude of this act, consider how difficult it is to pluck a chicken's feathers and then realize that an eagle's wings span up to eight feet!

The eagle is androgynous. Both the male and the female look and act alike. Sometimes the female is larger, but most often one would have to observe the female in the nest with the newly born eaglets to ascertain which is the male. He will make the first hunt after the eaglets are born. When there are no eaglets in the nest, both the male and female hunt and build together. There is no difference in their tasks. They build their nests together and they hunt together.

The eagle is monogamous. Once eagles bond, they stay bonded for life. Should one of the mates die, the other remains alone.

Eagles are great hunters. Eagles hunt in pairs. One eagle flies high, scanning the earth with telescopic vision. The other eagle flies low to the ground, screaming in a high-pitched voice. This scares the rabbits and mice into flight. The high-flying eagle dives to make the catch and they fly off together to feast.

Eagles are great visionaries. Among the Native people, the eagle is the most sacred. They fly the highest and see the farthest. Their vision allows them to amplify an object eight times larger and closer. They can also see very well at close range. Their feathers are used to pray to the Great Spirit, in that they can fly closer to the Most High than any other.

Eagles are great parents and teachers. When the little eaglets come to the nest, the mother and father eagle pluck the down from their own coats and pad the nest for the young. When it is time for the young to leave the nest and learn to fly, the parents lift the down from the nest and drop it over the side. The nest is not quite

I was raised in a white man's world. I lived a lie. My Indian father abused me. When I faced the truth, healing could happen.

—Grandmother Kitty

An Ojibway Tale

In the beginning there was no pain, suffering or death. In this village there was a vine growing from earth to heaven and spirits travelled up and down to council. A friendship between spirit and man caused jealousy, so the man asked to go to heaven.

Spirit carried man up and his grandmother chased after him and the vine fell and sickness struck the people.

The vine is trust in Spirit and believing in Spirit . . . Spirit will care for you.

—Kactus

so comfortable then and the baby eaglets get very antsy. The parents then sit on the side of the nest and "cluck" like a chicken. This is the only time the parents make this sound. It is a "challenge" to the little eaglets. It says to them, "I double-dog dare you to run up on my wings." The parents sit with their wings out-stretched and the young run onto their wings, where they bury their little talons and prepare for flight. Once the eaglets are settled into the wings of the parents, the parent birds fly the winds and practice taking off and landing. When the little eaglets relax into the ride, the parents simply "pop" them off their wings and the little eaglets fly. It is all they know. It is all they have been wired to do! Eagles always get A+ in flight school. Eagles live too high to make mistakes. An eagle either flies or dies— and eagles fly. You won't find a baby eagle at the bottom of a canyon because it failed to fly. Their bodies are only programmed for excellence in flight. Their parents make certain of that. While the eaglets are young and learning to fly far, the parents continue to swoop down under them and lift them back onto the winds. They continue to do this until their little muscles are strong enough for them to fly the winds alone.

Eagles are private in their mating act. They mate far out of sight of the naked eye. It is impossible to know just how high an eagle can fly. When the mating dance begins, they are higher than average flight. Suddenly the male flies straight up above the female, sometimes 3,000 feet higher. He then folds his wings and lowers his head. In this straight diving position, the male eagle soars straight toward the female, who is circling below. Just at the moment of expected impact, the male pops his great wings and the female flips over. Together they grab talons, lay their heads side-by-side, enfold their wings together and they mate, spiraling and free-falling thousands and thousands of feet. Just before they hit the ground, they release their embrace and fly away together to play again on the winds. May we all fly like the eagles!

I am a story-teller. The stories I tell are about life as I know it. I watch nature and learn its story. I track people and tell their stories. I track my own life and tell my own story. We are each a story in the making. Grandmother Caroline Avant is gifted with a wonderful imagination. Her stories enthrall her grandchildren and hold adults spellbound, for we know that when she tells a story, the Great Spirit is speaking through her and there is a lesson to be learned.

GRANDMOTHER JO JO

This chapter would not be complete without mention of the very finest story-teller I know. She is not a great story-teller because she weaves a tale more eloquently than others, although she rivals anyone. She is a great story-teller for our Rainbow Tribe because she has an unwavering belief in peace on earth. She is great because she has no ego. She is a living saint. Her name is Grandmother Jo Jo. She is Jewish. She is one of our truly great ancestors returned with white skin and a red heart. She knows more about the truly spiritual Red Road than most today. Finally, Jo Jo is a grand story-teller because she insists on peaceful resolutions to all stories and, she involves the listener as an active participant in her stories. Grandmother Jo Jo is a Ph.D. clinical psychologist. Day in and day out she listens to stories from her clients. In her "free" time, she runs the H.O.M.E. Foundation, which hosts retreats for children and elders, together. She also runs the Good Medicine School, where she teaches about the Good Red Road. Finally, Grandmother Jo Jo is the creator of the Paradise Gardens in Miami, where she is planting a forest of trees in the shape of the Medicine Wheel.

As fate would have it, I have just received a letter from Jo Jo. We had considered publishing one of her stories here, but knew it would lose too much in the translation. What makes her stories so great is the play-acting among the participants that give the stories life. Grandmother Jo Jo is very much like a modern "bag woman." Everywhere she goes, she carries prop bags of costumes and cue cards, just in case she runs into a handful of people along the road. Before you know what has hit you, you will find yourself wearing some ridiculous outfit and acting out whatever story happens to be on Grandmother's mind. She is so very pure and innocent in her presentation that all are convinced that whatever happens in the drama is bound "to be a direct message from The Great Spirit." In a very humble effort to capture her magic, we decided to simply bring a segment of her letter we received today. Each letter is equally as rich and endearing. We are pleased for you to meet our Grandmother Jo Jo, Story-teller consummate!

Spin a big energy around those who gather and then lift yourself high and hold the space for that energy.

—Cloud

I was the most insecure person you'd ever known, because the American government made me a stranger in my own land, and I hated them. I make no apology to God for that.

All I want now is a loving family. I want to be with the Indians again.

—Grandmother
Princess Moon
Feathers

[Excerpts from a letter, dated April 11, 1992, to

Cloud from Grandmother Jo Jo]

"In my everyday life, I am doing what I do the best— listening to people. I have two jobs now—seeing people, and hour after hour they come. I get the sense that I've done all of this before. Sometimes it comes over me that I've been seated in a huge armchair (as Abraham Lincoln—coming from a lowly background, impoverished up-bringing—saved and uplifted by books and the writing to and from such meaningful friends). I've done this before. The people come and become connected. I listen intently to their words, see them as struggling characters in their own drama, and offer suggestions, "games" they can try out to see if greater happiness and joy can lighten their days. I know when I've been helpful; when the little children reach up and hug me as they leave, or when the elderly people slightly bow their heads in leave-taking, as a gesture of great respect. When I'm able to get some eyes to sparkle and twinkle, where before they had been dull and down, I'm doing what I've been commissioned to do. Help bring hope. Help others be happier (both myself and others).

To replenish, I go to Paradise. (This is Grandmother's name for the forest she is planting.) We all come from the Garden, and to the Garden we shall return, like drops of rain flowing to the ocean.

And now for my story this time around. [Every letter from Grandmother has a story.] You see, Cloud, we Rainbow Warriors have walked our talk. It is our Heart Path. It is the way of the Spirit healers. And, so it came to be that I was inspired, lifted out of the darker times of my day, and, with pen in hand, rewrote the story of Dorothy in the Wizard of Oz. I rewrote it as a skit celebrating life for the children. Here are some fascinating glimpses, for all the characters in this story came together and formed a Council of Children. [This was our Grandmother Moon Feathers' last wish.] Let me share what happened. I did this improvisation with mentally disabled adults. Forever children they are! These are just some glimpses in a time of great laughter and merriment and high-flying. There was Dorothy, all lost and alone in a strange world, searching to return home. There was To-To, her devoted and loyal dog, reminding her that home was where the heart was and joy was in loving. There was Scarecrow, teased and tormented by others who do not care; who finds the way to be happy along the Pathway of Wisdom. There was Tin-Man who had become rigid and rusty by the tears of his own loneliness; who seeks a heart down the Pathway of Love and finds friendship through compassion (and giving out the jelly beans of forgiveness)! There was the Cowardly Lion, played by this angry, snarling man. He wanted to wear the "lion's tail" in the front and I gently taught him that the proper place was in the rear. It was delightful to watch him join in the play, be accepted by the others and change over to be truly courageous and protective of others. It came on the Pathway of Respect and Courage. (We planted our "respect tree" and our "courage tree" right next to each other in Paradise Garden.)

Well, at the end, the players gathered in the circle, creating a Council. (Together with the rabbit, grasshopper, turtle, butterfly, frog . . . who kept mumbling, "One day, one night." . . . crow and dragonfly.) A circle of twelve gathered. [A note about Jo Jo's play/stories . . . She always writes a part for everyone . . . even if it means amending the Bible!] The crow had to say, "Patience," and this was hard to do for the Spanish-speaking Maria who played that part. Yet, she practiced it and will now say it over and over in her everyday life. There were many words, thoughts, deeds of wisdom in our Council of Children. Cloud, they insisted that I be the grasshopper. Picture me wearing a white Davy Crockett hat and Groucho nose and mustache as the grasshopper. [Another note about Jo Jo's plays. The costumes don't always exactly match the part. She makes do with whatever she has in her prop bag!] My costume demonstrated that "everything is not as it seems" and that "life is an illusion." Life is definitely what you make of it! And so, the brown hat with antlers became the turtle. Absurd! It was so silly and so profound in our merriment! The Tin-Man became "Happy Heart Man" and he readily,

Give when you are asked. Unless I am asked, I say nothing.

—Grandmother Kitty

really did. I gave "Grandpa Jack" that part and it really fit. I had this tiny, empty peanut can and it took on a heart-beat (drum sound) all its own. Magic does happen! Scarecrow became "Happy Crow" and Lion became "Brave Lion" and everyone chanted, "You can do it! You can do it! YOU can do it! You can do IT!" And I thought of your very same words to me on the zip line at the Ranch. Yes! I can do it! Thanks for reaching for me, uplifting and bringing out the best in my story-telling skills. That is what you do best. Bring out the best in others! Through song and love, I changed the words in our final song to go like this:

We're a Council made of Children
Rainbow Warrior seeking Peace.
There's no problem that can stop us,
For Rainbow love is much too strong!
Oh, yes. The Great Wizard of Oz was played by The
Great Spirit . . . all around us . . . everywhere. It was
my final "message" in the play.

Most certainly, if one would want to become a story-teller, it would be good to spend time with Grandmother Jo Jo. She is all-loving. She is truly humble. She is a Master's master in the art. She gives lots of room for each person to become exactly who they are.

ENTERTAINMENT IS HIGH MEDICINE

A "born-again" full-blood Indian and his firey, red-haired Pentecostal wife came to inspect my display of medicine togs, tools and toys at an arts festival in Oklahoma. They stood with their arms crossed over their chests, shaking their heads in disgust. They were muttering under their breath. When I approached them, they looked me in the eye and said, "This is new age satanism." I was stunned. How could something so old as tomahawks, medicine bags, shields, children's dream catchers and hand-woven cloth be "new age?" I was deeply saddened to see a young full-blood so influenced by someone as to have put aside his own natural connection to Spirit. The things people are calling "New Age" are really just manifestations of a very old age coming alive again. In the old age religious belief systems have asserted that there are authorities outside of ourselves who know more about our reason that we do. The so-called New Age, with its gurus and channelled entities, is no different than the old age of priests, male dominance and preacher sovereignty. The old world is dying. It must come to an end. We must allow it to die as gracefully as possible, while ushering in the Light that is Divined to make our world a paradise for Spirit. We are Spirit's finest dance. We are here solely to provide total, awe-inspiring entertainment for Spirit. We are the servants of Spirit. We came here commissioned to assist in the passing away of the old and to herald the new. We are stars from the Stars, here to awaken all the other stars. Let us remember who we are. We must act like the stars that we are. We are on stage and the curtain is drawn. This is not a dress rehearsal!

It is not politics, religion or education that will lead the way. These are tired, old fear-riddled systems. Entertainment has the microphone. Unlike other social leaders, entertainers have the license to say and do pretty much as they please. They have license to be themselves, to dress as they please and everyone is interested in their opinion. This is a call to entertainers to realize the power held in their microphones and use them to create a paradise for Spirit. We grow what we pay attention to. When actors and actresses portray characters that are unfaithful, evil, conniving, cunning and bitchy, they can be assured that these characteristics will manifest in their lives. When more true stars in the entertainment industry wake up to the truth of their own Light within, they will refuse to accept roles that create a sick world. The same is true of the news. It is "the Industry" (a catch-all term for all media entertainment) that has created our current society. With the power of television, satellites and global link-ups, we can communicate with the world. America is responsible to hold high the Light of Love and Liberty for all. Instead, we have made shows like "Dallas" and "Dynasty" world famous. When we understand that we grow that which we put our attention to, we will no longer declare "wars on drugs." We will, instead, become fascinated with freedom and co-creation.

Even during times of economic depression, people spend money on entertainment. In fact, entertainment thrives when the economy is depressed. People seek entertainment to help them feel better. We need more films like *Field of Dreams*, *City of Joy*, *Hook*, *Beauty and the Beast*, and *Forrest Gump*! We want to leave the shows feeling good. We want to be filled with wisdom and hope and courage. We want to come away from entertainment saying, "YES!" Ideally, we want to be a part of the creation of our own entertainment. Entertainers hold a mighty microphone. This has always been true. In the old days, before radio and television, the minstrels and travelling medicine shows would roll into town and the people would gather. The simplest tune would set people to dancing. Old feuds would be forgotten in the light of music and entertainment. It is said, "People that pray together, stay together." It is even stronger to say, "People who play together, stay together." Truly, play and laughter create a bond that is strong enough to endure many differences.

When we told our Pentecostal friends at the art festival that

On the Business of Creativity . . . We must make a difference. Breath of life is not enough.

—Colonel Lyn

we were "Sworn to FUN," they really thought us "lost." What is fun is surely sinful! They didn't stick around to discover that FUN stood for Friends Uniting Nations. Of course, it also means good, clean fun! If what we do is not fun for us, it is best that we not do it. Think of all the things that would fall away on our planet, and how much happier we would all be!

We need to come together and play. We need to come together! We have proven our ability to come together for war. Now let us come together to celebrate. We need to come together. Any system that sets itself apart is based in fear. We have developed a federal security system that is actively engaged in killing everybody (including presidents). We have a federal drug administration that has all but recommended motor oil for dietary use and an economic system that has tried to convince us that life and peace is bad for the economy. We call ourselves intelligent beings and yet we are dangerously close to making our planet totally uninhabitable by anything other than concrete and asphalt. We, as humans, are at the very top of the list of the most endangered species. "Smart" has come to mean "good at business swindles and corrupt politics." Intelligence is not the same as having a brain. Some forms of life have no brain at all, but they demonstrate more intelligence than humans. Even a virus won't trash out its environment except in an attempt to save its own life. True intelligence is the force of life, skan, expressing itself in harmony with all other forms of life. In the words of my E. T. connection, "If earth's inhabitants had any idea what cooperation meant, the longest distance between two points would not be a committee. Nor would countries march endlessly from one war to the next."

We are here to help participate in the transfiguration of this planet into the glorified home of Spirit it is designed to be! Those who do not get on board will be reassigned. It is our job to bring in more Light. It is our vision of physical form that inspires the creation of the universe. The entertainment industry has been given the commission to lead the way in bringing about heaven on earth. Maximum freedom to create our own individuality brings us closer to the truth of our oneness. Oneness does not mean sameness. It is one in Spirit. Just as all of creation is unique in all the world, each grain of sand and each tiny blade of grass, so are we all very different. Our government and social systems have striven to force us into sameness. While the dress code for the

My dance is a tangible, physical display of energy at work.

—Mahisha

When I'm asked to perform, I just ask and wait and sometimes the idea is just there. Sometimes it comes in the form of dreams and with them comes the basic story line that is to be danced, taught or shared.

—Mahisha

corporate is uniform, the dress code in entertainment is "be as unique as you truly are." We dress for success when we manifest on the outside what we truly are in Spirit. Unless we find freedom in expressing our own "song," we will feel fear and lack of trust in ourselves. When we lack trust in ourselves, we lack trust in God. This, in truth, is the basis of the fall from grace. Excellence, the hallmark upon which our nation is founded, calls for each one of us to be excellently ourselves. We must enjoy the pursuit of excellence. We must truly enjoy being fully ourselves, denying ourselves no wind of emotion; no natural urges. We must celebrate and communicate. We must celebrate the amazing diversity of our excellence. Above all else, know that the Great One wants to be entertained. Let's show God a good time!

The Good Medicine Show is always the grand finale at any gathering. All participants in the circle sing or dance or perform a skit or make music or recite poetry. An entire day is spent in preparing costumes and rehearsing. The elders are most happy with this celebration. When we see the face of our elders so enjoying wholesome, family entertainment, we know that Star Maker is also very happy.

A Final Note: We have sat and watched kittens play for hours. We have laughed and giggled as we are entertained by puppies. We sit by the babbling streams and watch tiny fish and sit for hours watching wind blow across grassy fields. All of nature exists for the pleasure of itself. One day I watched a bird nose dive to the earth and come out of her dive just before crashing into the concrete. She was simply entertaining herself. It is time for humanity to step back into the circle of the All-That-Is and truly become the stars that Star Maker intends us to be.

THE GIVE-AWAY

Money first appeared on the planet in ancient China. It seems that there existed certain farmers whose abundance was so great that they had enslaved their own peoples to make them carry their baskets of grain to the roadsides for barter. This enslavement angered the Great One, so overnight there was money. It was given as a symbol of how much grain a farmer had in his barns. The symbol was light-weight and could be given on the roadside and redeemed at the farmers' barns. Money had only one intention: To free the slaves! It was intended to be on the planet for only two hundred years, a sufficient amount of time to bring about freedom for all. Money still has only one intention: To Free The Slaves. It still has not done its job. The farmers of ancient China were so greedy that they kept the money and the slaves. It is still so today. Of those to whom much has been given, much is required. If the wealthy do not give of their material abundance, it will be taken from their souls.

Our ancestors knew the importance of giving away. They knew the Law of Balance. A cup that is already full cannot be filled more, unless what is in the cup is given out and more room is made. Nature abhors a vacuum. When we empty ourselves, we create a space into which more abundance can flow. Our modern day world has cultivated a life-style of stockpiling material wealth. The one who has the most wins the game. This is feeding the physical body. For most, the spiritual body is starving. When a young athlete is outstanding, it is common to give her trophies and banquets and special dinners and presents and lots of accolades in the newspaper. All the attention goes to the "star"

When you truly understand giving, you will laugh at sacrifice.

—Cloud

I have to face it sometime. I hate the government and I don't apologize.

—Grandmother
Princess Moon
Feathers

and the other team members go without attention for their efforts that enabled the "star" to excel.

Those who understand the give-away know that when they have been blessed, it is good to "give away" to those who have not been so blessed. The truly "rich" person is the one who can "give away" the most, not the one who hordes the most. When an athlete has been outstanding and received awards, it is good for the family of the young woman to host a feast for all her friends and their families. It is good for the family to give gifts to the other teammates and say to them, "You have helped our daughter excel in sports. We give you this gift with the prayer that the Great Star Maker will richly bless you and bring you your dreams." In this way the balance is kept. The "Star" recognizes the "Star" in everyone else and acknowledges it. When Grandfather's son was elected Chief of the Oto, the family sponsored a "give-away" feast. When a healing is done, the family sponsors a "give-away" as a way of showing thanks. We have been blessed with the life of our grandmother. Now we sponsor "The Give-Away" feast and gifting as a way of saying "thank you" for her life. In order to receive, we must give. We give, and then we receive, and then we give again. This is the cycle of abundance. It is honorable to give away. We honor by our giving. If we want to make money at something, we must first give it away.

The Bible talks about the giving of one-tenth as a tithe. It is said that what we give from a good heart returns to us tenfold. In some cases, the return is seven times seventy. The church enforced the ten percent tithe without understanding the true honoring that it is to give. Then along came the government and imposed a tax. Now we are "taxed" up to 51% of our income. This is a gross violation of sacred law. It is time to return to the understanding of the Give-Away. We must learn to fertilize what we most value. We will grow what we put our attention to. If we give 10% as a matter of law, we fertilize having laws to tell us what to do. If we give "the best that we have" to friends and family, we fertilize abundance for friends and family.

Rather than fall victim to a system of taxation that maintains four out of five black children on welfare, it is better to open our homes to a homeless person. We have done this many times over the years and always we are the blessed for having done so. The Ranch is home to many. Several people have told us that they have endured the toughest challenges of their lives because they always knew they could come home if they needed to do so. This knowing sustained them and gave them courage to attain independence.

It is not a good thing for any government to provide food and shelter for our people. It is a good thing when we "the people" have our freedom of choice and we use our resources to support ourselves. Great changes are coming in this decade. We will see many changes in the governments and the power of the people will increase. There will be a moment in this decade, before the year 2000, when the people will be "The People" again. We will dream together again, and our beautiful Earthship will be lifted to Her place as a Starship. She will be known as "Most Beautiful." When this happens, we the people will give away the seed of creation that Star Maker has planted in us. We will give this seed unto all the worlds. We will run, but we will not be weary. We will walk and we will not be afraid. We will see rainbow light flowing from the plants and trees, and our own bodies. We will sit down with the coyotes and the snakes and all will be friends. The child within each of us will truly rule our heads. We will lead with our hearts. Money will no longer be necessary, as we share our gifts and talents with all around us. Those who oppose this law will be reassigned to another place in the galaxies, because a great age of light and love is divined for our beautiful Mother Earth. For those of us who find our greatest job in giving, we will have made for ourselves heaven on earth. This is the intention of the give-away: to free us from slavery and make our own Earth into Heaven.

In order to introduce people back into the giving stream of life, we play some of the following games. The Birthday Give-Away is simple. The person making the passage into another year hosts a celebration and gives gifts to all her friends. Each gift is a medicine gift that she cherishes or that she made especially for this occasion. The gifts are given to reflect the joy that was gained in friendship. The host also feasts the guests and provides unusual entertainment. This is a turn-around on the usual birthday party.

The Harvest Give-Away is a give-away to the Mother Earth for bringing in a good harvest. All who partake of the harvest gather for several days of grooming, fertilizing and caring for the land in a special way. The Mother Earth is treated to a special

Go where you're welcomed.

Give when you're asked.

—Cloud

altar, or a new pathway, or a new gathering place for children. The Give-Away can be anything that brings joy to the Earth and enriches Her in some way.

The Warrior's Give-Away is a must at all encampments. When the circle first gathers, each puts his or her name into a pot. The names are drawn out on the first evening together and kept secret for the entire week. During the week each person "stalks" and "tracks" the person whose name they drew. They watch them and listen to them and look always for their beauty. At the final gathering a great Give-Away is done, in which each person is gifted a warrior's name and a gift appropriate to their spirit. This is a moving ceremony in which the meaning of giving in order to receive takes on very special meaning. Both the name and the gift become a special reminder to rejoice in giving, to love giving, to want to give . . . and the resources to do so will always be available.

EARTH ETIQUETTE

I was four years old when I first remember learning Earth manners. I had gathered a small bouquet of periwinkles for my mother. The periwinkles came from the church yard. Mama explained to me that the small flowers belonged to the Mother Earth and our preacher man was the gardener at the church. It was wrong for me to take flowers from the mother without first asking the preacher. It was wrong to take the flowers without first paying the mother. She said it was like someone cutting off my hair without asking me. She made me take the flowers back to the church and explain to the preacher what I had done. She helped me plant new seeds to replace what I had taken. At the time, it seemed like a very big thing.

On New Year's Eve, 1988, I sat in a circle of women on the Big Sur coast of California. We had gathered at the home of Ted Turner to celebrate our passage into a New Year. One of the most beloved women in the circle was Barbara Pyle, vice president of CNN and head of the documentaries division. Barbara is a work force of a hundred people packed into one dynamic woman. She is responsible for some of the most amazing documentaries ever done on our Earth Mother. Barbara has spent more time in the jungles and deserts than she has ever spent in cities. She has been exposed to every possible type of dysentery, in her efforts to live close to the global community that she has come to love. We have Barbara to thank for such films as *The Day of Five-Billion* and *Hurricane Irene*. Her entire life is dedicated to global communication; from deforestation and overpopulation to world hunger and desertation of our planet, Barbara has given her life

May the mountain's own

great spirit

make your life a singing

stream.

May the twelve new moons

now coming

bring a purpose to your

dreams.

May a rainbow touch your

shoulder

with a promise of its glow.

May the sunlight fall upon

you

as you walk in many snows.

—Traditional Native
American Prayer

blood to Mother Earth. On this particular New Year's Eve, she would literally do so. We sat long hours chanting and praying together. We were calling in the Spirit of Gaia, our Earth Mother. When Her Spirit arrived, we all felt an overwhelming energy enter the room and Barbara became suddenly transfixed. Within a period of two minutes she transformed into the Earth Herself. She took on the persona of an old, old crone. She began to bleed and wretch. We saw, before us, the persona of our Mother Earth etched in the face of this beautiful young woman. And then She, Gaia, was gone. As quickly as She had come, She was gone. Barbara seemed stunned and "spent." In that moment I understood the importance of polite and proper etiquette in dealing with a very tired Mother Earth. She has grown weary of the treatment She is getting. She is tired of having Her life blood drained from Her body. She is tired of having poisons poured into her arteries. She is sick of breathing polluted air. She is weakened by drinking water that is full of lead. She is appalled with the plundering and raping of Her beautiful body. She is tired and old and distrustful. She is like an old crone that has been without love and nurturing forever. We must now treat Her with extreme respect. She is stronger than we are. We may become extinct. She will live on. Her wrath can be quick and mighty. Her love is even stronger. The choice is ours. We will either bask in Her beauty and abundance, or we will crumble under Her wrath. She calls her children together. She calls for us to share our resources and care for our resources. She demands that we "own" the Earth with our love. Roses grow best out of human feces. From our refuse, we must grow our own paradise.

When I was sixteen my mother taught me a lesson I shall always remember. I had come home from school with some juicy gossip about a school mate who was pregnant. It was the talk of the town. Mother listened to my rantings and then invited me to follow her into the pasture. There she forced me to kneel down and smell an old dried "cow pie" left by the cows. "How does it smell?" she asked. I begrudgingly responded that it didn't smell like anything. She then picked up a stick and broke it open. "Now what does it smell like?" she asked. It, of course, was rank and smelly and so full of ammonia fumes that my eyes watered. Mother gently stood me up, looked square in my face and said this thing: "Honey, remember this. Shit left unstirred, soon quits stinking." We have made a mess on our good Mother Earth, but out of our "mess" we can grow gardens. It is time to learn from our ancestors how to pay proper respect to Mother Earth.

Mahena is Hawaiian. She is one of the most beautiful women on earth. She practices the ancient Hula dances of worshipping the spirits of earth and sky. Each member of her circle is responsible to honor the spirits on the islands. Her assigned waterfall is two miles from civilization. Once a week she walks the two miles into the jungle and pays homage to the spirits that keep this beautiful waterfall. We were allowed to assist her in her task. Along the way she sang and spoke to individual trees and outcroppings of rocks. She gathered beautiful Tee leaves and flowers. She came singing to the place of her waterfall. Here, she raised her arms in celebration and greeted the waterfall as though it was her own mother. In truth, it is, and Mahena loves her mother. She spoke to the waterfall and told of her experiences over the past week. She spoke about the things that were on her mind. She knew that the spirits would be excited to hear all about her family. She then stripped down naked and played in the waterfall. She giggled and laughed as we joined her. We sang and screamed with delight. We could feel the spirits laughing and enjoying our company. It was the kind of enjoyment that comes with expecting a special visit each week. The spirits responded with the strength of love that let us know that Mahena's visit was the most important part of their week. They anticipated her coming and, after each visit, they reflected and remembered her visit until they started anticipating it again. The spirits of this waterfall loved Mahena! And, Mahena loved the spirits here. After we played, we prayed. We prayed in the presence of spirits who truly loved us and appreciated our visit. The rocks love us. The plants love us. The trees love us. All of nature loves us. We could feel it. The truth of our appointment as caretakers of our Mother Earth became a complete reality. Before leaving, we each made a gift for the spirits of the waterfall. We left our bundles of flowers and our altars at the foot of the waterfall. Mahena said that they would be gone when she returned the following week. Mahena told us that all the beautiful places on the islands had someone just like herself that came once a week to care for it. What a splendid idea for the whole of our earth!

Brooke Medicine Eagle travelled with me for four years. She always said that she struggled to love people as much as she loves the Earth and Her animals. I am privileged to this day to have

Few of us would deny that the planet is in crisis. We have reached the end of a great pendulum swing into despair, destruction, violence and injustice. We face the crisis of chaos. Will the planet swing back towards balance and harmony, or will the forces of destruction take earth into the sea of boundless chaos? As we spin gynergy, the path of the planet is changed. We bring the energy of "She" into our being, and through the channel of our being we release this gynergy into the realm of the material and spiritual reality of Earth at this time.

—Spider Redgold

It is not, "I Am," but rather "We Are." We are: The People . . . The Mystery . . . The Earth Mother.

—Grandmother Kitty

Brooke as a model for honoring the Earth. Everywhere this woman goes, she sings to the Earth. Any trip is longer than usual, because Brooke is drawn like fleas to a dog to any and all beautiful possibilities of places to stop and build an altar. She squeals like a child with the delight of a trail through the aspens or a creek to follow upstream. Any rock in the middle of a stream is to sit on and sing to. Every mountain is a reason to stop and play her flute. Every trickle of water from the rocks is a place to stop and bless herself and the earth. Every budding berry bush is a place to stop and eat like the bears. Every hot spring is a place to bathe and every star-lit night is made to sleep under. Brooke is truly a "child of the earth." She loves the earth with a passion strong enough to call her to travel the world inviting others to join her in a dance to the Mother.

Natalie loves the earth, too. She took us to see the pictographs left by the children of our ancestors. To this playground in the lava, we took offerings of corn and a special medicine bag. Natalie also took us to see the Valley of the Gods, Waipio Valley. Her son, Devin, loves caves as much as I do. We always carry our flute and play for the cave spirits. Some people are afraid of caves. They say that spirits live in the caves and we should never go in them. It's obvious that spirits of our ancestors live in the caves and they really like company. At least, they like my and Devin's company. We always linger at the door and ask permission to enter. We both have to feel it's right before we go in. And, we always leave a gift. Many times we take food for the Old Ones. We like to ask for special wishes in caves, because we know that our ancestors are listening there. What we ask for in caves is always a secret. I once received a new body in a cave on the rim of Waipio Valley. The cave had called to me on the mainland. I made the trip to the Big Island just to go to the cave. Skye helped me find the cave and stood as a dog soldier outside. Inside, I was taken by a dance that lasted for what seemed like hours. When I came out I was so energized that I ran through the jungles for miles. I was given the body of a teenage boy. At the time I was 44. I experienced physical transformation in my energy and again understood the powers of regeneration that are held in the hands of Mother Earth.

Natalie and Pua first took us to the Vagina Cave in Hawaii. It took days of preparation. We were to fast, pray and prepare a gift to leave with "The Lady." It is said that this sacred place is the female organs of Pele's body. I carefully carved a beautiful canoe to take with me. In it I placed a medicine bag with many sacred totems of my dream. We hiked into the jungles to reach the door that led into the belly of the earth. From this place, we announced ourselves and asked permission to enter. Pua stood close by to insure that our energy was welcomed in the cave. One of our companions was not welcomed. For a quarter of a mile or more, we climbed precariously down into the belly of the earth. We walked along narrow lava ledges, using flashlights to lead the way. Deep in the belly of the earth is a womb, or chamber room. A shaft of light shines down from far above. The lava has formed an amphitheater here, with a perfect altar. High above this theater is another altar. This altar is a woman's vagina, perfectly formed. It is about sixteen feet in length. In this place we worshipped creation. I sat at the clitoris of Nature's sculpture and was "taken" by an ancient ritual of praise for Woman, First Woman, Mother of Creation. A beautiful crystal appeared out of the Spirit World and was laid beside me. I carry it with my Thunder Rock. I was told to show it to no one. All things that hold a mystery, have power. As long as we do not know, our curiosity holds us to attention. It is good to be curious. I am curious about this crystal.

Each time I visit the Goddess Pele, I make Her a gift. The last gift I made was a carved, feathered serpent. My gift signalled this time in which the circle of Light Workers gather to Dance The Dream Awake. Some say six is the magic number for manifestation. One is really all that is needed: Just one person who comes believing. However, I placed six winged serpents around the North American continent. Our continent is responsible to "lead the way into the Reign of Peace on Earth." One feathered serpent went south to the Goddess Pele. One went north to Canada. One went east to New York. One went west to Big Sur, California. One went to the center at Milfay, Oklahoma, and one travels with me. In all of these places, the Rainbow Circles of Children of Light gather and direct their energies to healing our planet.

Let us pay proper respect to our Mother. Let us awaken in the morning of our lives and sing the sun up. Let us cheer when Light floods into darkness. Let us cheer the sun for a job well done and wave "good-bye" in the evening. Let us welcome the moon and sing Her beautiful songs in exchange for Her guardianship in the night. Let us wave to the stars and know ourselves to be stars as

Mother Nature is kind to us. Live with nature. Go with the flow . . . live every minute NOW.

—Grandmother
Princess Moon
Feathers

well. Let every flower grown wild remind us of our invincible spirit. Let us give thanks for each beautiful thing on earth and let us find beauty in each thing that first appears ugly.

It is Easter. Today we stand rooted on our Mother Earth and reach with our left hand into the Father Sky. Our action is one of reaching into, and receiving from the Great Mystery, our First Mother. We bring down this receiving into our hearts. With our hearts, we see with our strong eye and, from this "seeing," we speak from within the Great Mystery. Receive these words from First Mother, Holy Spirit, Grandmother God:

> You are all My Children. I love you each the same. You are each very precious. You are each unique and beautiful. You are free to choose your destinies. What comes your way, comes at your own bidding. You will rise or you will fall according to your own expectations. You and you alone can change your expectations. None is more fortunate or unfortunate than the other. All struggle between ecstasy and agony. You need not struggle anymore! You have each been given a gift. That which is given is always received, somewhere. That which is not given, is always lost forever. Every second counts in eternity.
>
> Your ancestors came to give you life. They came that you might live more abundantly. Go the extra step. Do what they could not do. Dream together of a world that calls all creatures "Family." See your borders and boundaries dissipate. Blend into each other's lives. Touch each other's Spirits. Be polite. Respect each other's individuality. Study and appreciate your differences. Note these differences as that which makes each thing beautiful unto itself. Appreciate yourself as beautiful.
>
> Appreciate the earth and all that is in Her. Pay Her for what you take from Her. Ask Her permission to take. Take only what you need for yourself and your own families. Allow others to do the same. Replace something that will grow and render fruit for all that you use. Announce yourself properly and insist on being welcomed, into houses, buildings, fair grounds and woods. All places are homes to someone. Treat all of the

earth and sky as home to Spirit.

Dare to remember your beginnings. It was you who stood within the great darkness and called forth the Light. It was you who set the sun blazing in the heavens. It was you who hung the moon and flung the stars to the farthermost corners of the universe. It was you who rounded the earth in the palms of our hand. It was you who called forth the waters above the earth. It was you who hollowed out the valleys and bulged up the mountains. It was you who waved your hand over the land and brought forth fishes and fowl and beasts to roam the forest and the woods and the winds and the seas. It was you who first thought into being the red flowers and the green grass. It was you! You were, and are now, One with the All-That-Is, First Mother, Great Mystery. All of life came from you and returns to you. Those who are invisible are as much part of you as your own fingers. The "other" outside of "yourself" is yourself. All is One. The "other" promised to awaken "this you" NOW! Wake Up! Your time has come to help the All vision Heaven on Earth. Listen to the spirits of the stars. You are a star, in a star, on a star, that is moving inside the Great Everlasting Star. You are now sharing the "I" of the great "I Am." It is you! You are the promised Messiah! Awaken! A simple child's trust is all that is required. The scientists are the last to know the truth; not the first. The child knows. You are the child. Give birth to yourself. "Greater things than these that I do, YOU WILL DO!" said our Brother, ourselves. Now is the time.

Earth's warning cry is,

"Listen! Heal yourself first."

—Mahisha

Enjoy your every breath! Enjoy being excellent. Play! Rejoice! Laugh until the lights go out! Then laugh some more! Become the laughing star!

Love,
Your Grandmother, Yourself

HONORING
CO-CREATION

"Know yourself as one with the creating force and you will know that, truly, you own the earth."

Ruth Beebe Hill, HANTA YO.

What goes around comes around. We reap what we sow. One with the Creative Force, we create our own lives. Ancient tools have been left for us to use. They are deeply encoded in our bodies, minds, and spirits. Thus, we are also capable of shifting our lives. To truly own that we are responsible for the co-creation of our lives and the world around us is to own the earth and each other. It is our sacred duty. The Grandmothers and the Grandfathers say so.

Within the circle of co-creation we must understand these four energies: *Intention, Attention, Attraction,* and *Appreciation*.

Intention ignites the spark that starts the circle spinning. It defines the game that we play and sets us in motion. Always it is good to remember original intent. We come to notice that, originally, all behavior has a positive intention. We want to be loved, we want to make a contribution, we want to feel secure, we want to experience pleasure. Original intent seeks to serve us in a good way.

Our old barn cat, Lion, has been a great teacher of intent.

It had been a steaming hot summer in Oklahoma, but it would soon be followed by a cold, snowy winter. The mice were unusually busy on The Ranch. We decided to get a "barn cat" to help out with the mice. That seems like an ordinary idea to anyone living in the country. However, for us, the idea of making a cat sleep in the barn defies our bent for totally spoiling all our animals. However, we bucked up and firmly planted our intention upon getting a "barn cat" to deal with the mice.

The want ads listed two locations for "free kittens." We arranged to see both litters. Stop one brought us into direct contact with three of the cutest little black kittens on earth. We couldn't decide, so took all three. The next stop again connected us with three of the cutest little red kittens on earth. Again, we couldn't decide and took all three. We arrived back at The Ranch with six little kittens ready to take up residence in the barn.

Our plan seemed immediately foiled when we realized that these little ones would have to endure the bitter winter in the barn. It was with some degree of guilt that we prepared their winter bed, put out food and water and played with them for hours. Then we left them in the barn and went to bed.

We were awakened early the next morning with yowling like none other. We raced to the barn to discover dead kittens scattered everywhere. The one little red kitten who survived came screaming across the yard dragging his back leg. We were horrified. Our young pit bull had found those "strangers" in the barn and proceeded to get rid of them. She got to wear a dead kitten wired to her collar for three days, just long enough to learn never to repeat such an act. Over her fourteen years she never again dared look at a cat.

By now we were sorely aware that we had gotten way off base from our intent. First of all, the kittens would take a year or more to develop an interest in mice. Secondly, our excess of six versus one came back to haunt us. We intended to get one cat. We ended up with one cat. The surviving red kitten quickly got named "Lion" and was brought inside to heal. He stayed there all winter.

In late spring we neutered Lion, who was by now quite spoiled. It would be impossible to describe the look on his face over the whole process. He simply couldn't believe that such a regal being as he would be forced to endure such a process. He took off for a couple of days to protest. Then three, then five, then a week, then two. Soon Lion was gone only to be sighted every month or so. He would show himself from a distance and let us know that he was still around, but took on all the traits of a truly wild lion. This went on for seven years.

In the eighth year, as the severe winter winds blew in again,

Once we set a target based on our own internal guidance, we are naturally drawn toward it.

Lion began to come closer and yowl and invite our attention. We put food out for him and gradually moved it closer to the barn. It took a full two weeks to coax him into the barn to eat and live. It took another four months to actually touch him.

We would begin our day by feeding our horses, llama, and donkeys.

Then we carried fresh water and food to Lion in the barn where we climbed up on the hay to his nest. There we cuddled and purred and prayed together.

Almost eight years before we had set an intent to have a barn cat to help with the mice. It took the better part of a decade to see that intent fulfilled. Lion is a strong teacher of the profound truth of intent.

Teachers of psycho-cybernetics use the analogy of a signaling device on a torpedo missile once it has been set to a mark. Knowing human beings are success-oriented, psycho-cybernetics emphasizes the importance of intent and having a clearly defined target. Once we set a target based on our own internal guidance, we are naturally drawn toward it. When a behavior moves us away from our target we get an internal signal. When we align with targets that match the resonance of our soul's desires we receive internal feedback for our target and needed course corrections. This is an amazing gift.

Our most recent example is the purchase of a five hundred acre ranch twenty-five minutes from our resort and training center. It became clear to us that we wanted a very private place with lots of space, natural running water, a beach, trees, optimum grazing and play room for all of our animals. We also wanted land within easy driving distance of our family and training center in Oklahoma. We made sure we both got a big internal *yes* for our intention, put it forth, and let it go. Very soon we heard of a place about two hours from our center. Further than we imagined, yet it fit all of the other criteria so we offered to pay the asking price. Much to our surprise, the sellers decided they didn't want to sell after all. Having had some practice with setting intentions by this time we were able to say, "oh well," and continue to hold the intention.

We left the land that day and drove to the biggest tree we could find. There we once again put forth the prayer that we would be led to exactly the right place for us and perhaps a tree such as the one we were under would mark our finding. Led by a series of wondrously synchronized events we found our dream spot that is better than anything we could have imagined and completely matches the purest essence of our intention.

Intent is everything. An intent set is a seed planted that will bring a harvest in spite of our distractions and detours. The sages of all time know this thing: Intend well. Project intention into that place that serves Divine Will and always ask that All be served in the highest possible way.

The greater the alignment with a vision, the greater the energy for manifestation.

Intend well, and then give *attention* to the true intention. It is said that energy flows into our attention. We grow the thing that holds our attention. When the local bank builds a miniature model of their vision for a new bank, puts it under glass, and displays it in the lobby, they enhance the energy of manifestation. Folks that come into the bank linger to see the model. They imagine it already built and they begin to feel themselves walking up to the new structure. The employees see it every day and align with the vision. They share the vision with their families. The greater the alignment with a vision, the greater the energy for manifestation.

We love garage sales. One of our best finds was a large, antique sign with the words "Little Dude" doweled in it. We brought it home to The Ranch and hung it by Miracle Pond. All who passed saw the sign and wondered about it. It was our point of focus for our western town, Little Dude. Within a few short years "Little Dude" began to manifest on The Ranch and now is home to a few wonderful people and lots of animals. Our first sign still hangs by the pond. It is still the focus point for all that our western town will become.

To manifest, we must stalk and capture attention.

Masterful physicians turn their patients' attention toward health. They ask about their abilities before the "dis-ease" occurred. They discover their patients' dreams for activity following recovery. Then they use all of their resources to hold their patients' attention on health, vigor, and re-creation of life. It is said that the true recovery happens when we keep ourselves entertained and happy while the deep healing takes place. Ancient healers and teachers have used medicine objects, herbs, dances, songs, and rituals to hold attention to their desired outcomes. Corporate moguls position products with symbols and slogans that have mass appeal: "Just Do It," "No Fear," and "Take the Challenge."

Manifestation is the mastery of marketing. We must first get the attention of the energies that are required to help us build our dreams. When we discipline our attention, we hone our

What we truly love creates feelings strong enough to attract the building blocks of our dreams.

focus. A disciplined focus drives manifestation. The one with a disciplined focus is addicted to completion. Success is guaranteed in the attention we give to our desires. Strong attention is the catalyst for passion.

An old farmer up north of our ranch has a passion for boots. He owns lots of land. Years ago he started collecting old boots and putting them upside down on top of his fence posts. His boots got the attention of friends and neighbors and they joined in his passion. Soon people began bringing old boots to the farmer's land from far and near. Today you can drive for miles around his ranch, and every fence post has a boot on it. The old man's passion for boots attracted miles and miles of boot-topped fence lines.

Passion is the energy of *attraction*. The Law of Attraction is key to manifestation. Everything moves. Everything vibrates. Thoughts attract vibration and feelings increase it. The faster the vibration, the faster the manifestation.

While thoughts are an important part of creation, feelings are more powerful. The relationship between our physical body and emotion represents the single most sophisticated technology available to us. Love is the strongest of all emotions. What we truly love creates feelings strong enough to attract the building blocks of our dreams. We must not only envision our dreams, we must feel ourselves living inside them. We must experience our successes in order to attract them to us.

We shift our bodies' experiences by shifting our point of view. Each thought is accompanied by its own set of chemical reactions in our bodies. When we think a fun, exciting thought, our bodies make ready for the fun. We emit endorphins. Our hearts quicken. Our stomachs feel a flood of excitement. Our eyes soften and widen. We see more clearly. Our hearing is enhanced. All the world is more beautiful. Our emotions quicken.

According to the "Wiggle/Squirt Theory," each time we think, we move vibrations. We move our bodies in response to these vibrations and our bodies squirt chemicals to support our movement. If we think "downer" thoughts, we lapse into "downer" postures, which in turn, activate our brains to release inhibitors. Bad thought, bad vibe, bad result.

We are the masters of our thoughts and our feelings. Our level of mastery over our co-creative process is the mark of our success in life. The old adage, "If it feels good, do it" has value. We've got to feel good to manifest good. This is a secret of manifestation. We must love to be loved. We must forgive to be forgiven. We must dance to be a dancer. We must sing to be a singer. We must build to be a builder. We attract what we feel. Our emotions are our "Town Crier." What they call for, we get.

A thousand years ago someone moved beyond his own fears and we are the result. Five hundred years ago someone chose to forgive a wrong and we are the result. Three hundred years ago someone chose to trust and have faith, in spite of overwhelming odds, and we are the result. One hundred years ago someone chose to tell the truth no matter what and we the result. A few years ago someone took a risk, with a smile, a kind word, a phone call, flowers, and we are the result. Future generations will result from our every thought, feeling, and action.

Thoughts create our feelings. Feelings attract form. Thoughts guide energy. Feelings drive energy. It is the template of vibration that creates the reality. When we are on the desert and yearn for water, we do not pray for water. We, instead, become the water. We feel our bodies drenched in rain. We dive into pools of clear, cool water. We feel our long, wet hair fall on our shoulders. We smell the sweet, wet rain on the prairie grasses. We must place ourselves inside of all that we pray and become the prayer. Feeling is *us* moving energy in our bodies to create our external reality. Prayer is about creating a feeling and that feeling interacting with the energy that already exists in our bodies and in our world. Whatever we create we experience in our bodies before the world ever experiences it. Knowing comes after the feeling of having our outcome. Then the manifestation of all that we want appears around us. To ask, believing, is to be engulfed by our answer.

Jesus tells us to become again as little children. To become again as a little child is to come believing. It is to have insatiable curiosity and a worldview of surplus and abundance, love, trust, and anticipation of joy. It is to be openhearted and available to act on intuition. We are told that our intuition is 10,000 times faster than our logic. Statistics indicate that our bodies are each composed of approximately one quadrillion cells. Each cell has some 1.17 volts of electrical potential. Thus we have 1.17 quadrillion volts of electrical potential that we guide each moment with our intention and attention. To co-create our dreams with all the energies of the universe, we learn to become again as little children.

We finalize our Circle of Co-Creation through the act of *appreciation*. "Thank you" is one of the most powerful words in any language. We are told by our elders that there is no energy

We have 1.17 quadrillion volts of electrical potential that we guide each moment with our intention and attention.

more attractive than appreciation. The influence of appreciation changes lives, stops wars, heals hearts and bodies, and brings peace.

At the turn of the twentieth century there existed a small town whose major employer was a state institution. In the old days it was called an "insane asylum." An old lady worked in the cafeteria and had all of her adult life. She was just four months from retirement when a little eleven-year-old girl named Annie was brought in. Little Annie acted like an animal, and in those days, it was considered proper to treat people the way they acted. Annie growled, and hissed, and clawed, so she was put into a cage in the dungeon. Attendants hosed her down, threw her food, and basically treated her like an animal.

This treatment was not acceptable to the little old lady serving lunch in the cafeteria. However, she felt her influence to be best served by doing what she did best. She valued children. She appreciated their struggles to grow and mature. Thus, the little old lady took her lunch breaks down in the dungeon with Annie. She sat at some distance and quietly ate her lunch. Annie growled and hissed and clawed at her cage. The old lady remained calm and simply sat with Annie. Before leaving she would push a brownie or cookie close to the cage so Annie could reach it. Over time Annie quieted down and the old lady moved closer to the cage. Over a four-month period Annie and the old lady quietly shared lunch every day. They never spoke. They never exchanged names. Annie grew calm and clear and quiet.

The attendants of the asylum thought that the cage was working well since they did not know of the old lady's act of appreciation. The old woman retired and little Annie was moved back upstairs. A couple of years passed before the authorities came to tell Annie the good news. She was well enough to go home. The only problem was that Annie had no home. She was an orphan. It was Annie who first suggested that she be allowed to stay on at the asylum as a trustee. She reasoned that she knew well the woes of being a hurt child and she could help other children. Annie's appreciation of the condition of childhood mental illness provided her a home until she was seventeen years old. She then left to find her way in life.

Many years passed and one day throngs gathered outside Buckingham Palace. On this day the British Royal Family would present a humanitarian award to a young woman who had inspired millions. The young woman was lead to the balcony where the Queen Mother awaited her. The young woman had to place her hands on the lips of the Queen Mother as she spoke. The young woman's name was Helen Keller. "Miss Keller, please share with us the most significant influence in your life." Helen Keller moved close to the microphone to pronounce her answer. "My teacher, Ann Sullivan, was the most influential person in my life." The great teacher of Helen Keller had herself been a child of darkness. Ann Sullivan was the "little Annie" once banished to a dungeon in an insane asylum.

We could end our story here. However we push it forward to revisit a day in Chicago when Helen Keller was invited to speak at a small luncheon in Chicago. A group of affluent business men asked her to inspire them to service. They called themselves "Lions." Helen Keller challenged these original members of the "Lions Club" to "restore vision to our planet." Many years later we see that small social fraternity became the largest social organization on the planet and the only non-political group to hold a voting seat at the United Nations. This is because they have made more friends with more countries than any other group in the world as they have provided glasses, eye care, and surgery for those who need help, and worked to restore peace on earth and health to our earth and our communities. It is impossible to calculate the impact of Helen Keller's simple challenge in Chicago that day, and it was but one day in her life. Again, we could end our story here, but there is more. We must return to the origin of our story to complete the circle.

One day one little old lady chose to appreciate a small child by sitting quietly with her in a dungeon eating and sharing lunch. One small act of appreciation by a nameless little old lady continues to influence our world toward peace. Let us be always in a state of appreciation.

In our training circles on The Ranch we often debrief participants in an activity using our "brag stone." As the stone is passed each person "brags" first on themselves and the contributions they made. They then "brag" on one or more members of the group. This appreciation expands the recognized talents of the circle. Appreciation is fertilizer. It grows things.

Intend well. Focus attention on the desired result. Attract the result by *being* the desired result. Appreciate the magic and mystery of co-creation. And, repeat the circle so that we can all co-create peace and pass it on.

One small act of appreciation by a nameless little old lady continues to influence our world toward peace.

257

HONORING OUR CHAMPION

My friend Bert is one of the greatest football coaches the state of Oklahoma has ever known. He shares with us some of his magic in the "Growing of Champions." He used to watch game films with his football players by spending most of the time pointing out and replaying what they had done wrong. Missed block, poor effort, lack of hustle—most of us know the list. He began noticing the team's performance continued to go downhill and that folks didn't seem to like showing up for film night. Huh. So he tried a new plan. He began watching the same films and pointing out what was right. He would rewind excellent plays and say, "Now look at that great block. That's what we call hustle. Look at that focus!" and something started to change. The team loved coming to film night and they started to improve. Bert coached himself moment by moment to grow the strengths, to notice the talent, to continually encourage the champion in every player. His team started to win before they ever took the field. He repeatedly won state championships.

Bert also celebrates his own champion. One lazy Oklahoma afternoon we were in a fiercely competitive, fun-filled game of horseshoes. I was competing against Bert which means I was standing at the same end of the horseshoe pit. Early in the game Bert hit a bull's-eye ringer. Before tossing his second horseshoe, he took a long pause and smiled. Ready to move on with the game I asked him what he was doing.

He said, "I'm having an awards assembly!"

"An awards assembly?"

"Yeah. Didn't you ever have those in school for attendance or grades or participation in something?"

"Of course."

He said, "Well, I'm having one for myself. I have awards assemblies all the time. That's how I grow my champion. You ought to try it."

He then took a deep breath and tossed another bull's-eye ringer.

We water the flowers rather than the weeds in life.

From Bert I continue to learn the power of personal awards assemblies. I love rewarding myself for hitting the mark I intended. I have awards assemblies over little things and big things. I know supporting the growth of the champion in myself energizes me to grow the champion in others.

For twenty-three years we at The Ranch have devoted extensive energy to exploring human excellence. We call this process the "Excellence Principle."® Simply stated, we track excellence and grow it in others and in ourselves. We water the flowers rather than the weeds in life. We know energy flows into our attention so we power the good with our attention to excellence. We identify, empower and utilize natural talents, strengths and strategies of success. These can be found everywhere. Finding them requires that we stay present, in the present moment.

We highlight the specific components of excellence and help individuals and teams recognize their unique abilities to contribute to outstanding performance. We identify and streamline success strategies. Excellence, when tracked, can consciously be repeated again and again and again. A behavior twice seen is a pattern, three times — a habit, four times — a compulsion, and five times — an obsession. We coach leaders in the skills needed to turn talents into peak performance. Excellence is a fun obsession. We are in the business of "growing champions."

Years of in-depth research by Gallup surveyors, cited in *First, Break All The Rules,* by Marcus Buckingham and Curt Coffman, and *Now, Discover Your Strengths,* by Buckingham and Donald O. Clifton, supports our belief in the incredible power of identifying and growing strengths and talents. They report findings from interviews with 80,000 managers in over 400 companies and further studies of over two million people. Guess what. Great managers build on a person's unique strengths rather than trying to fix weaknesses. We must help ourselves and others identify our talents, build strengths and

enjoy outstanding performances. If we want to motivate, ener-
gize and inspire ourselves and others we only need focus on
strengths and grow them. We must grow our innate talent —
our champions.

We have a ranch foreman, Mary, who blesses our lives in
every way. You may find her training horses, tilling, planting or
tending the garden, mending a teepee, leading a tour, readying
a lodge, tending a fire for a purification lodge, working with
children, caring for lots and lots of animals, solving a complex
problem, belaying on the ropes course, handling our recycling
center, wielding a chain saw, rescuing abandoned animals, honoring an elder, offering medical expertise or writing a book. She
is a woman of many talents. At one point she was only working
for us part-time and attempting to do another fulltime job. I
went through some knee jerk reactions to tasks I felt were being
performed below expected standards. Tensions rose, and dis-
cussions ensued about releasing her from her job at The Ranch.
Then one day I asked myself, is she being given the opportunity to utilize her talents? Does she have the resources she needs
to succeed? The answer on both counts was a big *no*. I decided
to practice what I preach. I first gave her a strengths/work style
preference survey we use with our clients and discovered her
work style preference was an Analyst. A perfect match for our
preferences. Yet we had not been using, appreciating and growing her strong analytical skills. We made a financial investment
to provide a full-time salary, benefits and lodging. We asked
that she only work for us. We began to utilize her natural talents. From day one of the new arrangement she has proven,
unequivocally, that people thrive and excel when matched with
their strengths and provided the necessary resources.

I have the pleasure of working with people in many set-
tings. Corporate board rooms, ropes courses, sacred ceremonial
fires, large concert halls, under the shade of huge cottonwood
trees, by the sea, on horseback, in churches, in the dark of night.
Wherever I am, I find people's incredible gifts popping up. I see
the delight in people's faces and hear the enthusiasm in their
voices. I feel their excitement when their natural talents are
noticed and utilized. We all love to give our gifts. Conversely,
when we work with individuals or teams who express feeling
dispirited, unmotivated, grumpy, cantankerous, "victimized,"
angry and otherwise "bummed," one hundred percent of the
time we invariably discover their talents and strengths are not

being recognized or utilized. Period. To assist them we share with them the Excellence Principle. They get it. They make team pacts that help them remember. They encourage and remind one another. They stumble, forget, backslide, and they keep coming because innately they resonate with the truth of tracking what is good. Their hearts tell them so.

Our elders beseech us to follow our hearts. Sometimes breaking old habits and opening our hearts can be quite challenging. Many of us had strong role models who assisted us in finding what is wrong, versus looking for what is right. We have been schooled to value our minds to the point of ignoring the intuitive voices of our hearts. Our hearts naturally see the good. They move us with love instead of fear. The rewards of a heart path abound. The Institute of Heart Math®, a nonprofit research and educational organization, offers astounding information regarding how the philosophical or metaphorical "heart" and the physical heart interact. They have shown the impact of feeling love, compassion and gratitude on underlying physiological conditions. Their discoveries are founded in scientific research and emotional wisdom. Growing champions is a win / win for everyone, even if you are focusing on someone else's strengths. It is a Sacred Circle. It feels good to grow champions.

Step forth and share with the world your unique soul imprint.

To be who we are, *champions*, conceived as perfection, is our vision, our birthright and our choice. It is, perhaps, the most important choice of our lives. Step forth and share with the world your unique soul imprint. Because we are all energy, and part of one large cosmic whole, the true tone of All-that-is can only be heard when we each sound our own distinctive note. When we dare to express our natural, authentic selves we can live the message of "Love One Another" because we have the opportunity to honestly know one another.

Believing this to be true, how do we truly know ourselves? How do we know our talents and strengths? How do we discern our internal guidance from programmed fear-based tapes? How do we connect with that deepest place of knowing that resides within our souls? How can we identify and follow our personal preferences, rather than reacting based solely on what we think others would want us to do? How can we live our lives, at ease with ourselves, and demonstrate reverence for all life?

We meet these challenges by staying in the present, practicing the "excellence principle" and trusting the grace of God. We spend time in stillness and leave room for the wisdom of our internal guidance. We practice listening to our internal guidance. We follow our internal guidance and carry with us our sense of humor. We dance with the songs of our spirits. We bask in nature's lap. We know that God is love and love is God. We know we are created in God's perfection. We know how it *feels* when we are truly at ease with ourselves. We feel the vital life force of Spirit flow through us when we are natural and authentic and comfortable in owning our true personal power. We choose reflections of love whenever possible in our family, in our friendships, in our environment and in our world.

Be the change you want to see in the world.

When we stand present within our own spirit, we meet each moment with greater joy, resiliency and strength. As Spirit moves through us we are energized. We can simply *be* and allow our ever-present homing device, tuned to our soul's deepest aspirations, guide us, one breath at a time. We are centered, even with our deepest sadness. As our uniqueness peeks forth we see one another's uniqueness and within that reflection we find our similarities. When we are true to ourselves, love or rejection taps in us a deep sense of honesty and security. We move in the world based on our own sense of knowing and any response becomes simply feedback to help us move forward on our desired path. We welcome fun, laughter and tears. Judgments, inherent in the labels of success or failure, are simply feedback as we attune to the homing resonance of our highest path. We navigate in the present. We look for the positive intention in behaviors that are hurtful. We find additional ways to fulfill those beautiful intentions. Spirit's countenance radiates from our faces. We live the questions into answers, and we have faith that our heart's purest intent will be realized. We fuel our vitality and manifest loving responses from within the deep wellspring of our being. We are safe. We are portals for love.

Many brave models inspire and encourage us on our path. Gandhi was once asked, "What is God?" and he replied, "God is Truth." He was then asked, "What is truth?" And he replied, "The answer is equally simple, truth is the light of the soul's aspiration, and when you surrender to it wholeheartedly, it will take you under its wing and you will become invulnerable." He also reminds us, "Be the change you want to see in the world."

The following are gifts that have come to us. They inspire us and grow our champion.

Nelson Mandela, in his 1994 Inaugural speech said:

Our deepest fear is not that we are inadequate.
Our deepest fear is that we powerful
beyond measure.
It is our light, not our darkness,
that most frightens us.

We ask ourselves, Who am I to be brilliant,
gorgeous, talented, and fabulous?
Actually, who are you not to be?

You are a child of God
Your playing small doesn't serve the world,
There's nothing enlightened about shrinking so
that other people won't feel insecure around you.

We were born to make manifest the glory of God
that is within us.
It's not just in some of us; it's in everyone.
And as we let our own light shine,
we unconsciously give other people permission to
do the same.

As we are liberated from our own fear,
our presence automatically liberates others.

Our friend Constance passed on this Theresa prayer:

May today there be peace within.
May you trust your highest power that you are exactly where
    you are meant to be...
May you not forget the infinite possibilities that are born of
    faith.
May you use those gifts that you have received, and pass on the
    love that has been given to you.
May you be content knowing you are a child of God.
Let this presence settle into your bones, and allow your soul the
    freedom to sing, dance, praise and love. It is there for each
    and every one of us.

A champion grows champions. The Circle is sacred.

TREASURED RESOURCES

Allen, Paula Gunn, *The Sacred Hoop*, Beacon Press, Boston, Massachusetts, 1986.

Hill, Ruth Beebe, *Hanta Yo*, Warner Books, New York, New York, 1979.

Lee, Scout, *The Excellence Principle*, Metamorphous Press, Portland, Oregon, 1990.

Lee, Scout and Summer, Jan, *The Challenge of Excellence*, Metamorphous Press, Portland Oregon, 1990.

Mails, Thomas E., *Secret Native American Pathways*, Council Oak Books, Tulsa, Oklahoma, 1988.

Mails, Thomas E., *Fool's Crow: Wisdom & Power*, Council Oak Books, Tulsa, Oklahoma, 1991.

Medicine-Eagle, Brooke, *Buffalo Woman Comes Singing*, Ballantine Books, New York, New York, 1991.

Sheehan, Kathryn and Waidner, Mary, *Earth Child*, Council Oak Books, Tulsa, Oklahoma, 1991.

Scout Cloud Lee and the staff of Vision Us, Inc., base their operations at The Ranch just west of Stillwater, Oklahoma. Founded as the Center To Explore Human Excellence, this 40-acre training facility has been in operation for over twenty years.
  Individuals and teams come from around the world to rejuvenate, learn, laugh and increase their productivity.

The Ranch hosts corporate leaders and other groups for trainings, retreats, meetings and family camps. Here in nature's beauty, leaders take the time to vision, communicate and practice precision strategies of success.

Using the Challenge of Excellence Ropes Course at The Ranch, facilitators apply the

267

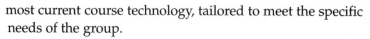

most current course technology, tailored to meet the specific needs of the group.

An outdoor pavilion that is also a massive earth drum easily holds 700 people under one roof.

Built in honor of the Native American heritage of Oklahoma, the Village at The Ranch has a very large fire circle

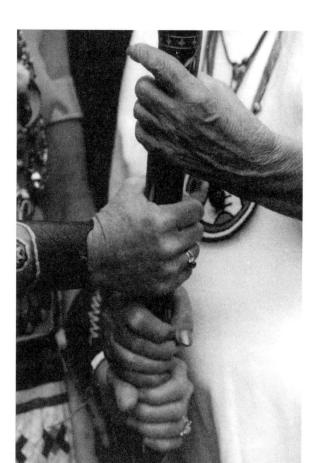

surrounded by 4 sweat lodges, tipis, a Wichita Grass Lodge, a Cherokee summer lodge, a Seminole chickee, the Star Lodge, the Little Bear Lodge and the Wilderness Chapel.

Little Dude is The Ranch's Western frontier-style apartment complex for today's "settlers."

More information about The Ranch can be found online at www.visionus.com.

Scout Cloud Lee, Ed.D., former tenured professor at the University of Illinois and Oklahoma State University, and has been awarded numerous federal grants for her research in peak performance and human excellence. She is author of eleven books and hundreds of articles on these subjects and has been featured on documentaries and television specials by all major television networks.

She is currently CEO of Vision Us. Inc., an organization- and team- development firm, founder of The Magical Child Foundation, a non-profit promoting global peace through play, and faculty member for the Institute for Management Studies. A singer/songwriter, author, keynote speaker, personal coach, corporate trainer, rancher and teacher, she is noted for her outstanding ability to track patterns of excellence and assist people in developing them.

In 2002 Scout carried the Olympic torch on its way to Salt Lake City for the Winter Games. This honor symbolized the theme of her life's work: "Light the Fire Within," as she seeks to inspire others to live their dreams and share their unique gifts.

Carol Ann Washburn Lee, Ed.D., (Annie), is an educator whose contributions to the field of experiential (adventure-based) education have been featured on major television networks throughout the U.S. and internationally. In 1979 she joined with Dr. Scout Cloud Lee to start a consulting and training business. She expanded their success by establishing training consulting bases in San Diego, California and Kauai, Hawaii.

Annie is co-creator with Scout of the "Excellence Principle" which emphasizes learning through positive kinesthetic experience (learning by doing). She currently serves as vice president of Vision Us, Inc., and president of the Magical Child Foundation.

Scout and Annie are co-founders of "The Ranch" a training and retreat center on the prairie west of Stillwater, Oklahoma, where they conduct their experiential learning retreats. Here they blend powerful practices from various cultures—Native American, Christian, Australian Aboriginal, ancient Hawaiian, and more—to bring about changes in people, in organizations, and in society.

For more information online, visit www.visionus.com

Scout Cloud Lee (l.) and Carol Ann Washburn Lee (r.)

Council Oak Books takes its name from a great oak tree that still grows in the center of Tulsa, our home city. Here the Locapoka Creek Indians established their tribal meeting place and rekindled their ceremonial fire after the long journey west over the Trail of Tears.

Since Council Oak's founding in 1984, the circle around that sacred fire has expanded slowly with each season, like the widening rings of the ancient Oak itself. Here is a meeting place for the telling of stories that speak directly to the human heart. Our books are meant to inspire the sharing of knowledge in the quiet, contemplative space beneath the great Oak.

Though rooted in the center of the North American continent, we publish books from people and places all over the world—books that, like this one, cross cultural lines to bring together ancient traditions in new ways. Drawing from history, we publish for the future, presenting books that are destined to become "classics," as they break new ground and point the way to a better, more peaceful world.

To request a complete catalog of Council Oak Books, e-mail: order@counciloakbooks.com.